DECIDE NOW:

THE GOOD LIFE or the BEST LIFE

I find L Jay Mitchell's ideas about human identity, our deep "relationality", purpose in living, and spirit, to be tremendously profound and remarkably practical. Here is one truly exceptional individual's distillation of the wisdom of the ages. Moreover, the author brings to life some of the best thinking in contemporary social theory and research while dispelling some of the most harmful academic misconceptions in psychology and elsewhere. Personally, I take away from reading this book a renewed sense of the unrelenting courage and humility needed to face life's uncertainty and tragedy and still find a truly "Best Life," for which I am grateful.

—FRANK C. RICHARDSON, Ph.D., Professor of Educational Psychology (emeritus), University of Texas, Past president of the Society for Theoretical and Philosophical Psychology, and co-author of *Re-Envisioning Psychology—Moral Dimensions of Theory and Practice*

Educators, therapists, youth counselors, and parents, are flooded with books and articles offering advice and wisdom. In his new book, *Decide Now: The Good Life or the Best Life,* L Jay Mitchell does not just give advice and instead—in his wisdom—inspires us to ask the right questions. What is the Good Life? What is the Best Life? And how can we move from Good to Best? Mitchell shares his dreams, draws upon remarkable life experiences, and engages the mind and heart of the reader who craves deeper meaning, authentic living, and the path to higher ground and fulfillment. This book belongs in the hands of everyone who wants to face squarely the challenges of living and leading with integrity, wholeness, and authenticity.

—JOHN C. HUIE, Ph.D., Educational Consultant and former Executive Director of the North Carolina Outward Bound School

L. Jay Mitchell has awakened a curiosity inside me to learn more about myself and the relationships around me, motivating me to strive for the best life that I can have. His insight on self concept will have you thinking about who you are versus who you want to be. I recommend this book to any reader who is willing to take a closer look at what makes you who you are, forcing you to decide now; stick with the good life or choose a different path that will lead you closer to the best life!

—SUZETTE CARLUCCIO, Author of *Run Away with My Heart: A Mother and Daughter's Journey toward Letting Go*

This work is a flower that has grown in the garden of an elder, L Jay, who has allowed life to plant in his mind beautiful seeds of thought, which he has fertilized with experience guiding the youth and to bring the best out of them. L Jay examines how our identity and our perception of identity is central to the way we navigate in what sages from indigenous wisdom traditions call the river of self (or the source of who we are). Using practical know-how the author demonstrates how to avoid the stormy misconceptions that make it harder to know ourselves. Above all, he assists us in making sense of the self while helping us to gain wisdom, which he identifies rightly as the best life.

—KYKO-TZU, Ph.D. Author of *The Furrows on My Forehead: A Collection of Wisdom Poems and Prose*

DECIDE NOW

THE GOOD LIFE or the BEST LIFE

L. JAY MITCHELL

Copyright © 2014 by L. Jay Mitchell

All rights reserved.
No part of this book may be reproduced in any form by any means
without the express permission of the author.

Print Edition ISBN: 978-0-9905127-0-7
Kindle Edition ISBN: 978-0-9905127-1-4
EPUB Edition ISBN: 978-0-9905127-2-1

LCCN 2014945021

Published in the United States of America by TAS Development, LLC
Printed in the United States of America by CreateSpace
Cover and Interior Design: Kathryn Campbell

CONTENTS

Acknowledgements

Sometimes, a book can only live inside a person for so long. Then, it has to be written. That has happened to me. The students who have attended my schools/ programs over the years have enlivened my life. Unbeknownst to them, they have been my teachers, mentors—and in some cases—postgraduate professors of life. I thank every one of them for the inspiration that they have given me to write this book. Of course, my wife and children have been faithfully supportive. Their frank recommendations and timely encouragement allowed me to stay focused and complete the process. I am already deeply in debt to them for many wonderful things. Their assistance with this book is a welcome addition to the mountain of gratitude that I owe them.

I thank my associates for their support of the book's content and its laborious process. They put into action many of the principles explored in each chapter. Brent Slife has been an inspiration to me for years as a courageous proponent of Strong Relationality and moral choice. I admire his intellect and brilliant contributions to the world of psychology. He has helped me hone some of the explanations of rather complex concepts to be more accessible to readers. I was privileged to have him write the Foreword.

I cannot too effusively thank my editor, Jessica. Her dedication has matched my own. Her professionalism and attention to detail have been a godsend. I could not imagine completing the writing process successfully without her.

Foreword

When I first met the author of this book many years ago, I was skeptical. I was exhilarated by our conversation, but I had trouble believing that people like him really existed. Here was an elegant man talking in an exceptionally humble manner about big ideas and even bigger applications. My own experiences had proven to me that genuine elegance and humility rarely went together, but big ideas and feasible applications were an even rarer combination. Was this guy to be believed?

Now, after some 15 years of collaboration, I'm so glad that I answered this question positively. I have come to know L. Jay Mitchell as one of the most insightful, highest integrity individuals I have ever met. Our collaboration has spawned important presentations at national psychological conferences as well as articles in noteworthy psychological journals. Yet, the most significant focus of our work together has been two groundbreaking and highly successful programs for troubled youth: a wilderness academy and a therapeutic boarding school for young women. L. Jay not only cobbled together the funds for these large programs, but also innovated a large portion of their treatment interventions. These interventions include some of the most creative and effective programs I have witnessed in my over 30 years as a clinical psychologist and professor of psychology. It is no wonder that he was well-known as a pioneer in the field of wilderness therapy before I had even met him.

I am excited that he has decided to funnel these intellectual insights and the practical know-how into the book before you. The reader is in for a real treat because L. Jay tackles one of the most important issues of our time—who we are. He is right that our identity and our perceptions of our identity are central to a whole bunch of vital life issues, including whether we truly flourish, whether we have quality relationships, and whether we experience real joy. It is a great sadness to me that so many people never attain any real life satisfaction or what some ancient writers call "the peace that passes all understanding." They, unfortunately, get lost in a host of common misconceptions about the self.

One of the many virtues of this book is that L. Jay gently corrects these misconceptions that are sometimes fostered unwittingly by the so-called experts on the self: psychologists. As he points out so poignantly, these misconceptions cluster around the tired notion that who we are, not to mention how we should perceive ourselves, originate from some interaction between our nature and our nurture. Too often we are told that our identity or our self is some amalgam of inborn factors and the way that we were raised, in which case there is nothing much we can do about the self. All we can do is discover who we are and live into this fixed identity.

This book, fortunately, takes a completely different tack. It assumes—and cites convincing evidence—that what you *believe* about yourself is pivotal to your identity. This tack is a hopeful one because it means that *you* actually have some say in whether you truly flourish, have good relationships, and experience authentic joy. The nature-nurture-only crowd would immediately tell us that your innate biology and your past development determine what you believe about yourself. Intriguingly, however, L. Jay cites fascinating research that turns this conventional notion on its ear—our chosen beliefs might actually, at least in some important cases, trump our DNA and our past experiences.

He then goes on to cogently demonstrate that we have a kind of agency about these beliefs. The influence of our biology and our environment is important, of course, but we *also* have possibilities within these nature-nurture parameters, possibilities that allow us to claim some agency over these beliefs. If this is true, and a growing number of researchers believe that it is, then it is a game-changer for the self and our identity. This book draws out many of the significant implications of these new ideas.

Just to whet the reader's appetite, allow me to single out two implications that L. Jay explicitly challenges: the priority of "feeling good" and the uniformity of the self. The first is the common notion that the most important life objective is our emotional satisfaction. Professionals and laypeople alike routinely confound this kind of satisfaction with happiness, well-being, and peace. Most surveys of the public seem to point to the priority of good feeling, and many researchers of the positive psychology movement focus on it almost exclusively. L. Jay gives good feelings their due, but he rightly challenges this notion as the main goal of our lives, replacing it with "a life of rich meaning and purpose, a life of quality relationships, a life of giving and receiving love." Anyone who has striven to do even the last—giving and receiving love—knows that this situation does not always result in "feeling good."

I am also relieved to see that this book discusses a second implication of this new understanding of the self and identity. For a long time, the self has been understood as if it is basically uniform, or at least *should* be uniform. The "personality" tradition of psychology has contributed to this understanding, often treating the self as though it is one entity, one set of feelings, one system of thoughts, and so on. L. Jay, on the other hand, understands that humans have mixed feelings and conflicting thoughts. He proposes that a better understanding might be that we consist of "mini-selves," with one personality when we attend football games and another personality when we attend church. Indeed, as he describes so powerfully, we might even harbor *simultaneous* mini-selves in our identities that conflict with one another. His ideas do not deny the continuity we experience between these mini-selves, giving us our sense of a unified identity, but I think he's quite right that this unification has been overly emphasized, leading us to wonder why we suddenly "blow up" in some situations and are "not ourselves" in others.

As much as I would read this book for its provocative ideas alone, its true strength is that L. Jay Mitchell does not just describe these important implications; he informs us practically of what they can mean for us in our own lives. If there is anyone, in my experience, who is the master of applying these conceptual insights, it is L. Jay Mitchell. His experiences in both his wilderness academies and his boarding school have led him to devise these thoughtful applications and creative practices. The book, in this sense, not only helps us understand the practicalities of these ideas, it patiently moves us through cognitive exercises and thought experiments so that we actually *experience* their richness and benefits. Readers who are willing to buckle their chinstraps are in for a very intriguing and enriching ride.

BRENT D. SLIFE, Ph.D

Clinical psychologist, university professor, and member of seven editorial boards for professional journals. Editor-elect (of the APA's Journal of Theoretical and Philosophical Psychology*)*

Introduction

This book is about getting a grip on who we *think* we are and who we *want* to be. It's about trading in the proverbial "Good Life" for the Best Life. We think that we *know* what we have in life and who we are. However, in reality we are more and have more than what we may often suppose. Our life is full of what we cannot see. This book expands our vision of who we are, and unveils the life we do not see. We will come to understand that we are the life we live, and we live who we *think* we are.

We have unconsciously assumed an identity—a way to fit into the world. No matter what friends, experts, or even scientists, say about who we are—we passionately act out our perceived identity like an Academy Award-winning actor. Values, hopes, and dreams are embedded in this identity. We unconsciously embrace them. We judge ourselves by whether we attain them. Nevertheless, this is an *assumed identity.* To assume means to *not* know for sure.

The same can be said about the "desired life" that we pursue. Our desires are intertwined with our perceived identity. We want to be happy and fulfilled. However, we can only assume that our path leads to this desired life. Again, we do not know for sure. Many of us have sought assurance by pursuing the proverbial Good Life. It is the life-path now in vogue. We assume that its large number of followers assure us that it is the best path. In doing so, we have to chose a perceived identity that fits this Good Life vision.

Is there something better? Do we have the freedom to choose or create a better identity? Yes! We can learn what we do not know, but only if we want to. This book explores what we have not known about who we are, and where we are going. Seldom do we take the time or make the effort to expand this knowledge. Our motivation to do so arises from provocative life experiences. These experiences provoke us to ask questions and seek answers. The experiences come in many forms and at different times in life. A powerful dream provoked me to ask my questions.

THE FARMER AND THE TRACTOR

When I was fourteen, I had a dream that changed my life forever. Instead of my usual dreams about girls, this one was about tractors, Volkswagens, and farmers. In spite of the strange subject matter, its emotional and mental effect on me continues to this day. It began with an old farmer walking into town and being disoriented. For whatever reason, he hadn't been to town in 35 years, and everything looked radically different. His old tractor had given up its life, and no amount of mechanical rejuvenation would revive it. He needed a new one, and he needed it now! Like many sprawling little towns, the outskirts were lined with car dealerships. In fact, the first business establishment that he walked by was full of little buggy-looking cars called "Beetles". This was indeed a strange sight. Out of curiosity, he walked on in.

He was met by a gentleman wearing a fully-colored Madras sports coat, an orange shirt, and a white tie with black V's sporadically spaced here and there. His smile was friendly in spite of the buggy eyeshades covering most of his face. The salesman walked up to the farmer and said, "Can I he'p ya fine something?" The farmer stood up straight and replied, "I want a tractor." With the truth of heaven shining down on his eager face, the salesman spoke loudly, "Why, y'uve come to the ri-ot place. I got more'n ya can count." The farmer looked around in amazement, because he didn't see one tractor in sight. The salesman took him by the arm and headed over to a brand new, red, Volkswagen Beetle. The farmer told him that he didn't need one of *those* "things". He wanted a *tractor*. Offended, the salesman dropped his chin and whispered, "You ain't been to town in a while. This here *is* the newest kind of tractor." So the farmer perked right up.

In my dream, the Volkswagen was alive and could understand their conversation. Of course, he was fresh and new, and a little naive. The salesman started his pitch with the farmer while the Beetle listened carefully. "Dey've made a lotta impuvements on tractors, especially dem Germans. Looky at 'dis. You gots extra seats so your wife and grandkids can ride wif ya. And do ya see 'dis? Windshield wipers, just amazin'. You even gotta radio to keep you innertained. And ya can't overheat this baby, 'cause she is air-cooled. Gas mileage! Oh Lawdy! Thirty-five miles per gallon. Ya can't beat that. If'n it gets cold, just turn on 'da heater, and you're toasty. Winders let ya see 360 de-grease. And yessir, a 3-year warranty if anythin' goes bad. Tractors! Dey've come a *long* ways."

The Beetle was almost vibrating with excitement. It was like a bird dog looking for a job—for something to do. It had been confused up until now as to what it was, and what to hope for. Now it *knew*. It looked at the farmer, hoping with his whole carburetor that he would take it home. The farmer's eyes were big and vacant. This was truly amazing. How fortunate he was to have stopped at this Beetle-tractor store. He reached into his back pocket and pulled out a fat wad of one hundred-dollar bills. He peeled off twenty and gave them to the salesman. There was no delivery fee. He could actually drive it home! His wife was going to be so proud. The little Beetle was elated.

When the farmer drove up his driveway, he could see his wife on the front porch shielding her eyes from the sun in order to get a better look. Before he could park in front of the house, his wife frowned, grabbed the screen door, and slammed it as she went back inside. Oh well, *she* didn't have to plow the field. He couldn't wait to hitch up the plow and get started. Somehow, in my dream, he actually hooked up a plow to the Beetle. He headed out to the field and started on the first row. The little Beetle was enthused, no, *more* than enthused. He gave his whole chassis and drive shaft to the job. All night long they used the Beetle's lights, alternating between normal and bright. The farmer only had to fill up the tank with gas one time during the entire night. When the sun peeked over the hill in the morning, they had completed two rows. I could feel the contentment, peace, and fervor of the Beetle. He knew who he was and what life was all about. For three months, the farmer and the Beetle worked like untiring beasts. The farmer changed the oil, and washed and lubricated the little machine. But at the end of three months, the Beetle died. The farmer's wife said, "I told you so." The dream ended abruptly.

DREAM AFTERMATH

In the morning after the dream, I looked in the mirror and asked myself if I was a Beetle or a tractor? Who was I? How could I *know* how to treat myself and other people? The farmer and the Beetle meant well, but in the end, the Beetle died. Their good intentions did not save the Beetle's life or the farmer's time and money. They were both deceived by the salesman, and as a result, their lives were ruined. I was concerned that I might really be a Beetle, but was acting like a tractor. I wanted self-fulfillment, not self-destruction. I knew that I could not be true to myself if I did not know my real identity. I needed to get a grip on *me.*

The dream dramatically raised questions that haunted me throughout years of inquiry and searching. **Does it make any difference who I believe I am?** Will I just end up being "me" no matter what I believe? If I believe a lie about my identity, will it make any difference? How can I live the Best Life if I don't know who I am? How can I tell the difference between the Good Life and the Best Life? If I act against my nature, will I self-destruct? What is my nature? Who can I trust in answering these questions?

This book entertains these questions in depth and suggests some strategies to answer them. In seeking answers provoked by my dream, another question emerged. How can you and I *create,* not find, who we really are in order to live the Best Life? This is the "soul" of this book.

Have you ever heard someone say, "Accept me for who I am"? What does that mean? We will explore different ways of thinking about who we are and who we can be. Obstacles in our path will be identified and resources will be revealed. In doing so, we will discover that our identity is not just a fixed thing inside of us, but a matrix of connections to others in life. The quality of these connections determines who we are and whether we can possess the Best Life. We will engage arguments for and against the importance—and even the existence—of self-concept. For example, many people believe, "I am who I am, and it doesn't matter what I think. I can't change the real me." Resolutions to these conundrums will be proposed. I will advocate that who we *really* are is substantially constituted by who we *think* we are. In addition, we can live the Best Life by not choosing the status quo, but consciously choosing to create ourselves.

The Best Life is what we all want. It connotes satisfaction and joy in living, but many have died never finding it. Why is it so elusive and often camouflaged? There are many mismarked roads on the way to this coveted place, and not all of the roads take us there. Like in *Alice in Wonderland,* we must be careful in choosing what *looks* like a rabbit hole. In fact, the Best Life is not a destination—it is a continuous creation. We may be living what we hope is the proverbial Good Life, while we privately desire a better life.

SELF-CONCEPT AND THE BEST LIFE

This book is about the nature, misconceptions, and reality of self-concept as well as insights and skills to create a Best Life self-perception. We will begin our exploration by thoughtfully considering the obvious as well as the hidden elements of the life we are now pursuing.

Please know that this book has a bias just like every other book. The bias is that humans have inherent worth. We are all connected and deserve equal consideration. The quality of our relationships determines whether we live a Good Life or the Best Life. The Best Life means that we consider the well-being of others to be as important as our own well-being (or even more so in some contexts). We build quality relationships by treating others virtuously. That means we live on the high road. We bring into our relationships, integrity, love, courage, and honor. We seek after a life of altruism.

In other words, life is not primarily about "feeling good". We will not analyze what feels good, when we can feel good, how to feel good, or where we can feel good. We will not pave out a path of sensual hedonism. The Best Life includes feeling good, taking care of our emotional and physical well-being, and pursuing our interests. However, the quality of our relationships is the most important. In fact, the Best Life may require us courageously and honorably to be uncomfortable at times. The Best Life is priceless. It is not something cheap or free. I refer to a life of rich meaning and purpose, a life of quality relationships, a life of giving and receiving love. It requires giving up the Good Life for something better.

There is general confusion about the nature of a self-concept or self-perception. We will examine competing ideas through stories and discussion. Let me introduce a few blanket statements to get your brain rolling. These propositions are the topics and themes of the following chapters:

- Our self-concept affects our well-being, health, and helps us acquire the Best Life.

- We are not a static, fixed self to be discovered somewhere inside of our body.
- The true self is a "relational" being, not a separate being.
- We have a moral choice in being who we are. We are not biologically determined or pre-programmed to not have choice.
- We are responsible and accountable for our choices.
- Choices exist, but the availability of choices is limited. We are responsible for increasing the availability and accessibility of our choices.
- The real self constantly changes with or without our conscious permission.
- We are inevitably drawn to be who we think we are, in spite of everything else.
- Incongruent beliefs about self-concept create internal contention and unhappiness.
- We are led to the Best Life by consciously mediating unconscious internal conflicts.
- We are a composition of our values demonstrated in our relationships.
- Our values are the most difficult part of us to change.
- We aren't forced to believe anything. In spite of the evidence, we believe what is most useful to us.
- Science is a constantly changing group of theories that are always in a state of flux.
- We are more than our genetics and our environment. What could that be?
- Epigenetics may explain how our beliefs can trump our DNA.
- Our worldview significantly biases our self-concept.
- The mind is not exclusively the brain, and the brain is not exclusively the mind.

- Your self is a combination of "mini-selves".
- Consciously uncovering the mini-selves within us helps organize our self.
- The past has not entirely made us what we are today and does not determine our future.
- Strong Relationality is a relational mindset of ideas that can enrich our worldview of the Best Life.
- Human brains are programmed to operate with unconscious biases that need to be recognized and accommodated in creating a self-concept.
- There are strategies to integrate our conscious and unconscious thoughts.
- We can consciously get a grip on how we unconsciously change.
- You may find the discussion of these propositions not only provocative, but usefully life-changing. You *can* have the Best Life. You need to know what you do not know.
- Notes and additional resources can be found at the end of each chapter. Some chapters may request that you engage in simple cognitive exercises. Doing so will enrich your understanding beyond what passive reading can do on key topics. Now, go ahead and turn yourself inside out (a relational notion). And stay away from tractor dealerships until you finish this book.

CHAPTER 1

Why Perception of Self Matters: An Overview

Have you tried to change, but you just can't? Even after committing yourself to change, have you ever felt like something was holding you back? Knowing what to do can be like saddling a horse but never getting on. It's probably *who you* think *you are* that stops you. To be the "perceived you", your beliefs and actions must fit the character that you have conjured up in your mind. *Your self-concept controls your motivation and permission* to choose what to do or not to do. That includes everything you do. It creates the boundaries in which you give yourself permission to operate in life.

Perhaps you have been to a county fair or amusement park where you go from booth to booth looking for entertainment. Most of the booths offer challenges or competitions like throwing rings on bottles, shooting hoops, or throwing balls at heavy bottles. And then, if you win, you get a stuffed toy. You can usually find a booth where someone tries to guess your age, and if they can't guess within two years you get a prize. I went to one of these booths once, and I remember the attendant scrutinizing me from head-to-toe. Of course I expected a prize because everyone always told me how "young" I looked. Well, I didn't get a prize. My actual age was a fact, but the real issue was how old I looked to a specific person. Someone's *perception* of me determined whether I got the prize or not.

Instead of my age, what if the question was "**Who am I?**", and if they guessed correctly I would get a prize? The answer to the age question was on my driver's license. Sure, the license reveals my name and age, but where is the proof of who I am? What evidence could prove whether they were right or wrong and whether or not I would get a prize? My driver's license also reveals my address, height, weight, sex, hair, and eye color. Would that be enough? How about DNA test results? Maybe I could provide a birth certificate, marriage license, diploma, social security card, proof of employment, voter registration card, tax return, immunization record, and arrest record. If they somehow could guess right about all of this information, that's still not who I am. That information doesn't define me. However, if I was asked to tell them the answer, what would I say? It would be more than a litany of facts. Somehow you and I are more than the "facts". Beliefs—especially our own beliefs about who we are—actually become a part of who we are.

YOUR SELF-PERCEPTION REALLY MATTERS

You may feel more comfortable answering true or false questions because your answers are *clearly* right or wrong. The answer demonstrates that you know a "fact" or that you are a lucky or unlucky "guesser". However, life offers up questions that are beyond yes or no answers. Some answers are not a matter of fact. Instead, they are judgments, opinions, preferences, or perceived meanings. For example, take the question, "What is the moral status of the United States?" Is the answer an absolute fact—an irrefutable piece of knowledge that once revealed is incontrovertible? Absolutely not! No matter who attempts to answer this question—scientist, politician, minister, student, male or female—no one seems to have the absolute, "right" answer.

Anyway, who has the status to conclusively decide the "correct" answer? The proposed answers would probably cover a variety of characteristics about the United States. Supporting an answer may require correct "facts", but these facts are not the answer. In the end, everyone can have an opinion and a perception about the economic and moral status of the country. But who is right? I suppose we all have an opinion about that too.

"Who you are" falls in this category where some facts are gathered and an opinion is formed. The answer to the question is not incontrovertible because you are not a "simple" matter. Instead, you are a complex, interacting combination of many things. Just like the economic and moral condition of the United States, you are in a constant state of flux. You change every day. Sometimes we want a bottom-line answer that is quickly available and fits nicely into a box.

You may be tempted to take information that appears obvious or common sense and conclude "this is me". Do not read this book hoping to discover the one simple, hidden truth of "who you really are". I hope to puncture the fallacy that you are a fixed thing. Using various disciplines of thought, including neuroscience, philosophy, psychology, social psychology, religion, and lots of "opinion", we will look at the self from many perspectives. Your **opinion** of who you are really matters, even if it takes time and effort to discover.

Oh, does it really! You may think that since you cannot completely identify and encapsulate the truth about your identity, why try? "I've made it this far without knowing or perceiving what constitutes my 'self', why worry about it now?" That is a "self" misconception that could limit your access to the life that you want. You may not have been consciously ruminating and researching who you are, but your unconscious mind works on this question constantly. In fact, you have a complex amalgamation of beliefs that your mind has already formulated about who you are. You currently have a self-concept that you are already committed to. It is simply out of your consciousness most of the time. So then, why does the question require constant mental effort?

THE ROLE OF PERMISSION AND MOTIVATION

You can't effectively function in the world without acting out the answer to this big identity question. You would be paralyzed without an answer even if the answer continued to evolve. Your unconscious mind cannot help itself from thinking about and seeking answers to who you are. Like food and oxygen, you can't live without it. Let me explain. Much of what we consider "living" is a combination of thinking, perceiving, sensing, behaving, and emoting. When breaking down a day in your life, the description will essentially consist of a combination of those things.

Consider the following example: "I *went* to my friend's house because I *missed* her so much, and we *sat* and *talked* for a while. She did not *look* me in the eye, and it *seemed* like she had done something *strange*". All of the words in italics are examples of how "I" experienced life in that short timeframe. The important question is: why didn't I think or act differently? Why didn't I make different choices? The answer, of course, is complex. And some reasons are more governing than others. Who you perceive yourself to be may be the most controlling reason of all. You acted and perceived things consistent with who you *thought* you were.

Why? Because your perceived identity (your self-concept) gives you PERMISSION and MOTIVATION to think, perceive, behave, feel, and even BELIEVE whatever you experience. Yes, in other words we are defining the perceived self or identity as: that which *permits* and *motivates* you to act and believe one way and not another. This self-concept permits actions that are consistent with your self-concept, and it rejects actions that are inconsistent with it. You must have permission within yourself to act and think as you do. Your perceived identity limits your options and will continue to do so unless your perception changes. Let me provide a few examples.

THE "LOSER"

I knew a boy who could not give himself permission to be successful. This kid grew up in a family neighborhood with buddies who were his teammates on various athletic teams. This boy was a gifted athlete. He had speed, power, and coordination. Everything he did on the baseball field seemed smooth and effortless. He was always the team's best player. However, he would get in a "lights out" groove of hitting and pitching, and then fall apart. I remember him hitting a prodigious home run and being swarmed by the team at home plate. In the dugout he was full of excuses for hitting it out of the park. "That is the worst pitcher ever! That ball was too hot to be legal! I just closed my eyes and swung!" He would not take credit for being a good athlete. When he got dangerously close to looking so good that he could not doubt himself, he would self-sabotage. The rest of his life looked the same. He could not embrace success of any kind. He quit baseball because it challenged his committed identity of "I'm a loser". Succeeding undermined his entrenched self-concept, and he would not give himself permission to be somebody fake. He believed that it was better to live in the real world of being a "loser" than pretending that he was someone else. After all, pretending to be someone else is a fantasy.

Perhaps you are wondering, where did the *entrenched* identity come from and why didn't he change it? He had inferred from impactful past experiences that he was a loser. Even though he resented it and suffered the consequences, he stayed stuck. The experiences did not create the loser belief. Rather, his *interpretation* of the experiences did the creating. As you can see, because he had exceptional talents, he had to work really hard at being a loser. He probably would have been shocked to know what a success he was at being a loser.

Why didn't hitting home runs convince him that he was a winner? Everyone else could see it. Was he successful at being a loser because that is who he conclusively believed himself to be? Other parts of him wanted something different, but the ruling "I am a loser" self-concept was the most powerful. Perhaps you know someone like this at home, at work, at school, or in your social circle. Powerful identity beliefs are strong enough to ignore or distort contradictory facts.

THE WARRIOR

Self-concept dramatically affects relationships with family and peers. Here is an example of how self-permission to change part of an identity can be life-changing. A Native American woman gave birth to a beautiful little girl, and for various reasons she gave her up for adoption. A wealthy family from Western Europe loved her enough to cross the ocean and become her adopted parents. As a result, she grew up in the sophisticated culture of European boarding schools. Unfortunately, she suffered incidents of violent abuse from male strangers. She became paranoid and emotionally closed. Her parents sent her to an emotional growth program in the United States, hoping that it would help her heal. At the program, she actually met the first Native American that she could remember. The meeting was profound, and she wept while staring at this young man of her race. She was encouraged to experience Native American culture in a wilderness setting. While in the program, she had a daydream or vision about being with her birth mother prior to being adopted. In the dream, her mother drew her close and whispered in her ear, "I give you the warrior blood of your ancestors." She felt her mother's breath being blown into her ear, nose, and mouth. At that point, she blacked out. When she awakened, she felt peculiarly different. Her posture and gait changed, and she held her chin higher. She became more assertive and visible in groups of people. The paranoid feelings came less frequently.

In this exceptional example, she became her mother's blood daughter. She was a warrior. Her perceived identity changed, not her DNA. Her newly-adopted self-concept empowered her and enabled her emotional healing. She had permission and motivation to begin living like the woman-warrior she now believed herself to be. She did not have all of the finished traits, skills, and attributes of a woman-warrior. However, she had the vision, motivation, and the permission to fulfill her new perception. Barriers and walls were removed and new choices became accessible to her.

THE HIKER

Self-perception permits or prevents us from trying out new behaviors. Our self-concept and not our abilities can restrict us from even trying to do something. Keep that in mind as your read this example. A young man found himself on a challenging wilderness trek. He had been raised in the city and had never camped out overnight. The outdoors was an unknown world that he had only read about or seen in the movies. His life was full of technology and urban endeavors. On his third day of the trek, he told the group leader that he had to quit. He actually said, "This isn't me." His guide and group members encouraged, cajoled, and even begged him to keep going. Hours passed and he sat stubbornly waiting for someone to take him to a car. He kept repeating, "I'm not a hiker." Finally, the guide showed him a map and the "easy" path that they would follow. The guide apologized for not acknowledging his statement, "I'm not a hiker." He then told the young man that his experience would change. Henceforth, they would only walk and not hike. He reminded the young man that he had walked thousands of miles in his life, and that he was actually a walker not a hiker. This bright leader asked to be corrected if they started hiking instead of walking, and that he would immediately switch back to walking. Amazingly, the young man got up, put on his pack and started walking (or was it hiking?). He had permission from himself to walk, but not to hike. He was startlingly committed to the reality of his self-concept: "I am an urban teenager, not a wilderness guy". How simple yet amazing!

INTERPRETING TRAUMA

Sometimes self-concept can be powerful enough to even minimize potential trauma. I know of two teenage girls who at different times and places suffered violent rape from a stranger. I won't go into the details, but how terrible that any young person suffers death threats, pummeling, and sexual abuse! But the effect on these two adolescents was strikingly different.

One girl, in her own words, had become a "whore" and a "nobody". Her life was filled with promiscuity and drugs, and she abhorred herself. The rape traumatically validated a budding belief that she was worthless. She interpreted the experience as a representation of her "identity". She concluded that no one would treat another person like that unless they were worthless or deserved it. She stayed true to the "worthless" belief, even though she hated the consequences. She could not understand her conflicted emotions.

The other girl had a remarkably different and unique response to her rape. Yes, it was painful, frightening, and outrageous. However, she interpreted the meaning of the rape as a validation of her attractiveness. She actually said, "I was too hot!" The rape convinced her that she was too attractive, and therefore too sexually desirable. Her response was to protect herself from future abuse. Her protection was a new hairstyle, less makeup, and less revealing clothes. She interpreted the rape as a reflection of how she looked and dressed, not whether she was a worthwhile or deserving person. This self-perception partially protected her from the potential psychological consequences of the traumatic event. As a result, she changed her appearance without questioning her identity.

Please note that the traumatic rapes did not create "determined" psychological symptoms that we might expect everyone to suffer. The severity of the trauma was determined by each girl's unique self-concept. One girl's self-concept prior to the rape devastated her, while the other's perception helped protect her. One harshly validated her already budding, negative self-worth. The other's self-concept as an overly-attractive person protected her from self-degradation. This might partially explain how some POWs and other victims psychologically survive ordeals better than others. A healthy self-concept can help you weather the storms of life.

You may remember other examples of how self-concept grants or denies permission to act or believe. You can be taught how to do many things, but if you do not have the motivation or permission to apply the skills, the learning can be wasted. For example, many people attend all kinds of seminars and trainings to learn how to act confidently. They are instructed on what to wear, how to stand, how to talk, how to respond to stressful contexts, and on and on. However, many participants just don't seem to get it. Why is that? It's because their identity or their perceived self just won't give them permission. If the skills or training are inconsistent with their perceived identity, no permission will be granted.

In this example, someone's self-concept may view confidence as a threat to their perceived self. Perhaps they perceive themselves as an "incompetent person". They are not necessarily happy or proud of who they think they are. However, if they begin acting confident, they risk drawing attention to their incompetence. Acting confident is inconsistent with their belief that they are incompetent. Consequently, the self-concept sabotages efforts at acting confident. They say to themselves, "Don't try to act like you know what you're doing when you don't. I'd like to do what the seminar taught me, but if I do, it could hurt me."

WHAT WE THINK MATTERS

Sometimes, permission is even withheld from learning skills or information because it is inconsistent with self-concept. How many young women have barely endured math or science classes because they embraced the identity that "girls can't do math"? Those same young women preclude themselves as women from considering careers in engineering or accounting. Many obese people cannot lose weight because being thin limits their strength and "identity" to carry the world on their shoulders.

Consider the person whose entrenched self-concept is being an "addict" with all of the beliefs, associations, and abilities connected to a particular addiction. Suppose they end up in rehab somehow. They are taught all kinds of reasons why and how they should give up the addiction. To get through the program they may say all of the right things. However, when they get out, it's back to addiction land. Relapse is so prevalent that some people actually consider it a "symptom" of addiction. Their addiction identity would not give permission to learn, believe, or act on what they were exposed to in rehab. The program may have been great, but you can't force anyone to believe something that they think is false. Self-concept beliefs appear to be the most powerful and controlling of all our beliefs. Incompatible beliefs—especially about self-perception—are cast aside. Self-concepts (including the addict), want to get out of life alive. Entrenched self-concept beliefs have survival instincts because they assume that they are the real "us".

SUB-IDENTITIES

There is good news and troubling news. The good news is that a congruent and well-formed self-concept empowers and protects you to fulfill the measure of your potential—to have the Best Life. The troubling news is that an incongruent and ill-formed self-concept can create frustration, failure, and a loss of the Best Life, or even the Good Life. What is meant by congruency and form within the self?

We seem to have factions or parts of ourselves that have their own little sub-identities. How they fit together creates our overall self-identity. They can compete and even contentiously conflict with one another. They can also adopt values that allow them to complement and enhance one another. When they have a cooperative relationship, they share fundamental values that create a congruent self-concept. The unity of the parts suggests that they are well-formed and together. When factions or parts have conflicting values and objectives, the overall self-concept is fractured and incongruent. We all have heard of "double-mindedness". That is the essence of personal incongruence. We often feel uneasy, frustrated, or anxious without realizing that our incongruent self-concept is the real problem.

The factions or parts usually create their little sub-identities unconsciously, completely out of your awareness. This is an ongoing process. One purpose of this book is to help you create a more congruent and well-formed self-concept. You can evaluate and improve the congruence and consistency of your self-perception to have more of the Best Life. How can we consciously discover our multiple, hidden beliefs and refine them in order to attain the Best Life?

Additionally, how can we more congruently align our factions or self-parts? There are many dynamics at play for both objectives. How can we trade up for the Best Life?

CHALLENGING THE GOOD LIFE

The proverbial pleasure-filled Good Life is compulsively self-absorbed and chills our virtuous connections with others. A life of self-serving connections starves our soul and stifles our potential. We want to enliven a self-concept that will desire and acquire the Best Life rather than the Good Life. In spite of the opposition, we can refine our seemingly entrenched life values and have more of the Best Life.

We can become troubled when we understand that changing our self-perception is not easy or simplistic. If we really had a "handle" on ourselves, this book would probably generate little interest and fulfill no real purpose. Have you ever tried to change a value or desire within yourself? Can you wake up in the morning and honestly say, "Yesterday, I hated boiled okra, but today I'm going to love it"? How about, "I loved music yesterday, but today I will abhor it"? Even more difficult may be, "I valued honesty in my relationships yesterday, but today I don't care about being honest". "I love my dog today, but tomorrow I think I'll hate him." What we value and love in spite of its quality or consequence is not merely a whimsical choice. When we set our heart on something, the heart has something to say about letting it go. A heart set on the Good Life resists the Best Life.

However, there have been breakthroughs in various disciplines about how our minds and hearts function and affect our relationships. This gives us hope that we can change and refine ourselves. I will rely on some of this knowledge to describe practical ways for us to create a Best Life self-concept.

OUR BELIEF SYSTEM

Our self-concept motivates us to have either the Good Life or the Best Life. Let's consider how this works. We've seen that a self-concept consists of a deeply-rooted belief system that includes our perceived self-worth, our most prized values, and the characteristics supporting both. This is our belief system, no matter how rational or logical it may seem to somebody else. We work tirelessly to create a self that is consistent with our chosen beliefs. Those beliefs direct our behavior to attain specific objectives. No matter what others think about our identity, or how others influence us, it is *our* beliefs that direct our actions.

We feel confused and conflicted if we pursue behaviors inconsistent with who we think we are. We feel comfortable validating our self-concept, even if it means not hitting home runs, not hiking, and being afraid of the opposite sex. We beat our heads against the wall when we try to escape from that belief system. We may suffer the effects of loneliness, rejection, embarrassment, or even punishment for acting out who we think we are. However, that is usually less painful than letting go of who we think we are.

Some part of the rape victim was not happy acting like a "worthless whore" in spite of believing that that's who she was. The athlete was troubled about being a loser. Parts within the addict suffered and fought for sobriety. Parts of the Native American girl were not happy being a victim. In other words, each person experienced at least two conflicting desires. While one desire was acted out, the other desires were dominated and frustrated. We all have a survival mechanism that will preserve who we *think* we are at almost any cost. We would rather suffer pain than lose our perceived identity because it feels like our identity is life itself. However, because we chose the beliefs constructing our self-concept, we can also change them. This process requires more than willpower and logic.

WHAT IS THE BEST LIFE?

This book is about the Best Life. Let me briefly mention why the Best Life is an upgrade from the proverbial Good Life. I'll focus on two distinguishing factors. First, the Best Life includes discovering and developing our talents, pursuing inherent interests, and enjoying the goodness and beauty of the world. Second—and even more important than feeling good and comfortable—is having quality, loving relationships.

A pragmatic definition of good mental and emotional health is the unhindered ability to give and receive love. This love is altruistic—meaning that we can care about others as much or even more than ourselves. The Best Life is freedom from hatred, jealousy, envy, revenge, or obsession. Instead, we are free to have compassion, empathy, integrity, courage, and forgiveness in our relationships. That is the heart of virtue.

We struggle to love everyone. It is easy and perhaps less virtuous to love someone who makes our life more pleasant. These are people we like because of what they do for us. They nurture us, encourage us, and bring zest into our lives. Our family, friends, mentors, and lovers fill this category. In other words, it is easy to love and care about people who serve our interests. Altruistic love includes people outside of that circle.

We are stretched to love strangers, those who are different, and certainly those who are our enemies. However, love is the primary virtue. We may be born with inclinations towards one virtue or another, but becoming a virtuous person requires effort, sacrifice, and discipline. We are not born with all of the virtues that we need. Acquiring virtue is not easy—which is one reason why it is so valuable. Acquisitions that are rare or difficult to acquire usually have the greatest value. Virtuous love is the most precious of all.

We love virtuously when we consider the other's interest to be as valuable as our own. We love others when we are honest, compassionate, courageous, and forgiving towards them. The list of virtues could go on, and they are virtuous because they are in some way loving. Virtue is what we all need to refine our nature and fulfill our destiny. We get it from each other, and many believe that we receive it from God or some greater Source. That is the true objective of the Best Life. What if our loving gestures are not accepted or even understood? That's okay. Virtue is honored because it requires effort and sometimes sacrifice. Somehow, virtue enriches, heals, and expands who we are.

LOVING VIRTUOUSLY

Loving our enemies does not mean having lunch with them every day or letting them abuse us in any way. Contact and communication may be limited with our enemies, but our intentions toward them, our hopes for them, and even our restraints toward them can be "loving". This can include tough love and other creative ways to give someone what they need. Not everyone will consciously give us love or openly receive our love. Their willingness to receive our love does not limit or affect our capacity to love. No feeling or act of love is ever wasted.

Fortunately, feelings of love and virtue cancel out negative biochemical reactions in our bodies generated by hate, jealously, revengefulness, and animosity. Those destructive biological reactions may not affect our enemies, but they can kill us by fostering cancer, heart disease, and other stress-related ailments. We need to congruently create a quality, virtuous self-concept. By doing so, we will have a life of relationships as good as we can make them. That life is priceless and can never be taken from us. At times, the other person may not contribute virtue to the relationship. Regardless, we make the relationship as good it can be. Their resistance does not take away the timeless benefits of our virtuous gestures.

Almost everything else that we value can be taken away. That includes our health, wealth, family, fun activities, power, beauty, and prestige. While these acquisitions can enrich our lives, they are perishable acquisitions that are easy to lose. If our mortal well-being is primarily dependent on any of those things, life can be filled with a desperate anxiety to hold on to what we can't control. The love-based Best Life can never be taken away. It can only be given up.

We are all unique, and our interests, talents, and opportunities will be different from everyone else. An exciting part of the Best Life is the personal journey of self-exploration and development. However, I am proposing that to fulfill our potential, and to make a beneficial difference in the world, we need to freely give and receive love. Our self-perception must give us permission to be a quality, loving person. We can create this identity or make it even stronger.

THE POWER OF LOVE

When I was a Judge Advocate General (JAG) in the US Air Force, I worked with many Vietnam Veterans. Morale was low because many American servicemen were spit on and spurned when they returned home. Some of them had lost all hope of ever having a Good Life, much less a Best Life. But there were exceptions. I received a postgraduate lesson on the Best Life from a veteran fighter pilot. He had been shot down over North Vietnam, captured, and was imprisoned for several years until the war ended. He had been a Prisoner of War (POW). I was fresh out of law school with a young family. I didn't serve in Vietnam, but I witnessed some of the human suffering from the war. This pilot shared with me his hard-earned lessons.

After he was shot down, he was captured, interrogated, and his wounds were superficially treated. He was then imprisoned. No, "imprisoned" is not a good word for being placed in an eight-feet-by-eight-feet hole in the ground covered by bamboo. He was repeatedly tortured and his life was constantly threatened. His leg was purposefully broken, and he didn't receive proper medical care. He was cut off from contact with the outside world and received false reports on the progress of the war. He didn't know up from down or in from out. His existence would seem intolerable for most us—beyond our strength to bear or endure. The water was filthy. His hole in the ground was pretty much just slippery muck. The food was meager when given, and he shrank into a living skeleton. Weeks turned into months, and months turned into years. However, he stayed alive. He was tempted to give up and die, but he *chose* to live.

Remarkably, he said that there were times that he felt freer than at any other point in his life. This was hard for me to comprehend. I was fascinated by this statement and wanted to understand. While in the hole, he created all kinds of number games and mind exercises to keep himself mentally busy. Miraculously, he kept his family relationships alive. Though physically separated from them, he found ways to give and receive love from his family. He had daily talks with his wife and children. He discussed his circumstances, and asked them questions about their lives. He even discussed what would happen when they were reunited once again. He imagined hearing their voices. They were far away, and yet in his heart and mind he felt close to them. He said he also loved God. He had a sense of how God could love him and yet allow him to live in pain and deprivation. He believed that God strengthened him.

Talking to his wife and God helped him curb the feelings of hatred and revenge that often surfaced. His captors were aloof and cruel. He often felt like retaliating and watching them suffer as he suffered. Fortunately, once in a while, he was assisted in some way by a compassionate guard. These infrequent acts of compassion kept him from generalizing and building irrational hatred toward an entire race of people.

He said that at times he would talk out loud to his family, or to God, and his heart would fill with so much love and gratitude that "sweet" tears would come to his eyes. He loved his family and God before the experience. But during the experience, he came to love them even more. That was the point that touched me. He escaped groveling in the pain, resentment, and filth of his physical circumstances. He said that never before, nor ever again would he have that much time to enjoy his family and embrace their love. Life outside of the hole—whether at home or at war—consisted of a myriad of activities and responsibilities. In the hole, he had no such distractions, and he focused almost entirely on his loved ones. In his words, they kept him alive and sane.

Love is powerful. Loving relationships are enduring, empowering, and sometimes just magical. When all else is lost, loving and virtuous relationships can bring a semblance of joy into your life. It can provide a sense of thriving even while living in a hole in the ground. A loving, virtuous life is the Best Life.

CHAPTER 2

Self-Concept and the Elusive Best Life

In order to transition from the Good Life to the Best Life, we must "recreate" our perception of self. In this chapter, we will explore the meanings of the Good Life, the Best Life, self-concept, and their relationships. Think of self-concept as an embedded belief system that defines our worth and our fundamental values. This perceived identity gives us *permission* and *motivation* to embrace the Good Life or the Best Life. We can't do anything without permission and motivation. They are the foundation from which we choose how to behave. Generally speaking, the Good Life is valuing the need to feel good above everything else. The Good Life is self-centered. On the other hand, the Best Life equally values our well-being and everyone else's. We can love others as much as our self, and sometimes even more. In the Best Life, the quality of our relationships is more important than just feeling good.

CHERRY PIES

When I was a child, I did a lot of daydreaming. I envied adults who seemed to have freedom to do whatever they wanted whenever they wanted. (This was before I paid taxes.) I perceived myself primarily as a "want-to-feel-good-person". I leaned toward the classic Good Life. I could not wait to be an adult so I could be free and fulfill the wonderful desires of my heart. I particularly enjoyed one daydream. In this particular daydream, I sat at a large table filled with a variety of beautiful, luscious pies baked to perfection. Of course there were several cherry pies—my favorite—and a few coconut cream pies piled high with whipped cream. My daydreams were exceptional because they engaged both my sense of smell and my taste buds. I sat at the table and looked around to discover I was gloriously alone. No silverware or napkins were there to hold me back. With gluttonous joy, I ate and ate those wonderful pies with my bare hands. Of course, in my dream I never got a stomachache. Later, I told my dad about the dream. He rained on my happy, little parade. He said that he remembered having similar thoughts as a teenager and actually ate two whole chocolate pies by himself in one sitting. They were his favorite. Unbelievably, he said that it made him vomit. As a result, he never ate another piece of chocolate pie again. I was devastated. So where was joy?

FIRST LOVE

Later on in my early adolescence, I fell in love. Oh, she was beautiful and heavenly: a 14-year-old with blonde hair and a turned-up nose. I would bump into her in the hallway at school and tingle all over when she looked at me—even if she frowned. Finally, I got up enough courage to say "hi", and a few days later I asked her how she was doing. She said "Fine" and then asked how I was doing. (Oh my gosh, this relationship was moving fast!) I remember wishing that I was an adult so I could be with her whenever I wanted. I started daydreaming about her. I was smitten. I could not imagine living without her. My heart could barely stand it. My life was planned out forever. I felt wonderful. Then one day as I was walking down the hall, I looked over at her locker. There she was between two open locker doors with another boy. They kissed. My heart broke. Tears came quickly to my eyes. I could barely go to school for a week. Where had my Good Life gone?

DEFENDING THE BEST LIFE

What is the Best Life—the life that we believe will bring us the most joy and happiness? It's easy to confuse the good with the *best*. As a child, I thought that I knew what would make me happy. It seemed rather simple: do what feels good now. However, I have learned that not everything that I sincerely desire leads to the Best Life. My desires can sometimes be deceiving. The vision of the Best Life is elusive for children, but I have also found that adulthood doesn't give us automatic wisdom.

Let's begin by exploring the idyllic dream of the Good Life. I have heard descriptions such as lounging on a beach, drooling over abundant assets and cash reserves, preening before a cheering crowd, lifting a beverage to a myriad of attractive friends, wandering through a beautiful home, painting the perfect picture, arguing before an admiring supreme court, or looking into the beautiful eyes of a loved one. Or maybe it is something simple like living one day without pain, never having to say goodbye, having enough to eat, not worrying about death, time to read a book, or getting your teeth fixed. Take a moment to see and sense your dream of the Good Life. Make it a movie in your imagination if you can. Now, imagine that it is more than a dream and you are stepping into the experience right now. Enjoy the beginning, middle, and end of the dream. When you finish, pause for a moment. Was it a compelling representation of the life that you desire?

Now let's take the next step. Ask yourself, "What will this dream get me?" In other words, why is the dream so attractive to you? Say to yourself: "If I had this dream in all of its fullness, it would give me ______________." Fill in the blank. Answer quickly from your heart—don't intellectualize and talk yourself into something. You have the answer already available—get it. Feel in your heart, mind, and body the sensations of getting what you really want. Perhaps what you want is not a material thing. Perhaps it is an "emotional state" in which you long to dwell. Whatever it is, think about it. Think about *why* you want it. Maybe you're curious about why you had to go through a dream to gain this insight? View the dream as a stepping-stone to get something more important. Clarify what you want. When, where, with whom, and how do you obtain it?

Acquiring the Best Life requires knowing what we want, and then doing what is necessary to obtain it. This exercise can help you identify what you really want out of life. It can be an essential step in identifying the Best Life. Are you satisfied with your vision of the life you wish to live? Or do you want something different? Now ask yourself, "What are my beliefs that led me to think that having the dream would really get me what I wanted?" You could not want the dream without somehow assuming that the dream was connected to your greater desire. For example, as a 14-year-old boy, I somehow believed that getting what made me feel good was the Good Life. I assumed that having more and more of what me feel good was the "Best Life". Whether it was eating luscious pies or just being with my girlfriend (that's what I thought would make me feel the best). Feeling good was the bottom line for me. I assumed that "feeling good" was what I really wanted: the true manifestation of the Good Life.

THE POWER OF HIDDEN ASSUMPTIONS

Often our assumptions about the Good Life go unquestioned. They appear as common sense or common knowledge. We accept them without giving much thought. That can be misleading. I no longer want to sit around and eat pies or forever look dreamingly at a girlfriend. (Although I do enjoy looking at my beautiful wife.) That may qualify as the Good Life, but it's not the Best Life. I have since learned a useful word: *insatiable.* It crushed my childish assumption. Webster's definition of insatiable is: "Always wanting more; not able to be satisfied"[1]. My lusty appetite for feeling good was insatiable, or never to be fully satisfied. I believed that if it felt good, more and more was required to have the Best Life. This is particularly true for bodily appetites and ego-based status. Pleasurable experiences are wonderful and necessary parts of life. However, disappointment and heartache occur when you try to build the Best Life on the number and quality of pleasurable experiences. The Best Life is not the proverbial, sensual Good Life.

Let's assume that all we want is the Good Life. How many luscious pies eaten qualify for the Good Life? How many days of high-intensity, glandular-inspired romance qualify for the Good Life? How many consecutive, increased, quarterly earnings in one's business constitute the Good Life? How many zeros to the left of the decimal point in your bank account constitute the Good Life? Winning or achieving the highest award may require a huge investment of energy and life itself. Once achieved, is that the beginning or the end of the Good Life? What's next that's worthwhile? What makes more and more—or even the higher quality of something—a step towards the Best Life?

PLEASURE TOLERANCE

"Pleasure tolerance" is a unique risk of insatiability. The more we experience a pleasure, the more we need next time to maintain that intensity level of pleasure. In the world of egotistical and bodily pleasures, reaching satiation is impossible. If the satiation of these desires is the apex of your Good Life, you'll never have it. In a world of paradox, we are often confused whether more is less, or less is more. Carefully evaluate whether your definition of the Good Life is the apex of something, or the perpetuation of the apex. In other words, are you seeking for a peak experience, or are you seeking to stay at the peak? If you are fortunate, perhaps it is neither, and you do not confuse the insatiable Good Life with the Best Life. Give your self-concept a break—don't expect it to do the impossible. Romance, business profitability, zeros to the left of the decimal point, and many other things can contribute to the Best Life. They add spice and texture, but striving for satiation doesn't even lead to the Good Life, much less the Best Life. Be honest with yourself. How much do you really need of what you want to have the Good Life?

DISCOVERING OUR HIDDEN ASSUMPTIONS ABOUT LIFE

We know that *what we believe* guides our behaviors towards the Good Life or the Best Life. Recognizing the *assumptions supporting our beliefs* about the Good Life or the Best Life help us know if we're moving in the right direction. Try this cognitive exercise for discovering hidden assumptions about your life. Take a moment and write a brief statement describing the life that you desire. After writing it out, ask yourself, "What else would I have to believe to make my desired life a reality?" Your answers to this question constitute your assumptions. Review the following example before writing. It will help you understand more clearly what I mean by an "assumption". As an example, assume that part of your desired life is "to maximize your potential abilities and personal gifts". What are necessary logical assumptions that are required to make this a reality? The assumptions will help you recognize why this part of life is desirable to you. The following are assumptions that logically support the need to maximize abilities and gifts:

- You must assume that you can accurately identify specific gifts and talents. If you can't do so, the desire to maximize is thwarted.
- You assume that maximizing the gifts is more desirable than just having the gifts.

- You assume that maximizing the gifts has a value equal to or greater than the effort required to maximize them.
- You assume that you have times, places, and people that allow you to maximize the gifts.
- You assume to understand what it means to maximize the gifts. In other words, does "maximize" mean to improve the gifts? Or does it mean to better use the gifts to accomplish other objectives?
- You assume that you understand what maximizing the gifts will get you. For example, does maximizing the gifts give you a sense of achievement or does it give you status by impressing other people?

Now let's see how the assumptions can direct us to the Good Life on one hand or the Best Life on the other. Remember that the Good Life focuses primarily on selfish interests and the Best Life focuses primarily on virtuous relationships. What we value as a gift or ability may reveal whether we lean toward the Good Life or the Best Life. Assume that we want to maximize the talent of eating three large pizzas without upsetting our stomach. We can agree that that tastes more like the Good Life than the Best Life. It's pretty obvious.

Now let's consider a more complex scenario. Consider maximizing the gift to sing. The gift of singing does not necessarily reflect the Good Life or the Best Life. We need to examine a few assumptions. What is valuable about the ability to sing? What if our primary desire was to attract friends who would admire and praise us? If our primary desire is to feed our ego, then we are leaning toward the Good Life. However, if our primary desire is to connect with people who enjoy good music, then we are probably leaning towards the Best Life. What if maximizing the gift of singing means demonstrating our potential for the sole purpose of attracting admiration from others? We aren't looking to maximize our singing potential, but we want to sing well enough to attract attention. That doesn't necessarily reveal our motives. We must ask ourselves: "Am I looking for an easy way to build my ego, or am I looking for friendships?" Our motives determine our commitment to the Good Life or the Best Life.

The most distinguishing element between a Good Life value and a Best Life value is how we treat others. Generally, most activities cannot be categorized as "Good" or "Best". The nature of the activity is often neutral when standing alone. The difference resides in the *intentions* behind our behaviors! Refer to your motives and assumptions as you write the description of your desired life. You can readily recognize whether you are moving toward the Good Life or the Best Life. Perhaps, you have mixed them up. Sometimes, you may want one, and other times you may desire the other. It's time to get off the fence!

Choosing the Good Life or the Best Life is a free choice based on personal preferences. No one can make us want either one. However, clarifying our motives and assumptions helps us make our decisions. We are moving relentlessly toward one or the other, minute by minute. Periodically re-evaluating our self-concept and our life destination can protect us from mindlessly wandering through life. As you move along in this book, you can clarify both your self-concept and your understanding of the Best Life. As you do so, you can more clearly understand what you really want and how to attain it.

We need to incorporate feel-good factors into our Best Life. That includes discovering and developing our talents, pursuing our passionate interests, and enjoying the goodness and beauty of the world. All of these factors may enrich our life and fulfill our sense of self. The Best Life is not about constant self-denial, self-sacrifice, and no fun or enjoyment. The Good Life does not have a monopoly on feeling good and enjoying the world. The Best Life incorporates all of this, but not as our primary objectives. Ideally, we mix having fun and feeling good with caring for and serving others. In fact, we give and serve better when we are joyful, refreshed, and invigorated.

RELATIONSHIPS AND THE BEST LIFE

The Best Life is about relationships. Having relationships is not enough. You have all sorts of them whether you want them or not. Your choice refers to the nature and significance of those connections. *The quality of your relationships is directly related to the quality of your life.* "Quality" here means the value that you place on others. High-quality relationships are those in which you highly value the other person. That motivates you to treat them lovingly or virtuously. Low-quality relationships are those in which you value others less than yourself, and you are motivated to use them for your self-interest without seriously considering their well-being. The Best Life entails a life of honorable connections, and the Good Life reflects a life of self-serving pragmatic connections.

THE SAMURAI

I assume that we all have enemies—people who are intentionally or unintentionally dangerous to our well-being. Can we have a quality relationship with them? How can we treat them virtuously if they are trying to hurt us? We cannot control their intentions or their behavior. However, we can influence the quality of the relationship because we are part of it. What difference does it make? Who wants to have a relationship with an enemy? It makes all the difference in the world, because it affects the quality of our self-concept, our very being.

Let me use an extreme example. Take two enemies at war who are trying to kill each other. Assume both enemies are filled with anger, vengeance, and hatred. They come to battle with these passions, and one wins. With inflamed, hate-filled passion, the victor exults over the kill. Now, assume that two enemies are battling. One of them is possessed with anger and the other is a virtuous Samurai. The Samurai is a trained warrior committed to the "Bushido Code", which is the "Seven Virtues of the Samurai". This warrior is motivated by love of family, home, and duty. He is fighting to protect his homeland and family, not simply to vent his anger. A Samurai's heart and motives are honorable, respectful, and virtuous. He has disciplined his heart and his body. The Samurai's Best Life includes respecting and honoring his enemy, even during war.

You may wonder how virtue could be important when one person kills another person. That question demonstrates why this example is extreme. A killing is always a tragedy. War is no exception. However, motives and the purpose for fighting affect self-concepts before and after the battle. For example, what can motivate the anger and hate-filled warrior to kill again? Anger and hatred are passionate motivations. What might he be angry about? Who knows? Is anger and hatred limited to the context of war? Certainly not! What value does the hate-filled warrior place on human life? He has already proved that he values his hatred more than human life in at least one context. How would you expect that hate-filled warrior to treat other people outside of the context of war? How would you feel if he was angry with you or hated you?

On the other hand, the Samurai embraces his loved ones and cherishes their safety. Their safety and well-being call him to arms—not a self-centered passion of hatred or anger. The Samurai can continue to be loving and honorable outside of war because that has become his nature. Additionally, the Samurai is not inwardly hounded by recurring anger and hatred. The biochemical reactions within the body stirred up by anger and hatred are self-destructive. The Samurai can wish his enemy well. He can hope that the enemy will do better in the next life where the ancestors dwell.

When we engage with others in contexts seeking a virtuous, loving connection, the relationship can benefit both people. Relating with others to primarily satisfy our personal appetites and passions is low living. Others become instruments to selfishly use. Love and virtue cannot nurture a relationship based on greed and self-interest. Therefore, one of the objectives of the Best Life is to discover *how* we can connect with other people to give and receive love. This intention can transform a difficult context like a conflict into something beneficial for all parties. The Best Life does not require us to have any particular context. We don't have to be where we most want to be, or be with whomever we want, or be doing what is most enjoyable. That is not required criteria for the Best Life. Seeking quality relationships can give us a portion of the Best Life wherever we are, whomever we're with, and whatever we're doing.

MEANING AND THE BEST LIFE

There is another asset that quality relationships add to the Best Life. Life without *meaning* is not a life worth living. You may be aware that the fundamental meanings in life are derived from your relationships with others. Meaning gives life purpose—something to live for. This "something" is what you end up valuing. We want to acquire those "things" that take us to what we most value. In a nutshell, pursuing and obtaining what you value ends up being the Good Life or the Best Life. Recent research validates the preeminence of *meaning* as the key to the Best Life.

This research takes meaning to an even loftier level. Results help distinguish meaning from happiness. Researchers have found that a life of meaning is healthier than pursuing Good Life happiness. It seems common sense that happier people are healthier than less happy people. However, research contradicts this belief. In this context, happiness was defined as feeling good in the moment. This was associated with selfish "taking" behavior and a hedonistic approach to life. On the other hand, meaning was associated with selfless "giving" behavior. Feeling good actually included not having to help others, and not having others interfere with a selfish, self-absorbed pursuit of happiness. But meaning was merging oneself into something greater than self, and that normally included caring for others.

Interestingly, happy people were found to have the same particular gene expression pattern as someone feeling lonely, grieving, or being threatened. Happy people were also grouped with lonely, threatened, or grieving people in being more susceptible to bacterial-based disease than meaning-oriented people. Meaning-oriented people had gene expression patterns to ward off viruses, which are diseases normally transferred through human contact. In other words, people with Best Life motives are more naturally protected from disease than others in a world of constant exposure to different people. For example, people in the happy category are more likely to get sick by just being around other people.

A life focused on meaning with a balanced menu of happiness-oriented activities seems to be the optimum. Of course, our "Me! Me!" culture reverses the order. Building a healthy self-concept and more rewarding life means going against the societal grain and swimming upstream. We are learning more about the benefits of a meaning-filled life rather than a life pursuing just happiness. A search for meaning is not the classic pursuit for happiness. Fortunately, joy and well-being ensue when we give our self to something higher.[2]

THE AIRLINE EXECUTIVE

Here is a real-life example of how mismatched values lead to severe consequences, as told to me by a colleague several years ago. An airline executive attended a leadership training seminar with other executives. In a variety of indoor and outdoor contexts, the executives engaged in various projects while rotating their individual roles and responsibilities. Their days were long and exhausting, both physically and emotionally. No one could complete their responsibilities without heavily relying on someone else's assistance and integrity. Circumstances were created to test each participant's commitment to project outcomes in spite of physical and emotional sacrifices required to get the job done.

Hidden opportunities to accelerate the project's completion and highlight an individual's potential "star status" were craftily integrated into the setup. Obvious shortcuts were created that required breaking project rules and misleading colleagues. This made cheating easy. In the end, the seminar exposed participants who lied and cheated to win. The project itself was a tool to reveal participant's values. Obviously, the training was not about acquiring skill sets, as much as revealing participant's values and their loyalty to relationships. The airline executive was a superstar at getting projects done. In the process, he also showed little respect for rules or loyalty to colleagues. I have often wondered if his boss used him in a similar manner.

The executive was shocked to starkly face how his self-concept (a "get it done", bottom-line executive) compromised what he thought were predominant values in his life. This disconcerting revelation was life-changing. He went home, resigned from his job, gathered his family, and went to another city. He started looking for a new life and a new self-concept. He left behind a high-paying position, colleagues jealous of his success, and promises of promotion. I never heard how all of this worked out in the long run. He recognized that his behavior and feelings during the seminar revealed a powerful conflict in his perceived identity and values. He discovered that his perceived "high-producing executive self" ruthlessly drove him and others to achieve business goals with little sensitivity to others. His behavior revealed that he valued his professional success more than his relationships with people. Over the years he had told himself that he was honest and loyal, but to what?

He uncovered two conflicting values. One set of values was to be financially successful, make big money, and be honored and revered in the business world. At the same time, a lesser set of values was to be a quality, ethical human being, a man who really cared about other people, particularly his family and colleagues. While he was cashing big checks and receiving company accolades, he could not understand why he was often uncomfortable looking in the mirror.

He had well-reasoned excuses, justifications, and explanations for breaking rules and manipulating people for his company's benefit. But in fact, it was not really for the company. It was for himself. He was a divided man. He wanted to be an ethical, caring colleague, and an exemplary father to his family. However, this was a secondary value, and he had to manipulate the meanings of his actions to reconcile both of his identities. He excused and justified his cutthroat behavior to believe he was a more caring and ethical than he actually was. His dominant value was winning. He unconsciously valued being recognized as winner, a high achiever. He wanted the Good Life.

The experience at the seminar was revelatory. Somehow, through the intensity and transparency of the experience, he clearly saw the deception within his divided self. Starkly confronting the divided parts was like jumping into a freezing shower. Seeing himself more clearly and more honestly provoked him to reevaluate himself and his values. He woke up and reprioritized his life-values. He reversed his priorities, choosing an ethical, virtuous self over the pride-driven superstar.

The point of the example is not to simply judge which self-concept was the "right" one. Someone might choose the superstar image and give no thought to the morality of the choice. The point is that he recognized his divided self-concept, didn't like it, did something about it, and he pervasively changed. Please note *what* changed. The priority of his values changed. Please recognize that both of his conflicting values were about the *quality of his relationships*. He was torn between valuing others to feed his ego on one hand, and valuing others because he cared about their well-being on the other. These are the conflicting values of the Good Life or the Best Life. Winning and being the best achieved the egotistical Good Life. Ironically, to achieve his precious accolades and honors, he gave himself permission to "walk all over" the very people who he relied upon to build his ego. Contrarily, valuing other people's well-being motivated and gave him permission to treat them ethically and virtuously, even if it cost him status and money. Relationships were at the bottom of both values. The conflict was all about the quality of the relationships.

WHAT THE AIRLINE EXECUTIVE TAUGHT US

Let's review what we gleaned from the airline executive's experience:

- We see again the permission and motivational power of fundamental values and one's self-perception.

- We appreciate how difficult it can be to change our perceived self-concept.
- Self-deceit is real, and it exists to justify getting what the Good Life wants.
- Incongruent self-concepts and values cause conflict in our life.
- Intense life experiences can starkly unveil our competing values and self-concepts.
- Reconciling competing self-concepts and values can lead to pervasive life changes including jobs, relationships, lifestyles, health, and well-being.
- How we value the quality of our relationships determines what we're willing to do to get the Good Life or the Best Life.

FINDING PEACE IN OUR SELF-CONCEPT

Knowing who we are requires a clear, honest sensitivity to our conflicting values and competing self-concepts. This confusion requires a resolution. Value-based conflicts are deep rooted and difficult to reconcile. We react to changing our identity in a similar manner to having our physical life threatened. We go into survival mode. This makes sense when we realize that changing our core values and identity requires giving up a part of our self. It's similar to thinking that a part of us has to die for another part of us to come alive. That stirs up a lot of emotions and resistance.

The airline executive example demonstrates the key to creating the Best Life. We can't overestimate the importance of having quality, virtuous relationships. Our self-concept depicts the type and quality of relationships that we value. The executive had to choose what type of relationship was most important to him. Did he primarily value relationships because they lauded his image as an executive superstar? If so, he had to value behaviors that would get him recognition. Ironically, they corrupted how he valued other people's well-being and gave him permission to deceive and manipulate them. However, the honorable self-concept was more other-oriented, seeking the benefit and welfare of others as well as self. With this concept, he perceived himself as an "ethical, virtuous person". He could not concurrently embody both personas.

Internal dissonance and anxiety was created by muddying-up his ethical conscience and trying to live a double life. He had to give up pretending that he could satisfy both sides of the fence. He was continually violating his conscience, and that had to stop. He did not give up wanting to be a great executive, but he gave up making it his number one priority. This discussion about our airline executive stimulates a few more useful questions for us to ponder and relate to ourselves. Why wasn't he able to see this conflict more clearly at an earlier date? How was he able to deceive himself into believing that he was honorable while he was behaving deceitfully? Why was his reaction to this revelation about himself so radical that he would quit his job, uproot his family, and step into the unknown?

Let's accept that we have a working self-concept and a sense of what we want as our desired life. As this chapter ends, we can be more sensitive to what permits and motivates us to make our most important decisions. We can come to grips with how we prioritize our values. We can honestly question how much we value quality, virtuous relationships. Do we need to amend or change our self-concept and more clearly prioritize our values? The following chapters will address how to navigate the path of change and the obstacles you may encounter by doing so.

NOTES

1. 2014. In *Merriam-Webster.com*. Retrieved May 8, 2014, from http://www.merriam-webster.com/dictionary/insatiable

2. McCraty, R (2003). Heart-Brain Neurodynamics: *The Making of Emotions*. HeartMath Research Center, Institute of HeartMath, Boulder Creek, CA, Publication No. 03-015.

CHAPTER 3

Are We Just Meat?

There are serious obstacles to obtaining the Best Life. One of the most pervasive and pernicious beliefs is that we can't change who we are. This belief takes away hope and effort to seriously change who we are, or who we *think* we are. This powerful belief affects you in ways you may not recognize. In this chapter, we confront this crippling obstacle.

You may wonder what "meat" has to do with self-concept and the Best Life. It's time to deal with the meat. So far, you have learned that self-concept affects how you live your life and what you believe is the Best Life. Hopefully, you are intrigued about creating your own self-concept and the expectations of what you can become. In particular, you may hope that you have a real choice about becoming who you perceive yourself to be and the "life" that you wish to live. However, as with most good "things", there are obstacles in obtaining them. The **Theory of Determinism** is a pervasive theory that has permeated our Western culture.[1] It threatens the right to *choose* your self-concept, or your Best Life. Determinism is all about the "meat".

Essentially, this theory asserts that your genetic makeup and your environment control everything that you think and do. In other words, in any given situation, because of your genetics and past experiences, you are pre-programmed to act and to think in a certain way in that situation. You have no choice to do anything else. If that is true, then your self-concept is pre-programmed and your idea of the Best Life is not a voluntary choice on your part. Therefore, why pretend that you have a choice and spend energy trying to do something that determinism says is impossible? Although there are several variations of the Theory of Determinism, we are addressing the deterministic themes that challenge moral choice and conscience.

INFLUENCE OF DETERMINISM

So what is at stake here? Paradoxically, scientific research suggests that people who believe that they have "choice" are happier and more fulfilled than those who do not.[2] So, really your health, joy, and well-being are at stake. Fortunately, although determinism is a favored scientific theory, some scientists disagree with some of its tenets and provide good reasons to believe in choice.

Perhaps you have not directly studied or thought through the Theory of Determinism. If so, you may think that the theory does not really influence you. As I will demonstrate, the assumptions and premises of determinism are implicitly influencing our entire culture, including you. If you have studied the theory and recognize its direct influence on your sense of responsibility and accountability for your actions, you are obviously caught in a dilemma. To believe in choice requires accepting personal responsibility for your actions. Determinism diminishes personal accountability for your thoughts and actions. Some people prefer to deflect responsibility from self and avoid accountability. However, most of these people do want to hold others accountable.

Do you wish to believe that you have significant choices leading to your Best Life, or do you accept the fate supposedly inherent in your body's biology? To help you decide, it's time to address the obstacle of determinism.

THE DILEMMA

René Descartes, a French philosopher, stated this dilemma a few centuries ago.[3] He wondered whether the human mind was merely a function of the physical brain, or if it had a non-body, non-biological component. If the mind is solely a product of the biological brain, all human thought would have to originate in the cells and tissues of the body, especially the nervous system. If the mind at least partially existed outside of the body's biological functions, then the mind could have thoughts originating from non-body sources, like the "soul" or a seemingly immaterial intelligence. His theory is still referred to as Cartesian Dualism. The implications of this dilemma affect almost every part of the human experience.

Let's review some of the limitations of determinism. Again, if our bodies (made of protoplasm, cells, and biochemical reactions) create our thoughts, we are at the mercy of our bodily functions. Some scientists explain our behavior as the materials of our body reacting to the laws around us. In other words, in whatever context we find the body, laws will act on the materials of the body, and we have to respond in a particular way. Our body's biology—including our brain—make us do what we do. We will also think according to what the bio-chemical reactions in our body make us think. This theory asserts that we have no choice to violate what the natural law requires the body to do including the brain.

For example, assume that you are in a store and discover a small item you really want but can't pay for. You are tempted to put it in your pocket and steal it. Natural law operates on your nervous system, brain cells, and bodily functions in its present condition. The affect of those laws on your body will determine if you grab the item as a "five-finger discount". According to determinism you have no *moral* choice about stealing.

If that is true, then no universal morals or virtues can exist. What we might call morals or virtues are biochemically created. Love, integrity, courage, compassion, etc. are nothing more than cellular excretions and secretions of the body. God, a Higher Power, or a Supreme Being, cannot exist because natural law is supreme in the world of determinism. The existence of God would mean that natural law could be overruled, and predictability of natural law would be compromised. Determinism implies that you are not free to choose your friends, your preferred colors, your favorite food or your most interesting subject to study. That stuff is all programmed. There is much more to this, but you get the picture. Determinism takes the meaning and purpose out of life. It also makes you whatever you are, no matter what you think or wish. In fact, it even *controls* what you think or what you wish. Now, let's get on with the meat.

THINKING MEAT

Many scholars including the renowned world historian, Huston Smith, passionately argue against determinism. Eloquently supporting his view, he playfully passes along an excerpt from a science fiction story that satirizes the proposition that humans are only their bodies. In this story, an alien explorer has come to earth to investigate. He returns to his commander and reports the following:

> "They're made out of meat."
>
> "Meat…"
>
> "There's no doubt about it. We picked several from different parts of the planet, took them aboard our recon vessels, and probed them all the way through. They're completely meat."
>
> "That's impossible. What about the radio signals? The messages to the stars?"
>
> "They use the radio waves to talk, but the signals don't come from them. The signals come from machines."
>
> "So who made the machines? That's what we want to contact."
>
> "They made the machines. That's what I'm trying to tell you. Meat made the machines."
>
> "That's ridiculous. How can meat make a machine? You're asking me to believe in sentient meat."
>
> "I'm not asking you, I'm telling you. These creatures are the only sentient race in the sector and they're made out of meat."
>
> "Maybe they're like the Orfolei. You know, a carbon-based intelligence that goes through a meat stage."
>
> "Nope. They're born meat and they die meat. We studied them for several of their lifespan, which didn't take too long. Do you have any idea of the life span of meat?"
>
> "Spare me. Okay, maybe they're only part meat. You know like the Weddilei. But I told you, we probed them. They're meat all the way through."
>
> "No brain?"
>
> "Oh, there's a brain all right. It's just that the brain is made out of meat!"

"So... what does the thinking?"

"You're not understanding, are you? The brain does the thinking. The meat!"

"Thinking meat. You're asking me to believe in thinking meat!"

"Yes, thinking meat! Conscious meat! Loving meat. Dreaming meat! The meat is the whole deal!"[4]

In other words, where does the intelligence come from to do the conscious thinking and loving? The alien finds it hard to believe that a piece of meat can think. That is a good question. Knowing that you are more than something out of the "meat-box", someone with choices to increase your intelligence and capabilities, someone that can choose at the crossroads of destiny, will enliven your being. You can actually feel hope and purpose in managing the expectations of who and what you can be. What is a life without hope? Determinism takes all of that away.

NOT A VICTIM

Think of the logical implications if your thoughts and your mind are exclusively driven by biology. How easy it would be to feel like a victim, powerless to make important moral or ethical choices because your material body is pre-programmed. But then again, some people wish to diminish their personal accountability and pass the blame to forces they cannot control—forces like determinism. Some people just want to hitch a ride on fate hoping it won't be too bad.

However, it is not logically necessary to believe that your life is biologically determined, and that you have no choice about how you behave. In fact, just believing in determinism can hurt you. The noted social scientist, Kenneth Gergen, reports that research shows that persons who believe they have a degree of control in their life (rather than being a pawn) are "better off—more optimistic, more effective in their performance, more likely to be leaders, more oriented to action, and so on."[5] Additionally, the esteemed researcher, Mertin Seligman, argues that a major cause of depression in human beings is indeed the sense of helplessness to control one's world.

I realize that determinism is a scientific theory. Perhaps you are not a scientist in the field of genetics or biology. Neither am I. I will not attempt to critique scientific literature to conclusively persuade you that determinism is a false theory. However, please keep in mind that not all scientists buy this theory, and that its **validity is a matter of opinion**. There are logical, legitimate reasons to believe otherwise, whether or not you are a scientist. I want to give you enough information so that you can responsibly believe in moral choice, and that you can responsibly create your own self-concept and Best Life.

DETERMINISM AND ACCOUNTABILITY

Let's take a look at the results of a scientific experiment that supports the importance of humans believing that they have moral choices in their lives. A group of students were evenly divided, and one group read an excerpt that promoted determinism, and the other group did not. All the students were then given hypothetical scenarios and were asked to choose appropriate punishments for each scenario. Those who read the excerpts on determinism gave less punishment than those who did not read the excerpts.[6] It appears that the students influenced by determinism felt less inclined to punish someone who "couldn't help themselves". They viewed the "perpetrators" as victims of their own biology. Imagine how these students could begin to view themselves, their own behavior, and of course their own self-concept. We could reasonably assume that these students could view themselves as *less* accountable for their actions, and therefore give less forethought to their next act.

WHAT CONSTITUTES A MAN?

We could list numerous examples of how deterministic beliefs about self-concept affect all phases of life. Let's touch on a few. Marriage counselors often see the effect of spouses believing in biologically determined self-concept. The belief itself can lead to marital discord. A couple was contemplating divorce, and the wife claimed that her husband's philandering could not be tolerated. She felt deceived, and that her husband was disloyal to her by committing adultery. He said that she did not understand him. He said that he was a man, and men were born to not "pass up skirts". It's just part of being a man. Why should she criticize him for being a man? He was a man when she married him and he would always be a man. What choice did he have? He claimed to still love her, but she didn't buy the explanation and felt used and deceived.

The counselor proposed a solution. Each spouse was to accept the other spouse's concept of what constitutes a "man". If she could agree with his self-concept that men can't help but "philander", she could be more tolerant and understanding if he made a "mistake". She could thereby soften her belief that he was being disloyal to her if he committed adultery. On the other hand, he was asked to believe that part of being a man was controlling his passions and emotionally protecting his spouse. This meant that he wasn't determined to philander, and that he could make moral choices. He could therefore accept more responsibility for controlling his sexual appetite.

These new beliefs required a shift in both spouses self-concept. The therapist hoped that each spouse—by changing their beliefs—would have more tolerance and compassion for one another. However, their beliefs were too deeply embedded to change upon demand. The proposed changes threatened each of their self-concepts. The proposed solution failed.

SOCIAL DARWINISM

The same counselor had another couple also contemplating divorce. This time the issue was money: who makes it and who should spend it. Interestingly, the husband and wife both agreed that humans were instinctively motivated to put themselves first. She wanted to spend the money that she made as she wished. He wanted to spend the money that he made as he wished. They could not agree on how to contribute their earnings to mutual expenses that benefited both of them such as rent and utilities. Each one argued that in life you had to (predetermined) take care of yourself first. Money meant freedom to each spouse, and they believed strongly that they could not give up their ultimate self-interests. They both were committed to Social Darwinism, the widely accepted theory that we are biologically driven to always put ourselves first.[7] The therapist had difficulty in convincing them that dividing expenses at some agreed upon percentage was not favoring one over the other. The couple divorced.

EFFECTS OF DETERMINISM

The potential effects of determinism and biologically justified self-concepts can be extreme. Hitler and his Nazi regime believed that Jews were biologically inferior to the German race. In fact, Jews were not thought to be genetically human. With this self-concept, the Nazis excused themselves from exterminating Jews on biological grounds. "We kill other animals and why not Jews if they threaten the purity of our race?"

Arguments of slavery follow the same ridiculous assumptions and logic. Even the perspective of "blue blood nobility" is clothed in the justifications of an arrogant self-perception. The blue blood was destined to rule, and those with other blood were destined to serve. Belief in our self-concept gives permission and motivation, and can even determine who we can kill or enslave.

In today's politically explosive world, various factions use genetics to justify changing or maintaining laws. For example, genetic determinism has allegedly explained criminal behavior, psychological disorders, and sexual preferences. Scientists agree that genetics contributes to many inclinations, personality traits, physiology and personal preferences. Scientists disagree about whether genetics is the sole and sufficient cause of these characteristics and behaviors. This scientific conflict leads to public and societal conflict.

For example, are criminals genetically determined to be criminals? Do they have a choice? Historically, some scientific theories have proposed that they are determined, and other theories disagree. Society will logically treat criminals who they believe have choice differently than criminals who cannot help themselves. Money is well spent on rehabilitation if criminals can actually change their behavior. However, why spend the money and effort if society believes their behavior is fixed? Our culture is split on this issue. Perhaps you have seen the television documentaries on our nation's "Toughest Prisons".

Let us view determinism from the criminals' perspective. Does it make a practical difference whether a criminal believes they are determined or not? We may think that beliefs cannot change a genetically determined behavior.

However, let us assume for a moment that a criminal really is determined. In this hypothetical the criminal believes they have choice. What will happen? We have to assume that criminal behavior will continue, but to what extent? The criminal may desire to stop their unlawful behavior and work hard at rehabilitation. Those efforts might reduce the number of crimes committed and their severity. We can once again appreciate the power of belief to affect even a determined behavior.

Let us turn to another example. Conflicting self-concepts among societal members can create fear and animosity. Let us take the conflict between homosexual and heterosexual self-concepts as examples. Let us put aside the religious, moral, political, legal, and financial conflicts surrounding this issue. I will not advocate for either side. I am only raising the issue to illustrate the powerful influences of self-concepts. Please do not slip into advocating for the homosexual or heterosexual side of this controversy. It is easy to do. Instead, think about the power of self-concept in complicating the resolution of the conflict.

Think about the survival instincts of preserving life. The drive to stay alive gives us permission to do almost anything. Now consider that a deeply held self-concept represents our identity, which can significantly represent life itself. We can feel driven to fight for our core identities like we fight for oxygen. If we lose our core identity, can we recreate ourselves to be someone else? That is for many an unknown, and we may fear the unknown more than anything.

Homosexuality can be perceived as a core identity. Likewise, heterosexuality can be a core identity. Both sides wish to survive and preserve who they believe themselves to be. Unfortunately, both side's core self-concepts are often threatened by the full expression of the other side's self-concept. Creating full space for the expression of one identity seems to require infringing on the identity of the other. What is the result? These perceived survival threats chill each side's attempts at empathy, compassion, and negotiation. Unconscious, strongly held self-concepts can create schisms in society.

Let us be more specific about the self-concept conflict between homosexuals and heterosexuals. Assume that some homosexuals' full expression of their self-concept requires them to be legally married or have a legally recognized union with their partner. If unable to have this marriage or union, their identity is threatened. When this happens we can understand the intense emotions and behaviors they experience to preserve their identity.

Does the same self-concept threat apply to heterosexuals? Yes. Many heterosexuals' core identities are wrapped up in being a mother, father, husband, wife, or a blood offspring of a traditional marriage. When these traditional identities are threatened by a change in the definition of family, their self-concepts are threatened. When this happens they understandably react intensely to preserve their perceived selves. The homosexuals and heterosexuals can view one another as enemies and threats to their psychological survival. That does not create a context for resolution.

Due consideration should be given the role of self-concept in this conflict. Effort should be made to determine what are the underlying assumptions of homosexuality and heterosexuality that affect self-preservation. These assumptions should be reviewed, tested, honored, and respected. In doing so creative resolutions may be found to preserve the most essential elements of each identity and allow them to co-exist. If this empathic approach is not taken, I fear that all other arguments will continue to be motivated by fear and animosity. Valuing and honoring one another, irrespective of our conflicting self-concepts, open doors to peaceful, compassionate, co-existence. Perceived self-concept matters to self and society.

CONCLUSION

You have had a glimpse of how determinism affects you and society, both directly and indirectly. You are affected whether or not you understand anything about the nature and depth of this theory. It so permeates our culture that you are affected by determinism outside of your conscious awareness. Choice or no choice is at the heart of actually creating a self-concept. Believing in determinism and no choice precludes the whole endeavor of continually creating who you perceive yourself to be. It also "determines" what else you can or cannot believe. Let's review the main ideas of determinism discussed in this chapter:

- Determinism means that you are not morally responsible for your thoughts and actions. Society can choose to hold you accountable by enforcing its laws, but you cannot morally choose to obey or disobey. You do what you "have to" do.
- Your thoughts do not affect who you are. Instead, they simply reflect what your protoplasm, biochemistry and genetics have determined you to be.
- Determinism requires you to be ultimately selfish and incapable of caring about others as much or more than yourself. In other words, true altruistic love cannot exist. Everyone's motives (including yours) are motivated first by selfishness. You cannot trust anyone to ultimately care about your interests ahead of their own interests.
- You have no unique creativity that is beyond your cells and tissues playing out their pre-programmed designs.
- A Higher Power, Higher Intelligence, God or a theistic being cannot exist to interact or intervene in your or anyone else's life. No influence outside of Natural Law is any influence at all.
- You don't morally owe anybody anything. Attending to someone else's interest is only a setup to get what you want.
- Being independent of others and not having to rely on their benevolence is a desirable objective.
- Life has no purpose beyond working out the biochemical processes of your body that have been set in motion. Life just is—no matter if you desire otherwise. Needing purpose in your life is meaningless according to Determinism.
- The Good Life is the playing out of your bodily processes and mechanisms. It is what it is!

YOU HAVE A CHOICE

There are more implications, but you get the idea. Now that you have a grasp on the powerful implications of determinism on your life and society's well-being, let's take the next step. There are persuasive arguments to believe in determinism. There are also persuasive arguments to *not* believe in determinism, but to believe in choice. You need to feel confident that believing or not believing in determinism is a choice and *not* prescribed by science. You can rationally and scientifically decide not to embrace determinism, but rather cling to choice. Examples are provided to support this. Remember that these examples and explanations are not exhaustive, and therefore references are given to further study determinism if you wish. As an afterthought, do you have a choice whether to study or not study more about determinism? How will that decision be made? **YOU ARE NOT JUST MEAT!**

The Appendix offers you three science-based theories that support believing in choice. I recommend reading these theories for those who need an educated, science-based justification for choice. The theories do not conclusively disprove determinism or positively prove that moral choice exists. However, they present logical arguments giving you rational reasons to choose choice. Refer to them as; Emergence Theory, the Theory of Epigenetics, and Myelination Theory.

NOTES

1. Doyle, B. (2011). *Free Will: The Scandal in Philosophy*. Cambridge, MA: I-Phi Press. This will provide you a history of the concepts and major contributors to the Theory of Determinism.

2. Gergen, K. (2009). *Relational Being: Beyond Self and Community*. New York, NY: Oxford University Press, Inc.

3. Descartes, R. (1996). *Meditations on First Philosophy With Selections from the Objections and Replies* John Cottingham, (Ed.). Cambridge, United Kingdom: Cambridge University Press. This is great resource for the original *Meditations* translated in its entirety.

4. Smith, H. (2001). *Why Religion Matters*. New York, NY: HarperCollins Publishers, Inc.

5. Gergen, K. (2009). *Relational Being: Beyond Self and Community*. New York, NY: Oxford University Press, Inc.

6. Gazzaniga, M. (2012). *Who's In Charge?: Free Will and the Science of the Brain*. New York, NY: HarperCollins Publishers, Inc.

7. Dickens, P. (2000). *Social Darwinism: Linking Evolutionary Thought to Social Theory.* Philadephia, PA: Open University Press.

8. Appelbaum, P. Law & psychiatry: Regulating psychotherapy or restricting freedom of speech? California's ban on sexual orientation efforts. *Psychiatric Services, 65.*

CHAPTER 4

Self-Concept and Your Worldview: How You Place Yourself In The World

DEFINITION OF WORLDVIEW AND ITS IMPACT ON SELF-CONCEPT

A worldview is all about how the world works. We all have a worldview because we all need a big picture of life in order to figure out how we fit in. Our worldview is built into our self-concept. You can't examine one without intruding on the other. They are interdependent.

When you clearly understand your worldview, you can understand how you maneuver yourself within that world. Your identity will make more sense to you. The logic behind your self-concept choices will be unveiled. You can also get a better sense of whether you want to change your worldview and self-concept. You can't change one without changing the other.

MATCHING YOUR WORLDVIEW WITH YOUR SELF-CONCEPT

Fitting in is important. Can you remember going to a new school, a new job, or moving into a new neighborhood? Remember how alert and aware you were to know how "things" really worked in your new environment. You were going to spend a lot of time there, and you needed to know how to work your way into this little mini-world. Your view of your new environment would control how you talked, acted, related, looked, and "showed up". In fact, how you viewed your mini-world determined how you would survive and thrive there.

Perhaps you experienced or observed the conceited, presumptuous, and narcissistic person first showing up at your school or work like they owned the place. In spite of being the new person on the block, they acted like it was *their* block. Disregarding the existing environment with its values and practices, they expected the environment to accommodate and tolerate them first and foremost. They took pride in being "themselves" wherever they might be. That meant trying *not* to fit in with the status quo—or in some cases disrespecting other people's roles and values. They found their worldview in the mirror. They *were* the world. We all want to be sincere and avoid hypocrisy, and yet we are not so ignorant to think the world will mold itself according to our will and desires. What was the result of that person ignoring how the little mini-world really worked? Not pretty! Not a good connection to life!

A high school coach had a quote on his wall, by who I can't remember. However, I remember the quote well. "The reasonable man adapts himself to the world. The unreasonable man adapts the world to himself. All progress depends on the latter." He lived that way and created a mess for himself. I bought into that for a while. However, after numerous "emotional concussions", I wised up. Obviously, we all want to change things around us for the better. However, most of us don't unreasonably think that we are God.

I'll share with you a classic real-life example. A teenage girl arrived at her new boarding school. She went through the orientation and learned all about the school's values, rules, and policies. She met the teachers, counselors, and administrators. Throughout the orientation, her new roommate escorted her everywhere, and tried to help her feel welcome. The new girl smiled politely, and asked all the right questions. When the formal process ended, the two girls sat in their dorm room. At this point, the smile disappeared, and she said, "Okay, tell me how this *really* works. Who runs this place? What are the rules? Who do I have to watch out for? Where can I get some weed?" Her resident roommate smiled and said, "What you've seen is what it is. People here try to walk the talk." Incredulous, Miss New Girl during the next week approached lots of other girls and asked them the same questions. She thought she was being set up and panicked. She couldn't calm down until she heard what she believed was the true inside story. Eventually, she found one girl who told her what she wanted to hear. She finally got advice about getting weed and who was "really" in control. Miss New Girl accepted the view of just one girl as the correct worldview or reality within the school. She didn't believe the other girls. She was looking for the school scenario that matched *her* worldview, in spite of all the contrary evidence.

She would not believe that the school operated differently from how she perceived the bigger world to operate. She searched relentlessly until she found validation for her macro-worldview perspective. She believed that her worldview was "reality". She had to search desperately to discover a school scenario consistent with her self-concept and how she fit into the world. To somehow fit in, she had to find a school reality that allowed her to be the same person in school as she had been in the outside world. If she couldn't match up these realities, then she would be forced to change her identity, and that was indeed frightening. Little did she know that the school was designed to mismatch her worldview. She eventually recognized and accepted the mismatch, and thereafter she was motivated to change her self-concept and adapt to this new worldview. It didn't happen overnight.

ADOPTING WORLDVIEW CHUNKS

We all have a worldview that was put together over time. We unconsciously put together our worldview in perceptual chunks of beliefs. Our worldviews contain beliefs about human nature, what it means to be human, and how we operate. That was the theme of my tractor/Volkswagen dream in the Introduction. Our self-concepts are interconnected with our worldview. We try to create ourselves to survive and thrive according to how we assume the world works. How we think the world works tells us who we need to be.

Worldviews consist of perceptions, mental constructs, and beliefs. We cannot escape them; they are like body parts, constituting much of whom we are. However, worldviews can change. Our experience of living in our worldview tells us when we need to "hold 'em or fold 'em" in the many contexts of life. In other words, our worldviews define our risks for us. Changing these fundamental beliefs can be as difficult and frightening as amputating parts of our bodies. We can't help but change our self-concept as we change our worldviews, and vice versa. To understand who you are, don't just look inside for a "hidden person"; look at your worldviews. You chose them, and they guide you like a map.

We find large chunks of our worldview all around us. They are packaged as cultural norms, psychology, politics, religion, biology, history, and from beliefs we derive from our personal experiences. I want to demonstrate how pervasively powerful these worldview chunks are in structuring our perception of self. I will choose a few common ones, and I'll demonstrate how believing different ones create very different self-concepts.

Some of these worldviews have academic labels, and if you have not academically studied them, you may feel they are not part of your worldview. Don't worry about the labels—focus on the ideas. You'll be surprised how some of them have infiltrated your worldview.

As we look at worldviews, we will again touch on the conscious and unconscious minds. Some parts of a worldview may be very consciously familiar to you, and you may remember thinking specifically about those beliefs. However, you may have unconsciously adopted parts of a worldview without remembering or thinking about it. We learn at or on both levels. Sometimes our unconscious thoughts are brought to the surface, and pop up as we consciously delve into ideas. In any event, you can be sure that your worldview is made up of consciously considered and unconsciously integrated chunks of existing worldviews. We have adopted them either way.

Our worldviews weren't created at one time. We didn't sit down and put one together like writing an essay. We put them together, bit by bit, over time. It is a part of our developmental process as we move through life. Our worldview typically gets more internally consistent and concrete as we age. We become dissuaded from seriously considering ideas that are rationally inconsistent with our worldview. We become more opinionated. Of course, as our worldviews become more concrete, so does our self-concept.

OUR INCONSISTENT WORDLVIEWS CREATE INNER-CONFLICT

We aren't perfect thinkers, and we have inconsistencies in our worldviews. This may be partially explained because we have conscious as well as unconscious beliefs. They don't always agree. Additionally, we have conflicting parts or factions within ourselves that want different things. These individual parts may adopt worldview chunks to support each of their interests, and the chunks may contain conflicting beliefs. This causes schisms in our self-concept, and dissonance in our life. As we consider some worldview ideas, notice if part of you is attracted to an idea, while another part of you wants to reject it. Over time as we create congruence in our life desires, our worldview and self-concept will become more compatible. We can have greater focus and increased self-assurance.

May I use a personal example? I was raised in a family and school culture where excellence and perfection appeared to be the pinnacle value in life. It seemed as if everything I did academically, socially, or on the basketball floor, was compared to some standard of perfection. My coach had quotes on his wall that he repeated often. "Winning is not everything, it's the only thing." "Nobody ever drowned in sweat." "Losing is like kissing your sister, there's nothing to it." There were more, and I never forgot them. Not even playing for the state championship was "enough". At home, it seemed that my mother was shocked and depressed if I wasn't the "best" at everything. She would even shed tears if I came up short. Yes, I grew up with a worldview that excellence and perfection were what life is all about. (Sorry about this imperfect book!)

After marrying and having children, I consciously noticed how fragile children's self-esteem can be, and I made a conscious attempt not to push my kids like I had been pushed. I emphasized that they needed to have fun and grow. I tried never to show any outward disappointment when they didn't do well. However, if you listened to my conversations about life and success, you would inevitably hear the words: "perfect", "excellent", "the best", and "great", sprinkled throughout my sentences. My kids listened, and they were bright. My third-party conversations, and my high achievement lifestyle, persuaded them that I loved high achievement, excellence, and even perfection. They also noticed that I did not use that language when I commented on their life and activities. They saw a mismatch, a conflict. (How could I super-value ultra-high achievement, and not see or expect that excellence in them, but super-value them anyway?)

I believe that they sometimes unconsciously questioned my affirmations that I loved them unconditionally, and that they did not need to be high achievers, to have my respect. Instead, they believed that because I did not push them hard, I did not value them, or believe they could be worthwhile without being excellent. In other words, they believed that I looked on them as being of lesser value. Believe me, this caused them and myself a lot of heartache.

I really did have two conflicting beliefs in my worldview. I unconsciously elevated excellence and high achievement as standards in my own life, while trying to believe that my kids should not embrace that stressful standard in their lives. I couldn't pull off both beliefs in my actions. The incongruence was devastating. I was shocked later, when I finally realized what I had been doing. At the time, I was clueless—ignorant of what was actually happening. That is what occurs when you have worldviews with conflicting parts. Notice how my worldview affected my self-concept.

Now let's take a look at some worldview chunks that affect us all. Some will have academic names or titles. Don't get hung up in the titles, just focus on the ideas. As you read, consider how your own worldview has taken on some of the beliefs. Notice how persuasive these beliefs are when woven into the structure of our culture.

We'll look at psychology first. Psychology tries to explain human nature and the "self". There is no consensus among psychologists about why humans behave and feel the way they do. However, some psychological theories have achieved sufficient status to affect cultural worldviews, and also your self-concept. Let's consider two of the most famous and culturally influential psychologists: Sigmund Freud and Carl Jung.

SIGMUND FREUD

Freud divided the self into three parts: the id, ego, and superego. These self-parts are not physical realities, but abstractions. They are proposed as real, but not *physically* real. In other words, you won't find them hiding behind your liver, kidney, or even your brain. No one has ever seen an "id". Brilliant minds have written thousands of pages about how these parts interact. I will only touch on their purposes and interactions.

Freud taught that you have an id, which is primarily motivated by an instinct to obtain pleasure (particularly sexual pleasure.) It does not like being denied.

However, thoughtlessly running around in society, chasing sexual gratification is frowned upon. (At least it used to be.) To restrain the id's insistent behavior, Freud proposed that you have a superego, which is like a social conscience. This part of the self works to please the demands of society, and it counters the id. The superego manages a self-image to please society. It would therefore frown on the id's plans for public groping because society frowns on it. As the mediator between the id and the superego, the "ego" works to mutually satisfy the conflicting desires of the id and the superego.[2]

Obviously, neither the id nor the superego can ever be fully satisfied as long as the ego is around. The ego exercises a labor of futility, trying to satisfy the id and the superego. Therefore, in a Freudian worldview, life is a continual series of compromises within the self, and no part is ever fulfilled. Imagine the implications to your self-concept if you believe this worldview. The Good Life would be a series of frustrating compromises, and never really getting what you want. Or, it may be a few crescendo experiences without societal blame or shame.

Imagine Freud's perspective as part of your worldview and self-concept. Your life would have to revolve around the interactions of these three abstract, internal parts. What if you have never read about Freud's worldview and the names of these parts? No problem, you are able to adopt the self-traits of his theory through societal influence. How so?

Many academicians in various disciplines have adopted some of Freud's views; particularly that sensual, hedonistic motivations, and social manipulation are predominant in our nature. Strategic, influential members of society are taught these ideas in school, particularly in high school and college. Politicians, educators, physicians, mental health professionals, pastors, and other strategic members of society have been influenced by his views throughout their educations. They have integrated these beliefs into their public and private service.

You are directly or indirectly surrounded by their services. Freud's beliefs about the human self are subtly inculcated into laws, therapies, sermons, fashions, literature, film, medical practices, and so on. That means that Freud influences you to some extent, whether you want to be or not.

How would Freud's beliefs about human nature influence your self-concept as a member of the human family? According to him, you are naturally driven by raw self-interest, primarily seeking physical pleasures and social acceptance.

No wonder you may have a hard time trusting or respecting other people, or maybe even yourself. Through this filter, other people are just tools or pawns to fulfill your always-selfish desires. In this worldview, life is a dirty contract: you use me and I'll use you if I get the best deal. You would primarily be attracted to people who are a source of physical pleasure or social status. Your id, superego, and ego paradoxically complement the materialistic "meat" theory of biological determinism.

Freud and Darwin's worldviews are complementary in that they believed humans are inherently selfish and self-serving. You can't help it! Human life (including yours) is about pleasing the meat while pleasing the public to maintain social status and avoid rejection. This together would create the Good Life. Do whatever feels good within the shadows of societal restraint.

Does this philosophy fit somewhat into your worldview? Freud's early 1900's theories have lost some of their luster, but the self-seeking, compromising frustrations of his fundamental ideas are alive and well. They continue to influence many people's worldviews and self-concepts.

CARL JUNG

Carl Jung was a protégé of Freud who escaped into his own worldview. In some ways, he seems to have escaped materialism but found other ways to complicate choice and responsibility. Jung's perspective may be more convoluted and complex than Freud's. Again, I will brush over much to focus on one of his universal, fundamental beliefs about human nature. First, he taught that the primary dynamic or causative factor in life is mental or spiritual—terms that he seemed to use synonymously. The self has a conscious and an unconscious. The conscious is your open awareness, while your personal unconscious is a configuration of beliefs that are denials or defenses. He posits that rejection of the conscious happens when you do *not* consciously notice something, or you notice it, but can't handle it for some reason, and therefore you deny it. This interplay of a person's conscious and personal unconscious is part of human nature.[3] However, the heart of his worldview is the "collective unconscious".

He posits that the past mental attitudes, feelings, prejudices, fears, and affections of the human race continue to exist in some unexplainable manner, and are collectively grouped into a mental/spiritual/psychic influence that act on all individuals. In other words, rather than exclusively focusing on the biological brain as the originator of ideas, he included the continuing relationship and influence of generations past as a source for our thoughts, emotions, and impressions. He believed, however, that consciousness itself was exclusively biological.

A category of these collective thoughts and feelings, he calls "archetypes". What are they? Humankind throughout history share common categorical experiences that are so generic and universal that they form a unique consciousness, and these shared experiences he calls an archetype. They are not individual creatures or beings, but rather the combined personality and characteristics of human experiences. Rather than biological genetics, Jung's archetypes ring of "mental genetics" passed along through the ages. For example, the combined experiences of mothers historically have come together in the collective unconscious, to form an archetype he calls the "Primordial Mother". She has universal mother experiences, concerns, and attributes. She and other archetypes are forever unconscious, and their lingering, combined experiences, and traits are so pervasive in human history that they have taken on a personality of their own. They are like subcategories of the collective unconscious.

Again, Jung's archetypes refer to mental or spiritual forces not actual beings. The Primordial Mother archetype could exude motherly characteristics and influences on people other than mothers. This could be anyone. What you need to understand here is that according to Jung, your self-concept is influenced and shaped by these archetypes. If you accept this worldview you cannot ignore or disregard their influences on you. They are part of your self-expression. Salvatore Maddi describes it as follows: "In addition, one must accept and value the collective unconscious. This means, among other things, accept experiences of the uncanny, of things beyond individual control. It also means identifying with humankind and all living things in an uncritical, appreciative way."[4]

Scientists criticized Jung's ardent belief in the immaterial, but for many people, his propositions were desirable and embraced. His worldview gives believers permission to believe in an unseen world of the ancestors whose combined lives continue to exert influence on every person in the present day.

He believed that these unseen, non-biological influences, help shape every person's personality, relationships, and moods. Jung stops short of proposing that we can ever control archetypes or the collective unconscious. Instead, humans must deftly and sensitively recognize and accommodate their influences.

Believing in Jung's worldview, your self-concept would include behaviors, emotions, and thoughts derived not just from your own mind, but also from all humankind. In fact, his view suggests that you are not a completely separate self, but you are also composed of your relationships with others. The Good Life would include a conscious awareness and respect for the present and the past. Jung's worldview expands Freud's boundaries of an exclusively "inner self" to a constitutive self. That means that you are partially composed of the collective unconscious and the archetypes. Freud proposed more of an exclusively inward view of the self.

Before moving on, realize that by using Freud and Jung as examples, this is not to advocate one or the other. The point is that academia's ideas are powerful and culturally pervasive. So much so that once inculcated in political, educational, financial, entertainment, and health industries, they infiltrate your life. We would all be surprised at the intellectual origins of many of our cultural beliefs and values that we tacitly accept. Being aware of the intellectual influences in your culture can help you better understand the source of cultural values and movements surrounding you.

Additionally, an enlightened cultural awareness creates more choices about your self-concept. How? You have not consciously considered and filtered all of your ideas about worldview and self-concept. Many of your strongest ideas have been unconsciously adopted. To empower your choices, bring your unconscious ideas to consciousness. Search to find the source of your worldview ideas, and view them in the context in which they were created. Evaluate the lives of their proponents, whether it is your parents or philosophers in order to distill a clearer understanding. You will inevitably run across divergent opinions about these ideas. Compare them and think about them to help you clarify the origin of your own worldview and self-perception. Ask yourself, "Should I keep them or not, and if not how do I replace them?" We will continue to explore that important question as we move forward. In the meantime let's take a look at another worldview.

THE INFLUENCE OF RELIGION AND SPIRITUALITY IN WORLDVIEWS

Religion or spirituality is another source for worldviews. As previously mentioned, science's worldview is so pervasive that some have called science a religion. How does religion affect a worldview? Religion is defined as "a set of beliefs concerning the cause, nature, and purpose of the universe [...] usually involving devotional and ritual observances, and often containing a moral code governing the conduct of human affairs."[5] In this definition, religion may or may not embrace a theistic or supernatural presence. This is a broad definition including organized or institutional religions, but also individual or personally conceived ideas, observances, and codes of conduct. This definition could include an atheist whose belief system proposes the non-existence of a god or higher power, but who may have other religiously-oriented beliefs. While using this broad definition, evaluate whether you have a religion, and also ascertain how religions, other than your religion, influence your worldview.

Certainly, science and religion have attained a worldview status, particularly in our western world culture, often called "modernity". I include religion's affect on our self-concept because of the data received by a comprehensive, worldwide survey reported in 2012. The Pew Forum on Religion and Public Life collected data from 2,500 national censuses, surveys and registers from 230 countries and territories, and some scholars say, it is the most comprehensive report on the world's religious makeup. Out of 7 billion people, 84% identified with some form of religion. However, the 16% unaffiliated group included not just atheists or agnostics, but also people who consider themselves religious, but are not followers of a specific faith tradition. The largest unaffiliated groups are found in communist countries like North Korea and China.[6] The United States has experienced recent growth in the religiously unaffiliated. This may include those people who view science and religious worldviews as incompatible and prefer a scientific perspective. In any event, religious beliefs and practices surround you wherever you go in the world, and they unabashedly affect your worldview.

What is religion's status in our Western world of modernity? Some modernists view religion as a useless world of mysticism—a step back into the Dark

Ages, and a world of witch-killing. Nevertheless, the statistics above suggest that the majority of Westerners consider religion useful. In fact, a religious worldview is politically protected in the United States. The First Amendment to the Constitution legally protects our right to religiously believe as we wish and prevents the government from choosing our religion. It also prohibits the government from impeding the free exercise of religion. Historically, the United States was one of the first countries to recognize free choice and protection of individual religious affiliation. However, religion appears to be losing its constitutional status and priority compared to other rights, such as equal protection of minorities and sexual preference.

Why is religion so politically and personally controversial? Religion is so powerful in creating worldviews that many countries have chosen a state religion, or have restricted the practice of religion in order to protect their regimes. Historically, we know that in doing so, these regimes attempted to impose their worldviews on their citizens. Think of the old Soviet Union in which the economic and political theories of communism were implemented to supplant the worldviews of organized religion. Religion was outlawed.

The subject of religion is obviously personal and sometimes provocative. I am not promoting or criticizing any religion. But I do want to give examples of religion's role in forming your personal worldview. In doing so, I apologize for any perceived judgments or critiques of a particular belief system. That is not my intention.

RELIGION'S CREATION STORIES AND WORLDVIEW

Examples of religion's impact on worldview and self-concept will be helpful. A common facet of a religious belief system includes a "Creation Story". This is an explanation of how the world—and humans in particular—came into existence. The personal and cultural implications of a creation story are woven into a worldview. We have already looked at science's classical Theory of Evolution. That is science's creation story. There are variations of this evolutionary story as we discovered. You are aware of the legal and public education battles between Darwin's classical Theory of Evolution creation, and

Christianity's theory of creation. Acknowledging the energy and passion of this debate only serves to validate our society's passion about creation stories and self-concepts. Creation stories spawn beliefs about human values, relationships, choice, agency, time, family, and death just to name a few. Think about your creation story or explanation, and how it affects your self-concept. Be sensitive to how your own religion (and other religions) has affected your worldview as we look at creation stories.

More than one institutional religion embraces the Adam and Eve account of the earth and humankind's creation. I will compare two accounts of this creation story and how they can contrarily affect an individual's self-concept and an entire society's structure.

In one version, Adam and Eve are created by a supreme being and placed on the earth in a beautiful garden. They have an existence with no death and no suffering. They are free to move about and enjoy the garden with one caveat: do not eat the fruit of the Tree of the Knowledge of Good and Evil. They are also told to multiply and replenish the earth. Eve partakes of the fruit and convinces Adam to do likewise. They are cast out of the garden and into a world of death and suffering.

In this creation story, Eve is the culprit and is blamed for the downfall of humanity. She was deceived, partook of the fruit, and persuaded Adam to partake too. As a result, they were cast out, and their offspring (all of humankind),must endure needless death and suffering. As daughters of Eve, women in this society continue to be blamed for Eve's action and everyone's suffering. Females are consequently labeled less worthy than males because of Eve's foolish choices. They are less favored politically, economically, socially, and legally. You can also imagine how this society's interpretation of creation affects a man's self-concept versus a woman's self-concept.

Another institutional religion also embraces the Adam and Eve story, but interprets it differently. In the Garden of Eden, they could not know joy because they could not experience the opposite (pain and heartache). Adam and Eve are again told not to partake of the Tree of the Knowledge of Good and Evil because it will lead to being cast out and suffering death. However, they are also told to multiply and replenish the earth. In this scenario, they cannot have children in their immortal state within the garden—they can only do so as mortals. They could only become mortal by partaking of the fruit. Adam and Eve knew the consequences of partaking or not partaking. Eve was the first to respond, and she chose to be the mother of humankind, even if that meant suffering and mortal death. The Supreme Being gave them a choice. Eve convinced Adam of the importance of eating the fruit, and fulfilling their destiny outside the garden. They were cast out, bore children, experienced the differences between joy and pain, and eventually they died, but with a promise to live again as immortals. The purpose of earth life was to be tested, develop character, and prepare for an afterlife more desirable than what they experienced in the Garden of Eden. In particular, they would not have to be alone.

In this society, women as daughters of Eve, are revered for their spirit of love and sacrifice. They are held in the highest esteem. Imagine how this interpretation of the Garden of Eden affects a woman's self-concept, a man's self-concept and society in general. How would you expect this to affect relationships between men and women? The two different interpretations of the same general creation story would lead to opposite societal mores on the status of men and women.

Religion can have other roles in creating a worldview and self-concept. What value do you have as an individual? Why should you take up space and breathe the air in this world, and how much do you deserve of each? People embracing a low self-worth don't expect much. Those who feel of great worth have a greater hope and more positive expectations. What guides them to a high or low self-worth? Which are you? Do you actually feel of lesser worth but wish it were different? How are your actions a reflection of your self-perceived value?

I have asked various groups of adults and adolescents, "What is the worth of a human being to you?" They normally tell me that people are valued for what they can do, or what they have to offer. In other words, a person's value is their utilitarian value. They tell me, "Everyone has something to offer the world." Sometimes their answers referred to individuals who had given much to them or society like great teachers, friends, musicians, parents, lovers, and so on. However, utilitarian worth can be used to devalue a quadriplegic, a hardened criminal, the aged, or an enemy. Finding utilitarian worth for these people can be a stretch. I suppose enemies can keep you on your toes, quadriplegics teach you to appreciate your health, and some criminals turn around and help society.

However, from this perspective, what is the relative utilitarian value to society of the disadvantaged, compared to the value of services society must give to them? From a utilitarian perspective, some individuals take more than they give. They would have a deficit value. This did not sit well with my groups. Most people intuitively wanted to value everyone equally. However, most of the group found that doing so was not logical. Where do you derive your self-worth and the worth of others?

RELIGION'S IMPACT ON WORTH IN SELF-CONCEPT

Are some people worth more than others? Are you worth more or less than someone else? Should you be treated differently? Your answer is part of your worldview and self-concept. Certainly, some people have brought you more joy and happiness than other people. Are these the platinum people, the high producers who deserve more love than others? Are there true "blue bloods"? This proposition disturbed most group members. The search for an alternative answer usually led to the concept of "inherent worth". Rarely did someone suggest that a human has inherent worth *without* some type of religious justification. Besides your intuition, how do you justify your self worth beyond your utilitarian value to others? If you are committed to utilitarian criteria, what is your Plan B if or when you lose your utility (job, looks, personality, physical skills, and so on)?

What is the religious rationale for self worth? In many creation stories, primitive to modern, a supreme power is the creator. The story's context reveals humankind's relationship to the Creator, and human worth was derived from the creator's perspective. Believers adopted the creator's criteria of worth for themselves and others.

Divergent creation stories set up unique and peculiar relationships between humans and the creator suggesting different values. Some religious beliefs are deistic, meaning that the creator created everything, and then wound up the world like a clock to function alone. There is not an ongoing personal connection to the creator.

Other beliefs establish humans as "supreme creations" of the creator, and the creator watches over them as a valuable possession. Another belief is that humans are like pets of the creator. In Greek mythology, Zeus and the gods found drama and stimulation in mixing their godlike lives with lesser humans. The humans were lesser because they did not enjoy the supernatural powers of the gods. Some religions have god-creators who watch over an unstable earth where humans must sacrifice other humans to create stability and safety from the god's wrath.[7]

Another religion views mankind as literal children of the Creator, and the relationship is more of a parent and child paradigm. Inherent value comes from the parent/child relationship with deity. If the Creator values them as family members, they all must be precious.

A variety of human/god relationships are suggested in these varied examples. Humans logically think of these various theistic beings with a sense of fear, abandonment, maybe awe, certainly respect, hopefully love, and often anger. These various types of relationships depend on whether we approach God as primarily super-powerful and emotionally disconnected or as primarily loving and connected.

Imagine the various perceptions of self-worth engendered by these different worldviews. If you believe in a god or creative power, what is your relationship with that source? How does it affect your sense of self-worth? If you do not have a religious view, what are your criteria for valuing yourself and others? Think of how individuals logically treat themselves and others based on their "origins". We consciously or unconsciously treat people according to what they're worth.

SACRED AND PROFANE WORLDVIEWS

Incorporating religion in general into your worldview adds a dimension to your self-concept that is not found otherwise. This dimension reaches beyond dogma and doctrine. I will introduce another definition of religion—one that is narrower. It translates into a mindset. The great religious historian of the Twentieth Century, Mircea Eliade, contrasts the effects of a "religious" view, versus what he calls a "profane" (naturalistic and non-religious) view of life. In doing so, Eliade defines religion as not just a belief system, but as the world of the sacred—an unseen and incomprehensible power.[8] A religious or sacred worldview recognizes this power while a profane or non-religious worldview would deny it.

Eliade sees religious-minded people purposefully pursuing and connecting with this power. For them the Good Life includes a reciprocal relationship with the source of this power, and the security or well-being found there. A profane person for various logical reasons dismisses this mysticism as something that cannot be proved, overly presumptuous, or a sign of weakness and neurosis. The profane person prefers to rely solely on their powers and those harnessed from the natural world like technology.

The distinguishing **effects** of the sacred and profane are as important as distinguishing their ideas. People with a religious perspective or sacred worldview live a reality in which they interface daily with a creator's sacred power. They acknowledge an inner human drive, a need to connect with Source. They are satisfied the sacred exists through reason, intuition, faith, and personal experience. On the other hand, the profane or non-religious group only bows to the power of natural law. What is the life **effect** of embracing one of these contrasting views over the other, and how do they individually affect self-concept?

How many times have you or someone else said, "That happened for a reason." What is the meaning of this statement? You can almost feel a tangible shroud of hope. Implicit is the faith that because of something benevolent beyond self, "It's going to be okay." That everything's going to work out for the best. Destiny for these believers includes a benevolent intervener beyond the self, something that can make everything (including us) alright. That's an example of an "inner-animated drive" to acknowledge the sacred.

At the least, many people hope that important things in human life do not just randomly happen because material particles bump into each other. Believers in the sacred want life events to have purpose and meaning. They want to see the past as worthwhile, the future as hopeful, and the present as a choice. Victor Frankl posits that purpose and meaning is stronger than any other human drive.[9] Your self-concept cannot be hopefully "meaningful" without a corresponding worldview.

Followers of the sacred are examples of Eliade's thesis. Religious followers have lives that can be filled with a plethora of essential meanings far beyond what a profane follower could possibly have. In the world of the profane, all things just happen by law. Life events are explained from a rational, law-based perspective. It just is. There are no other essential meanings attached to it.

Those who embrace the sacred or the profane experience life differently. For example, faith is not knowing for *sure*, and the profane person questions commitment to beliefs of uncertainty. A profane presumption is that only empirically based knowledge can be trusted. "It's better (not) to know truth than to create meaning out of fantasy." However, those of the sacred, argue that empirically based knowledge changes over time, and is therefore uncertain. The sacred believe that the meaning of facts and things are more important than the things or facts standing alone. The profane believer disagrees. In the world of the profane something just "is", and empirically speaking, so what!

However, Frankl says that humans crave meaning, and they must imperatively find or create meaning in life. Eliade and Huston Smith argue that historically the most compelling and fulfilling meanings come from religious, spiritual perspectives. We are left with the question, profane or religious, which is the most *useful* perspective for living the Best Life?

What are these essential meanings that people crave? Ceremonies and rituals (even in a profane society) demonstrate this human need to find meaning beyond the literal or material. There is no rational reason for throwing rice on newlyweds; no one is eating the grain or planting the seeds. However, throwing rice has a useful *meaning*. Football players at a university emerge from a tunnel onto the field, all tapping a statue as they pass. This little ritual has gone on for decades. What about New Year rituals including Times Square? Why break a bottle of bubbly on a ship before its maiden voyage? Why wear robes at graduations? Why would someone carry a rabbit's foot around in their pocket? Why value and cherish artwork? Aside from degenerate and prurient interests, what are the purposes of initiations?

As Eliade points out, even the practice of Freud's psychoanalysis requires a person to descend into unknown psychic depths to confront the pains and fears of prior traumatic experiences resembling religious initiatory descents into hell for transcendence. Yes, some of these profane examples smack of superstition. That is the point. Even in a profane society, the community and the self cannot escape the need for meaning and the need to connect to a higher source.

What practices in your business, school, family or social life help fill this need in you? Essential meanings enrich life, make life intriguing, and give hope and motivation. Meaning changes life from *surviving* to *thriving.* Meaningful experiences can be life-changing. The following example illustrates a neuroscientist's worldview and self-concept transformation from a sacred experience.

NEAR DEATH EXPERIENCES AND WORLDVIEW

Dr. Eban Alexander is an academic neurosurgeon, educated at Duke and affiliated with Harvard's two top hospitals. He is a scientist and a neurosurgeon with over 150 authored or co-authored peer reviewed articles for medical journals. His self-concept and worldview centered on being a scientist and a medical physician. His primary support system was family, and he called his religious life just above a "C&E'er" (someone who only goes to church on Christmas and Easter). He tells the story of his worldview change in his book, *Proof of Heaven.* "Modern neuroscience dictates that the brain gives rise to consciousness—to the mind, to the soul, to the spirit, to whatever you choose to call that invisible, intangible part of us that that truly makes us who we are—and I had little doubt that it was correct."[10]

In other words, he believed in biological determinism. However, in 2007, at age 54, his life changed. Possibly connected to recent travel in Africa, he contracted a formerly unknown strain of bacterial meningitis. The onset was furiously fast and violent. Within hours, he was taken by ambulance to the hospital. After various diagnostic tests and tracking his symptoms, his probability for survival was considered minimal. In his own words, as a physician, he describes his condition. "More specifically, given my diagnosis of acute gram-negative bacterial meningitis and rapid neurological decline at the outset, I'd had, at best, only about a 10 percent chance of surviving my illness when I was admitted to the ER. If the antibiotics didn't kick in, the risk of mortality would rise steadily over the next few days—till it hit a nonnegotiable 100 percent. [...] Even if I didn't die, the bacteria attacking my brain had probably already devoured enough of my cortex to compromise any higher-brain activity. The longer I stayed in coma, the more likely it became that I would spend the rest of my life in a chronic vegetative state. [...]During my coma my brain wasn't working improperly—it wasn't working at all. [...] If you don't have a working brain, you can't be conscious. [...] But in my case, the neocortex was out of the picture. I was encountering the reality of a world of consciousness that existed completely free of the limitations of my physical brain."[11]

He fell into a weeklong coma, and during those days, he worsened. The prognosis was death. Fortunately, his systems were carefully monitored. Clinical charts verified that his brain was not working. During the coma, he had what is commonly called a Near Death Experience. "During that time, my entire neocortex—the outer surface of the brain, the part that makes us human—was shut down. Inoperative. In essence, absent." As a neurosurgeon, he had helped revive patients who later described a Near Death Experience. In those cases, the blood flow and oxygen to the brain was interrupted for a short time (merely minutes). Their brains had not totally crashed. His had, and yet he had a Near Death Experience.

Miraculously, he not only survived, but also gradually recovered all of his brain functions, including his scientific acumen. That in itself is a medical miracle. However, that he could have a Near Death Experience without a functioning brain, (an active neocortex), was also a medical miracle. It should have been scientifically impossible if all consciousness, dreams, etc. are exclusively brain functions. He and his colleagues were clueless to explain his experience. Dr. Alexander and other scientists researched and assumed a variety of explanations, but none of them held water. He was adamant that he had the out of body experience, and that life goes on beyond mortality.

Another factor closed the case for him. He had been adopted. His birth parents were adolescents later to become high achievers in the world. He had two sisters he had not known prior to the experience. During his visit to the other world, he was escorted and taught throughout his visit by a kind woman. His description of what she taught him is limited, but much of his understanding came through observation and unspoken conversations with this person. After his recovery, he learned that one of his sisters had died a few years prior to the experience. The surviving sister sent him a picture of the deceased sister he had never seen or known. That's right, *she* was his guide and shadow during his journey, but she had never introduced herself. One of the gnawing doubts about his Near Death Experience was not meeting people there he had previously known. The experiences told him by patients and others always seemed to include visits from love ones passed on. His sister filled the gap.

This is quite the story, an almost laboratory-staged, biological view of a Near Death Experience by a neurosurgeon. It severely challenges the underpinnings of scientific explanations about human origin, nature, and purpose. As expected, the status quo has already begun to challenge Alexander's character, professional competency, and the medical implications of his experience. They scurry to defuse the possibility that the mind is not exclusively the brain, or that life exists after mortal death. The exclusively scientific worldview could be turned upside down.

Nevertheless, what did it "mean" to him personally. How did the experience affect his worldview and self-concept? In his book, he describes many beautiful and fascinating things he learned. However, there is much he left out. Adamantly and positively he believed he visited another world, and that life continues after mortality. He describes the effect on his present life back in this world. "It is my belief that we are now facing a crucial time in our existence. We need to recover more of that larger knowledge while living here on earth, while our brains (including its left-side analytical parts) are fully functioning. Science—the science to which I've devoted so much of my life—doesn't contradict what I learned up there. But far, far too many people believe it does, because certain members of the scientific community, who are pledged to the materialist worldview, have insisted again and again that science and spirituality cannot coexist. They are mistaken. [...] The unconditional love and acceptance that I experienced on my journey is the single most important discovery I have ever made, or will ever make, and as hard as I know it's going to be to unpack the other lessons I learned while there, I also know in my heart that sharing this very basic message—one so simple that most children readily accept it—is the most important task I have."[12]

This experience changed his worldview and his self-concept. He continued to respect parts of the science worldview, but not the part that denies the existence of immateriality, and not the part that states there is no higher being, and not the scientific proposition that consciousness is exclusively biological. Instead, his newly expanded worldview found a place for scientific beliefs, but science was not the foundational worldview. Paradoxically, his new view was more sacred based. This was true even though the Near Death Experience apparently revealed nothing specific about his church. Nevertheless, church attendance changed for him. "At last, I understood what religion was really all about. Or at least was supposed to be about. I didn't just believe in God; I knew God. As I hobbled to the altar to take Communion, tears streamed down my cheeks."[13]

His purpose and his focus changed. He ended with a message: "You are loved." Those words are what I needed to hear as an orphan, as a child who'd been given away. But it's also what every one of us in this materialistic age needs to hear as well, because in terms of whom we really are, where we really came from, and where we're really going we all feel (wrongly) like orphans. Without recovering that memory of our larger connectedness, and of the unconditional love of our Creator, we will always feel lost here on earth."[14]

Where does that leave us in comparing profane and sacred worldviews? You are surrounded by both worldviews. They influence you in many ways. Many wonderful people have divergent worldviews. The worth of a person does not depend on whether they have a sacred or profane view. Our emphasis is how those views affect the Best Life. Once you really settle on what the Best Life is for you, you can better choose which worldview fits you. However, changing a worldview is not like turning a light switch on or off. We can't make ourselves believe something that we unconsciously disbelieve.

Dr. Alexander said that he already seemed to know much of what he learned in the experience. You may read his story and agree or disagree with his changed worldview. However, just reading about it will probably not change your life like it did for him. It was not just the information he received, but also the experience itself that was critical. What worldview-creating experiences can you remember in your life? It need not be traumatic or life threatening. Perhaps there are several that have contributed to your present view. What made those experiences so meaningful and life directing?

Dr. Alexander created a new worldview and a self-concept that was an amalgamation of his science-based beliefs and his sacred beliefs. The sacred beliefs of love, connectedness, afterlife, and purpose became paramount. However, science based beliefs that did *not* contradict these fundamentals were maintained. Creating a worldview and a self-concept that can rationally integrate a set of contrary beliefs is difficult. For example, Dr. Alexander's experience prohibited him from subsequently accepting religious beliefs based on selfishness, revenge, domination, exclusion, and self-righteousness.

He would have a hard time supporting the Crusades or genocides in the name of a religion. The cloak of religion or the sacred may create meaning, but the meanings can be virtuous or destructive to body and soul. Profane followers don't trust some religious followers for many legitimate, historical reasons. The religious don't trust the profane, because the profane specifically reject and deny the authenticity of religious beliefs and origins. Therefore, the effect of choosing a sacred or profane worldview requires clarity on what you consider the Best Life. What do you value? A sacred view of life can encourage love, virtue, unselfish service and altruism more than a classical, profane perspective. In choosing a sacred or religious perspective you are free to avoid those belief systems that are not virtue oriented or devalue any human life.

Are you aware of how important understanding the meaning of life is to you? What worldview is most conducive to achieving your values?

NOTES

1. Shaw, G. (1903). *Man and Superman*. Cambridge, MA: The University Press.
2. Slife, B., & Williams R. (1995). *What's Behind the Research?: Discovering Hidden Assumptions in the Behavioral Sciences*. Thousand Oaks, CA: Sage Publications, Inc.
3. Maddi, S.R. (2001). *Personality Theories a Comparative Analysis* (6th ed.). Long Grove, IL: Waveland Press, Inc.
4. (Maddi, 2001).
5. 2014. In *Dictionary.com*. Retrieved May 27, 2014, from http://dictionary.reference.com/browse/religion
6. Religion & Public Life Project. (2012). *"Nones" on the Rise*. Retrieved from Pew Research http://www.pewforum.org/2012/10/09/nones-on-the-rise/
7. Maclagan, D. (1977). *Creation Myths: Man's Introduction to the World*. London, UK: Thames & Hudson.
8. Eliade, M. (1987). *The Sacred and The Profane: The Nature of Religion*. Orlando, FL: Harcourt, Inc.
9. Frankl, V. (2006). *Man's Search for Meaning*. Boston, MA: Beacon Press.
10. Alexander E. (2012). *Proof of Heaven: A Neurosurgeon's Journey into the Afterlife*. New York, NY: Simon & Schuster.
11. (Alexander, 2012).
12. (Alexander, 2012).
13. (Alexander, 2012).
14. (Alexander, 2012).

CHAPTER 5

Filtering Your Worldview and Self-Concept: Strong Relationality as a Tool

NEEDING A WORLDVIEW FILTER

We need to be careful with our worldview because it persuades us toward the Good Life or the Best Life. In this chapter, we will consider strategies on how to evaluate, manage, and change our worldviews to more accurately and clearly represent what we believe and value.

Our worldview and self-concept contain mistakes, misunderstandings, and internal inconsistencies. We're not stupid—we're just not perfect. For example, if our worldview proposes that we live in a "dog-eat-dog" world, then we perceive ourselves to be acquisitive beings, competing with everyone for everything. That defines how we would logically act to survive in a viciously competitive world.

While living in this selfish world, imagine watching a movie like *Schindler's List,* and being touched by the self-sacrificing characters that endanger their lives to help Jews escape the Nazis. Because it touches us, we add this unselfish characteristic to our "dog-eat-dog" worldview. Then what happens? We begin to have inconsistent behaviors, expectations, and relationships, as we try to be a "hungry dog" *and* a "benevolent rescuer". Life gets confusing and dicey. "Do we eat 'em or help 'em?" By incorporating both characters into our self-concept, we can't figure out how they can live compatibly within us. We need to better protect ourselves from mixing inconsistent ideas into our worldview and self-concept. Doing so will reduce stress, sharpen our focus, and allow us to become a "together" person.

This chapter gives us a method to protect ourselves from these internal mistakes. The method helps us attract compatible beliefs into our worldview while keeping out inconsistent beliefs. This allows us to prioritize and structure our worldview ideas. We do so by consciously embracing the fundamental beliefs that are the *foundation* for our worldview. As a foundation, they filter out incompatible beliefs. Likewise, they attract acceptable and compatible beliefs. The filter cleans up and maintains the integrity of our worldview.

We all have some type of worldview filter, but it was probably put together haphazardly. We will compare two well thought out, prominent filters, and compare them. I will recommend Strong Relationality (SR) as a worldview filter, because it is compatible with the Best Life.[1] In the meantime, think about the benefits of using an *existing* worldview filter, instead of creating one from scratch. You can tweak an existing filter according to your preferences, but you keep its fundamental beliefs and structure. Existing worldview filters are efficient, because their bugs and inconsistencies have already been removed.

OUR STATUS QUO WORLDVIEWS

We consciously and unconsciously choose the fundamental beliefs making up our worldview, our self-concept, and how we fit into the world. We have reviewed how two worldviews helped shape our self-concept. Yes, we can refer to science and religion as worldviews. They have powerfully influenced our culture. Both science and religion have their own worldview filter that keeps their worldview organized, intact, and consistent. We'll take a look at these distinctively different filters. They have similarities, but for our purposes I will focus on their differences. To set this up, let's consider a few more points.

As mentioned, some of our fundamental beliefs were adopted consciously, and some were adopted unconsciously. That includes science-based and religion-based worldview beliefs. We are all influenced by their beliefs. We are probably not even aware that some of them exist in our minds. This makes it difficult for us to consciously compare them with other potential worldview beliefs. This lack of awareness can lead us to adopt contradictory beliefs. When this happens we feel unsettled and disheveled.

We already reviewed some of the incompatibilities between science and religion worldviews. Be aware that all of us have consciously and unconsciously incorporated beliefs from each of them into our worldview. Some of those beliefs are not logically consistent with each other. We have also probably adopted beliefs from other well-known worldviews. That leaves us with chunks of religion, chunks of science, chunks of other worldviews, all mixed together with additional beliefs we picked up here and there. That can be confusing. We need a system to help us build a worldview whose beliefs are internally consistent. Without an orderly process, we can end up with a worldview looking like a collage of beliefs slapped together on the canvas of life.

INTERNALLY INCONSISTENT WORLDVIEW BELIEFS: WINNERS AND LOSERS

Let's take a look at how internally inconsistent, worldview beliefs can affect us. Let's use a hypothetical example. Imagine being raised to believe that "winners win" and "losers lose". As children, we try out our parents' worldviews. The assumption here is that we are born as winners or losers. This becomes part of our worldview. With this belief overshadowing us, we want to believe that we were born a winner. What happens when this engrained worldview belief is consciously threatened?

For example, imagine as we get older, that we are taught in school and in church that, "everybody is a winner". At track meets and spelling bees, everybody gets a ribbon or a little trophy. Our worldview about winners and losers is now threatened. We are confused. How should we act? Why should we work hard to be a winner if everybody is a winner? Think for a moment. If there are no losers, what is a winner?

What does this mean if we are competing to get into a college? If we apply to a college and are rejected, while someone else is accepted, are we really a winner? Are all college applicants winners? If so, then why are some of those winners rejected? We have two worldviews in conflict. In this example, the child unconsciously embraced the teachings of parents that winners win and losers lose. The child also learned that winners get rewarded. However, as they moved into the world, they were taught that everybody is a winner. Who then gets rewarded? Do they have to compete for rewards?

How would this confusion affect our self-concept? Being a winner was important as we grew up, and we didn't want to be a loser. We worked hard to validate ourselves as winners. However, this belief got challenged at school and church. We're taught that there are no losers, and so there is nothing special about being a winner. We might find ourselves trying less in school, because "winning" a high academic grade has nothing to do with being a winner. Good grades may lose their importance to us.

Assume that knowing that there are losers and winners in life has supported our self-concept and our self-worth up to now. If our worldview changes and there are no losers, we are left confused about who we are and what we should want to be. The meaning of losing a job, failing a test, or coming in last in a foot race, becomes confusing. Should we feel entitled or not? Having inconsistent worldview beliefs can make it difficult to know what motivates us, how we should act, or how we should feel after we have acted. Often, we consciously or unconsciously incorporate inconsistent beliefs into our worldviews, like trying to be a winner and a loser at the same time.

My point is that a simple but comprehensive worldview filter can help prevent these potential stumbling blocks. Foundational beliefs within the filter need to be carefully thought through and evaluated. This includes a decision on whether we agree with them, and whether we understand how they affect the rest of our beliefs. Of course, our worldview and our self-concept are intertwined, and therefore the worldview filter also acts as a self-concept filter.

The organizing filter creates efficiency. In considering whether to accept a belief into our worldview, we don't have to stop and consciously compare it with each individual belief in our worldview. That is a time-consuming process. Instead, we can determine if the proposed belief is inconsistent with the few, basic assumptions of our worldview filter. This shortcut saves time and minimizes errors in what gets into our worldview.

IMPLICATIONS OF A WORLDVIEW FILTER BELIEF

Let's see how this would work by evaluating the implications of a "filter belief". As an illustration, let's assume a worldview filter belief is, "I can never really know if something is true." Imagine how this belief dictates our interactions with the world. This worldview assumption affects our level of *trust* about anything we learn. We would be skeptical of everything we were taught. That is certainly not all bad. However, we will not believe that we can know for sure the truth of anything we learn. Imagine how that uncertainty would affect how we learn and what learning means to us.

Let's use this assumption as a filter. What beliefs are inconsistent with not being able to absolutely know the truth of anything? Here's one answer! We have to reject any belief proposing a *method* that could conclusively prove that something is true. No such methods could possibly exist according to the filter.

Let's consider a specific method. Would the filter allow us to accept, "I can believe what I see." We have to exclude this belief from our worldview, because it contradicts our filter. Why? Seeing is a proposed *method* to know for certain that a belief is true. According to the filter no such method exists, and that includes the method called seeing. That's how the filter helps shape a worldview. Once we understand the beliefs within the filter, we can more efficiently evaluate any proposed beliefs for our worldview. The implications of our worldview filter need to be clearly understood to work efficiently.

What happens if the filter's internal beliefs are inconsistent with each other? This causes confusion. A proposed belief we are considering could be consistent with one of our filter's beliefs, but inconsistent with another of our filter's beliefs. In that case, what do we decide? The filter is telling us yes and no about accepting a new belief. There's confusion. What do we do? As my coach used to say, "We have to punt". Consciously reviewing the internal beliefs within our worldview filter helps solve this problem. We can ensure that our filter's internal beliefs are consistent with one another.

We may not presently have a well thought out worldview filter. Strong Relationality is broad enough to encompass our values and preferences as well as an understanding of how the world works. This filter will help us to continually evolve a congruent worldview of beliefs, values, and desires.

STRONG RELATIONALITY AS A WORLDVIEW FILTER

Strong Relationality is a powerful organizing tool. Again, we must strongly believe Strong Relationality's filtering presuppositions to use it. Let me review some of these presuppositions for your consideration. Carefully evaluate whether you agree or disagree with them. If you don't believe the presuppositions, don't use Strong Relationality. Be aware that Strong Relationality is consistent with this book's bias that human choice and accountability along with quality, virtuous relationships lead to the Best Life. Strong Relationality filters out proposals to our worldview that would undermine the Best Life. Using Strong Relationality means incorporating our biases for moral choice and virtuous relationships as part of our worldview and self-concept.

Let's consider the name first. The term Strong Relationality is not mine. It was coined by minds much higher than my own. However, I have seen people scratch their heads at the name. Everyone knows that relationships are important in many ways. Someone asked me if Strong Relationality was distinguished from regular relationality by giving tighter hugs and firmer hand shakes. Does it mean for people to sit closer together on the bus, or to share popcorn at the movie? Not necessarily! Someone else asked if Strong Relationality was the study of marital intimacy. No! Not really! That would be the Freudian filter. The meaning is something quite different.

STRONG RELATIONALITY FUNDAMENTAL ASSUMPTIONS

- All things (including humans) derive their meaning and significance through relationships with others.
- Moral choice or agency exists. From a moral perspective, I could have done other than what I did under the circumstances. Moral choice does not include whether our stomach growls, or, we sweat in the heat. It does include choices such as being kind or mean to someone.
- Material and immaterial things can exist outside of our thoughts, including a god, spirit, and virtue/love.
- Humans are in relationship with everything (material or immaterial) in a here and now context.
- The most powerful and influential human need is quality, virtuous relationships and not independence from others.

- Humans inherently want to understand the meaning of things, including life events.
- Humans make most acted-upon decisions without using the scientific method. There are other ways of comprehending truth.

SCIENCE'S WORLDVIEW FILTER

Strong Relationality as a worldview filter will make more sense if I contrast it to another popular filter. Science has a worldview filter called Abstractionism/ Materialism, hereafter referred to as (AM). AM has foundational beliefs that create a foundation for science's worldview, and it screens beliefs that are inconsistent with science's worldview. AM consists of beliefs that are generally accepted as fundamental to the study of science. We will compare the beliefs of Strong Relationality to AM and notice how they must create two different worldviews. Let me first explain a little bit of how science's filter works.

AM defines the boundary of what is "real" for science's worldview. It is truly an all-encompassing filter. According to AM, nothing is real unless it is a material thing or a law that acts on material things. This is the foundational belief of AM and science has adopted it. This belief creates a boundary for what can be real. Let's view some of the implications of a reality only consisting of material stuff and laws.[2] The following are logical assumptions compatible with AM's foundational presupposition:

- Everything in existence must have a material substance that can somehow be observed by one or more of the human senses.
- Natural laws exist and influence all material things. Any real event only occurs when a natural law "acts" on a material thing.

These two assumptions are primary baselines for what is real in the science worldview. These foundational beliefs are essential to a scientific understanding of anything in our world. Laws and materiality are considered the most fundamental units of reality. For example, rocks are obviously material things and pass the AM test. An event takes place when rocks fall off a cliff. Gravity pulls the rocks to the ground. Gravity describes the law acting on the material rock.

Of course, AM allows humans to be "real" in science's worldview. However, only the material part of a human is real. A human event occurs when a law acts on a human body. Humans have no choice but to do what natural law requires. That brings us back to determinism as mentioned in Chapter 3 and discussed at length in the Appendix.

Pause for a moment. Most people intuitively consider immaterial things to be part of our reality in spite of science's worldview. However, AM denies the existence of love, integrity, or virtue because they are not material or recognizable laws. AM requires science to explain the idea of so-called loving behavior and feelings as a biological reaction to some law-based stimuli. The reality of love itself does not exist in science—it is only a name that describes certain law-generated behaviors.

LIMITATIONS OF SCIENCE'S WORLDVIEW FILTER

Of course, this creates a problem for scientists. If love doesn't exist, how does one know that any behavior is loving? Scientists have to speculate and construct a set of behaviors that they *assume* describes loving behavior. Those behaviors then become a "something" called love. Contrarily, Strong Relationality holds that love and other immaterial virtues actually exist as something more than the behaviors that demonstrate them.

Why would AM accept Darwin's Survival of the fittest theory as part of the science worldview? His theory is a material/law explanation of humankind's development. "Survival of the fittest" refers to an instinct that is considered a natural law. This law is believed to "drive" all human behavior to be exclusively selfish and survival-oriented. The science worldview believes that the primary law of our existence is the law to survive, and that we will do anything and everything to survive. It fits the worldview filter beliefs of AM.

How does that affect our self-concept possibilities? It means that humans cannot sincerely act altruistically, benevolently, or with moral choice. Why not? Natural law will not allow them to. We may have observed or experienced what we considered loving, unselfish behavior. Science explains that what looks like altruistic behavior is actually some form of "self-interest" to ensure the person's or the species' survival.

Science considers the existence of altruism or benevolence to be an illusion. They are immaterial, and they are not scientifically recognized laws. Additionally, love and benevolence are primarily "other-oriented" and not "me-oriented". This makes them contradict Darwin. That means that science requires our self-concept to be primarily selfish, competitive, and incapable of altruistic love.

Science's worldview does not include God or a higher power, because no one has proved the materiality of God, or that God is a predictable, natural law. The existence of an unpredictable God could overturn predictable natural law. God then becomes an obstacle to AM's and science's scheme of predictability in the universe. This is true even if God uses natural laws to do His work. God is unpredictable in how He will use natural law.

Science is desirable, because it claims to diminish unpredictability and allow us to anticipate what will happen in a context. If God can rule over natural law, AM's definition of reality would implode. AM and the science worldview have been trying to demonstrate a world of certainty and predictability that humans crave. To do so, AM has defined reality to fit into a tight box without including God, or immaterial realities such as meaning and virtue.

THE SIGNIFICANCE OF MEANING

Many of us view "meaning" as a part of our reality. The meaning of something goes beyond its material or literal existence. For humans, a material thing can represent something that is more valuable than the material itself. A rainbow is refracted light created by laws operating on materials in the atmosphere. However, rainbows also mean hope and beauty to many people. A rose is a material flower, but to humans it can also mean romance. A college diploma is just paper and ink, but its meaning to a graduate may represent their hopes and dreams. It's difficult to tell people experiencing these meanings that they don't exist.

Imagine a dear friend walking up to you in a room of people and slapping you hard in the face. Objectively, you will feel the sting and your face will show finger impressions. However, at another level you frantically search to understand the meaning of what happened. Was your friend angry, jealous, deceptive, or just mean? As you settle on a possible meaning, you begin to feel shocked, angry, hurt, or revengeful. The feeling corresponds to the meaning you inferred. Assume you interpret the slap's meaning as anger towards you. As you respond to the "anger" in the slap, another friend whispers in your ear that this person has a brain tumor, will die in ten days, and is going crazy.

What happens to your emotional response to the slap? With this new meaning, your feelings may change from shock and anger, to compassion and empathy. Your perceived meaning of the slap creates your emotional response—not just the physical slap. Yes, it stung your face. However, when your initial assumption changed, so did your emotions. Our emotional life is connected to the meaning attached to our experiences.

REALITY OF VALUES

Let's consider how AM and SR affect perceptions about the Best Life. In the definition of Strong Relationality, "Strong" denotes that presupposed relational values are real; they co-exist with us.[3] "Strong" also refers to humans' innate need for loving and virtuous relationships. "Strong" helps us understand that we don't just need and have one type of relationship, but that relationships have different qualities. Relationships are more than neutral connections to others. In other words, Strong Relationality proposes that the Best Life includes our ability to give and receive love, and to connect to others in quality, reciprocal ways. That's perhaps the greatest need of humans. The quality of a relationship is motivated and measured by the love and virtue within the relationship. What one person receives in the relationship does not determine the quality of the relationship. Quality is the synergistic combination of what each person contributed to the relational experience.

On the other hand, AM's Good Life is focused on the embodied self, the closed self, and independence. The independent self requires that the self's goals, desires, and wishes take precedence over the family, group, or community. From this perspective, the individual's preferences should not be restricted by external, moral systems, or traditions like religion. Unselfish acts and loving motives are filtered out as part of AM's reality. AM holds that relationships are merely important tools to get other things that are more desirable than the relationship itself.

Human choice and virtue do not exist in science's worldview. AM's presuppositions also help us understand why our Western culture values extreme individualism and independence more than cooperative, "other oriented" interdependence. The law of survival forces a person to always put self first.

Do you value your independence more than your interdependence? Are your independence skills better than your interdependence skills? Realistically, no one can ever be truly independent because humans are social by nature. We need each other no matter who we are. Do you work to exclude reliance on others, or do you work to create cooperation with others? Do you view interdependence as weakness and independence as strength, or vice versa? Be aware of how these two attitudes affect your self-concept.

Strong Relationality and AM don't disagree about everything. We must clearly understand that Strong Relationality also acknowledges the existence of material things and the phenomena called "laws". However, Strong Relationality recognizes that some things are immaterial. Strong Relationality recognizes much of what AM describes as real, but disagrees that materiality is the most significant part of reality.

WORLDVIEW FILTERS' METHODS TO BELIEVE

Furthermore, Strong Relationality does not agree that using the scientific method is the only reliable way to "believe" something. This means that Strong Relationality has a broader perspective of how to examine reality. Strong Relationality reaches beyond and recognizes that reality includes many things that AM would exclude. AM would not accept an immaterial thought as being real, and therefore thoughts should not affect one's biological health. Thinking is not a predictable, recognized natural law. Intuition and a higher power's answer to prayers would be excluded by AM and science. The human desire and need to be altruistic would be excluded. Although AM and Strong Relationality share some common observations, I want to stress their distinctive differences and demonstrate how following each one leads to dramatically different life results.

Let's use a chair as an example of how reality is viewed differently. For AM, the chair has a particular weight, measurable dimensions, color, shape, and type of material—such as wood or metal. All of these things can be observed through the senses. Laws such as kinetic energy, friction, and so on, could be described as forming the chair. That defines the reality of a "chair" from an AM perspective.

How would using Strong Relationality's presuppositions create a different perspective of what makes the chair real? Reality would certainly include all the material characteristics pointed out by the AM perspective. However, Strong Relationality includes relationship as real. Strong Relationality is designed to help us know how to relate to the chair. SR would evaluate this thing called a "chair" by its relationship to everything around it. What if the chair was situated in a pile of split logs next to a fireplace? Is it a chair or firewood? Why call it a chair if it will just be burned with the other wood? The word "chair" denotes a particular type of relationship. Should the other pieces of split wood be called "inferior furniture material"? So relationships determine if it is considered a chair or firewood?

This is not just a semantic distinction. The meaning of the object comes from its relationship to the other elements in its context. Does that mean that the chair is not made of fibrous material? No, but to meaningfully understand how to relate to the chair, the context must be appreciated. Do you burn it or sit on it? Both perspectives can be useful. However, AM focuses on just the object alone and what is "within it". Strong Relationality focuses on context and the object's relationships with things around it. Both perspectives are useful, but Strong Relationality provides a broader perspective of how you relate to the chair/firewood. That is a richer or thicker view of reality.

Now, let's use a human being as an example. Please view this person from an observer perspective. He is a 40-year-old attorney—married with children, who feels suspicious most of the time. How would AM view him? He has body weight, body structure, blood type, gender, organs, neuro-chemical brain reactions, blood and urine readings from lab tests, and so on. He is a 40-year-old biological organism acted upon by gravity, exclusive self-interest, electro-magnetism, biochemical reactions ,and so on.

Strong Relationality assumes that there is more to him from a practical standpoint. He gets up in the morning and heads to work. His wife kisses his cheek and says, "I love you dear". (He is a husband.) He walks into his office, and the staff scurry around and say, "Good morning Mr. Lawyer". He goes over to the courthouse to argue a motion. The judge hears him and says, "That is stupid and ridiculous." (He is a moron.) He goes to lunch with a group of his colleagues and orders three sandwiches, two orders of fries, and three desserts. (He is a pig.) He rushes to the ball field where his little leaguers are waiting for him. They run up and say, "Hi Coach!" He leaves practice and rushes to his psychiatrist for his weekly visit. She greets him with a handshake and asks him to sit down. She pulls out his file that says "Paranoid". (He is a diagnosis.)

Neither him nor you have a meaningful self-concept outside of a context. The real him showed up in every context. Like you he has different and varied relationships. They combine to give him a textured self-concept. It's in the action! His body was in all those different places during the day. However, he had multiple identities as he went from place to place. From a practical perspective, the best way to know him is not from just reviewing biological, psychiatric, and medical data. This data provides important information to consider, but it's not enough. We don't carry around our medical, psychological, and psychiatric files to exchange as a prerequisite to a relationship.

However, observing him in relationships throughout the day helps us know how to relate to him. It could even assist the psychiatrist. The Strong Relationality perspective would therefore be more fundamental in knowing how to connect with him. Understanding him not just from the skin inward, but rather from the skin outward, helps us know him, and who he is. Considering his self as an exclusively biological organism would leave out much of him.

EXPERIENCING THE DIFFERRENCE BETWEEN TWO FILTERS

Let's take another approach in helping us understand the practical difference between Strong Relatioality and AM. As an *observer*, you have looked at two objects: a chair and a human. By using an AM filter and a Strong Relationality filter you got two observer perspectives. I will ask you now to be empathic in order to get another perspective. Experience Strong Relationality and AM differences through the eyes of another human being. In this exercise, you will step into a fictitious person named Jane and experience being her as much as you can.

In this example, you will alternate between an AM and a Strong Relationality filter as you go throughout Jane's day. Remember that the AM filter focuses on the internally-oriented "material" self, whereas Strong Relationality focuses on the relational self.

You will experience not only her actions, but also feel her motives. Remember Strong Relationality's primary motivation is to care for and connect with others. AM's primary motivation is to satisfy the body's desires and to feel good.

Let me illustrate how each of Jane's contexts can have an AM or a Strong Relationality filter. Imagine Jane as a young woman being invited to three parties in three consecutive nights. All of the cool people will be at each one—with dancing music, live entertainment, and food. A good time is promised at each one. All of the parties are on evenings the night before a work day.

Here are a few AM considerations. Will the pleasure of the parties be stronger than the discomfort of being tired at work? Will the pleasure of the parties justify missing work and using up PTO or sick days for other future pleasures? Will she get in trouble for being late or missing work from partying hard, and if so, will the discomfort be greater than the pleasure of partying? If she has to reschedule other evening commitments, will she have more pleasure at the parties than at the other commitments? Can she keep her boyfriend on a string if she breaks a date with him to go to the party? Assume that she doesn't plan to attend, but she can't concentrate on work because she keeps thinking about the parties. If she doesn't go to the party, her friend Mary will get all the attention at the party.

Now, we will consider the consequences from a SR filter. There will be people at the party who she hasn't seen in a while and she wonders what will happen to their relationships if she doesn't go. If she misses work, will her assistant be overloaded and overwhelmed? If she goes to all three parties, will it help or hinder her productivity at work? She does need some kind of a break to stay fresh at work. Her boyfriend lost his job a month ago, and she has tried to keep his spirits up. Should she discuss the parties with him and discover his plans for those nights? Does Mary need a night out where she doesn't feel she is competing with Jane?

A DAY IN THE LIFE OF JANE

In this scenario, you will imagine that you are Jane, getting up in the morning and going through part of her day. As Jane, you will encounter a variety of situations and contexts. Experience the contexts from a Strong Relationality and an AM perspective. Find the easiest way for you to experience each context from both perspectives. This will require you to slow down.

Jane wakes up at 6:00 a.m., feeling a bit tired and anxious after going to bed around 1:00 a.m. She has a big day in front of her, and she needs to be on top of her game. Nevertheless, she luxuriates in her comfortable bed, still warm and cozy from her snuggling during the night. She remembers that her physician said she has a weak "nervous system", and she cannot function well without rest. Why should she even try to go to work? Should she just call in sick and crawl back under the covers? As she slips back under the covers, she remembers that she has no more sick days at work. At the same time, she smells coffee. She wonders how much the coffee will amp up her nervousness. She slows down and looks back at her bed. The coffee may generate a boost of energy, but she knows that caffeine will also intensify her stress.

There's still plenty of time to call in sick. With that thought she gets back into bed. As she relaxes, she sees the face of the 12-year-old girl who she is scheduled to meet in her office. The girl has been abused and is struggling to cope in school and at home. Her mother doesn't have insurance, and she may not be able to pay her therapist fees. Jane lies back down with a knot in her stomach. The mother agreed to have a percentage of her salary taken out by her employer and sent to Jane. However, the payout would take a few months. Jane can't afford to work without compensation, even from poor people. However, she believes she could help this girl, but she had planned not to take periodic payments from any client's employer. She tells herself that she doesn't absolutely "need" the money immediately as she gets out of bed again.

On the way to work, her cell phone rings. Using Bluetooth of course, she answers and hears the voice of her old boyfriend. She knew that he was engaged to be married in a couple of months. He tells her how much he misses being with her and how beautiful she is. He reminds her of all the good times and the great "chemistry" between them. He has to see her! His fiancée would never know. Jane feels adrenalin and excitement building inside her. It would feel so good to be with him again. Why not? What if someone found out? She would get a ton of grief. She knows his fiancée and how much in love she seems to be. Hooking up with him would hurt her deeply. She might even sense the deception without ever actually knowing about it. No, she better not see him again. It would not be right to treat him or his fiancée that way. She tells him she was glad that they broke up since he is clearly still a "player". "Don't call me again."

Let's debrief your experiences as Jane. Were you able to access both SR and AM for each situation? If so, did you notice that one filter was usually easier to use than another? Did you also notice that is was easier to start with one particular filter before switching to the other filter? You are unconsciously programmed to favor one filter over the other. Remember that you sometimes had difficulty "feeling" the motivation required by one filter compared to the other. At times, you found it difficult to apply both filters to the same situation. How did you perceive hooking up with the old boyfriend through the SR filter? These examples and this exercise help clarify how worldview filters help create our experiences of reality, and direct our simple decisions as we go through a day.

Hopefully, you are convinced that choosing a worldview filter requires not just a cognitive commitment, but also an emotional one. In fact, you will prefer the worldview filter that allows you to express and live your deepest desires and highest values. You can't change your worldview filter by flipping a mental switch—no matter how logically correct the change might seem. To change your filter, you must also change some of your desires. This is not easy!

SHORT HISTORY OF RELATIONALITY

Relationality applies to other science-oriented disciplines. Advocates include Nobel Laureates: David Bohm (1996) in Physics, Roger Sperry (2002) in Neuroscience, and Ilya Prigogine (1998) in Chemistry. Prominent scholars in the social sciences include: Bradbury and Lichenstein (2000) in Business,

James Bohman (1993) in Sociology, and Jay Greenberg in Psychology. These scholars advocate Strong Relationality as a healing for the ills of large corporations, societies, and individuals.

Imagine the impact of Strong Relationality if it was the dominant reality in these disciplines. Its effects on business could revolutionize compensation strategies, reward incentives, negotiations, management philosophy, committee collaborations, motivation strategies, and employee training. Psychology would experience paradigm shifts in diagnosis, treatment strategies, quantitative and qualitative research, developmental theory, group dynamics, marriage systems, and communications.

Dr. Brent Slife—world-renowned clinical psychologist, academician, and major contributor to the American Psychological Association—is a primary spokesperson for Strong Relationality. Most of he and his colleagues' peer-reviewed publications in prominent psychological journals about SR have been written to academic audiences. The fundamental concepts and usefulness of SR need an even greater audience. He and I have collaborated to that end by founding the Greenbrier Academy for Girls—a college preparatory and therapeutic boarding school for adolescent young women. Our therapeutic milieu of diagnosis and interventions, an administrative and peer culture, an academic program, family workshops, and a relational philosophy are all grounded, rooted, and established in Strong Relationality. After viewing several years of positive outcomes from quantitative studies, dialogue, and continual feedback from resident and alumni, the results have exceeded our expectations. However, we are still learning and progressing with Greenbrier Academy as a wonderful laboratory for SR. We have good and exciting reasons to continue.

Confusion in your self-concept is created when you try to live as if AM and Strong Relationality are not inconsistent. You may try to act as if you are only "meat" one day, and a relational being on another day. If so, how does it feel to flip-flop back and forth between Strong Relationality and AM? You are either "Numero Uno" or you place others on a platform beside you, willing to sacrifice for their needs. Unconsciously trying to create an inconsistent dual reality leads to confusion, misunderstandings, and inconsistent relationships. Are you flip-flopping? If so, be aware of it. You and the world will be a more pleasant and safe place when Strong Relationality is your worldview filter.

NOTES

1. Richardson, F. & Slife, B. (2008). Problematic ontological underpinnings of positive psychology: A strong relational alternative. *Theory & Psychology* (39.1).

2. Schick, Jr., T. (2000). *Readings in the Philosophy of Science: From Positivism to Postmodernism.* Houston, TX: Mayfield Publishing Company.

3. Consider the following list of philosophical features for what I am calling "Strong Relationality" as written by Dr. Brent Slife. He entitles this list, "Features of a Relational Ontology". *Ontology* is used here in a broad sense as "that which is most fundamental".

Relationality is less a system of thought and more a loose framework or even an anti-system for understanding engaged, situated activity (practice).

Relationality can be distinguished into its strong and weak forms.

Weak relationality assumes that all things occur as self-contained, purely local entities that influence one another causally across time and space. The identity of these things stems from what is incorporated "inside" this self-containment from the outside.

Strong or ontological relationality assumes a mutually constitutive, holistic relation in which all or most of the qualities of things stem from their relationship to other things. Identity is thus simultaneously individual, as a unique nexus of relations, and communal because all things have a shared being.

Strong relationality allows for instantaneous relations and influences that are sometimes considered "nonlocal" or "formal caused."

The historical legacy of moving from a strong, more animistic relationality to a billiard ball causality among self-contained inertnesses has resulted in the free will/determinism and mind/body problems.

Ontological relationality (hereafter, relationality) is best contrasted with ontological abstractionism where abstractions, such as theories, principles, natural laws, and propositions are considered the fundamental realities of the world—i.e., what's "behind" or "above" everyday appearance with practice as an extension of more fundamental abstractions.

Abstractionist frameworks typically value contextlessness atomism, and thinness of explanation and method, whereas relationality frameworks typically value contextuality, holism and thickness of explanation and method.

Abstractionism frameworks yield the "punctual self" as a kind of isolated point of consciousness and will, separated from and standing over against its context.

Relational frameworks yield a "shared being" as a unique and mutually constituted nexus of historical, situational, interpersonal and moral contexts.

The "other" is almost irrelevant to the abstractionist because the individul self is in spite of the other, whereas the other is pivotal to the relationist because the other is constitutive of the self.

Abstractionist frameworks imply that community and relationship originate from common abstractions, such as common beliefs, theories, principles, and values.

Relational frameworks imply that we are, in an important sense already in community and must not deny and live out this ontological relationality.

CHAPTER 6

Avoid Being Labeled: The Relational You

Sometimes we get pigeonholed. We get labeled with an identity, and that label sticks. We get put in an identity box that we struggle to escape from. A perceived identity can follow us unchanged for years. The label could be a medical or psychiatric diagnosis like a borderline, an addictive personality, or a disabled. It could be a personality trait like a "ditz", a "wild child", a "nerd", a "freeloader", a "bore", or a "player". We can get fixated into these objectified identities, and that is all that we (or others) see in us.

Strong Relationality views our identity as fluid and evolving, not some fixed thing. This chapter can help us avoid getting pigeonholed by anyone (including ourselves or even professionals). To create and grow our self-concepts we need freedom from labels. Our evolving identity can't be permanently pinned down as an objective thing. We need not be burdened with labels.

Let me demonstrate the futility of objectively capturing a person's identity. We can all breathe easier knowing that we don't need to identify ourselves by having a label on our foreheads. Let's take a person's "identity" into the courtroom and put it under the scrutiny of cross-examination. Strict rules of evidence govern what can be reliably considered as "admissible" to the jury. This process can be revealing. In this chapter, we will bring "pinning down" or labeling a person's "self" into this adversarial setting. We will see how difficult it can be to conclusively and objectively pin down "who" someone really is.

We will then look at how Strong Relationality provides flexibility and change into understanding the self-concept. No scientist, lawyer, or anyone else has been able to capture the "whole" person. The unacknowledged parts of us can be treasures.

IDENTITY IN THE COURTROOM

A famous psychologist raises his hand and swears to tell the truth. He is seated before the jury and is qualified as an expert witness. The judge peers over his glasses at the attorneys who are paging through their notes, and he admonishes them to move along. The child custody battle between Charles Lambert and his former wife, Clara, spilled into the courtroom five days ago. After spending tens of thousands of dollars on lawyer fees and psychological evaluations, they are now farther apart than when they began.

The animosity in the old courtroom corrupts any hope of justice that its walls ever had. Charles sits with his neck and head stuck forward, his jaw clenched. Clara sniffles and wipes away a tear, clasping onto the arm of her dear brother who sits ceremoniously beside her. Thank heavens that Jen, their 14-year-old daughter, is at least spared the contentious trauma of being in the courtroom. The divorce was of course founded on irreconcilable differences. Clara has her career, and Charles has a new squeeze. Jen is caught in the middle by loving them both.

The controlling law for physical custody rests on what is "best" for Jen. The sides have introduced evidence showing how one house has nicer bathrooms than the other house, one former spouse is a better listener than the other, one follows through with discipline more than the other, one spends more time with Jen than the other, one drank booze at lunch and the other one didn't, one helps with homework more carefully than the other, and one is not depressed like the other, and on and on and on. Today, Charles's attorney, Mr. Gotcha (Mr. G), wants to unveil the "real" Jen so that the judge and jury will decide that she matches up better with Charles than Clara.

The psychologist, Dr. Allsgood, is the professional hired to disclose the "real" Jen's **identity**, and persuade the jury that she should live with her Dad. He has tested her, talked with her, taken her history, and interviewed both parents. It seems that after all is said and done, Jen's future is ultimately in his hands. Most jurors are overwhelmed with his expert credentials, professionalism, and theories. He has conducted over 40 empirically-based psychological studies, written several books, and he spent over five hours with Jen. He has testified in over 60 child custody cases and got paid well for every single one.

Who could know the real Jen better, and who could more wisely decide with whom she should live? We barge into court to witness his cross-examination by Clara's attorney, Ms. Notsofast (Ms. N).

Ms. N. has a woman sitting just behind her right ear, and they whisper back and forth. This psychologist, Dr. Hermeneutic, also a renowned equestrian, specializes in the construction of the "self". Her excellent training and broad studies give her an in-depth comprehension of Abstractionism/Materialism and also of Strong Relationality. She has familiarized herself with Jen's case, including all of Dr. Allsgood's testing results and clinical evaluation. She also went to lunch with Jen a few times, watched her at her ballet class, visited her in the home of both parents, and has even ridden horses with her.

THE CROSS-EXAMINATION

Ms. N. Dr. Allsgood, what is the most significant point you have learned about Jen?

Dr. A. It's all important. Everything I said!

Ms. N. You testified that she has brown hair, a corpulent body, and a "budding" anti-social disorder. Are those equally important to your determination?

Dr. A. Obviously not!

Ms. N. Then please answer the question. What was most significant about Jen in your evaluation?

Dr. A. Well, I suppose the anti-social disorder is extremely important.

Ms. N. How do you relate the disorder to the custody question?

Dr. A. It is extremely important in considering which parent can best deal with her disorder.

Ms. N. Is it more important to deal with the disorder than with Jen?

Dr. A. The disorder is the most significant thing about Jen?

Ms. N. What qualifies a parent to deal with the disorder?

Dr. A. There are a lot of factors including the parents' ability to cope with her behaviors.

Ms. N. Which parent could best cope with the disorder?

Dr. A. The father.

Ms. N. Could the father be good in dealing with a disorder, but not so good in dealing with the rest of her?

Dr. A. Maybe so.

Ms. N. Why is dealing with the disorder more important than dealing with the rest of her?

Dr. A. The disorder causes most of the problems.

Ms. N. How do you disconnect the disorder from the rest of Jen?

Dr. A. Through objective testing.

Ms. N. Could Jen change something else about herself that would affect the disorder?

Dr. A. Certainly.

Ms A. Then, why do you try to isolate the rest of Jen from the disorder?

Dr. A. It's what I do professionally.

Ms. N. Did you clinically test and interview both parents to make your determination?

Dr. A. No. I wasn't able to test them, but I talked with them.

Ms. N. Isn't it true that you did not psychologically test either parent?

Dr. A. That's true.

Ms. N. Isn't it true that both parties to a relationship determine the quality of the relationship?

Dr. A. Yes.

Ms. N. Then how do you know in which parental relationship Jen would thrive if you only claim to professionally understand Jen and not either parent?

Dr. A. I evaluated Jen as I was asked to do.

Ms. N. In other words, your recommendation is not purely objective.

It is not based exclusively on pure scientific evidence! It was just your opinion?

Dr. A. It is my opinion.

Ms. N. Are you saying that Jen is a budding anti-social disorder no matter who she is with, when, where, and how she is behaving?

Dr. A. Yes.

Ms. N. How often does she need to act anti-socially to be an "anti-social"?

Dr. A. There isn't a certain amount. Everything is taken into consideration.

Ms. N. I'm confused. Could someone act at times anti-socially and not be an anti-social?

Dr. A. I suppose so.

Ms. N. Why did you do psychological testing?

Dr. A. As I testified, I used a wide battery of assessment instruments to better understand her emotional and cognitive functioning.

Ms. N. How reliable are those test results?

Dr. A. They are quite reliable and are used extensively by qualified psychologists throughout the United States. They have validity scales to rule out persons who just give random answers or are purposefully deceitful.

Ms. N. Would you rest your professional reputation on the reliability of those tests?

Dr. A. Well nothing is perfect. However, along with most of my colleagues, I rely heavily on the results of these psychometric instruments.

Ms. N. Then, why did you do a face-to-face clinical evaluation? Weren't the testing results sufficient for your professional opinion?

Dr. A. Why no! I needed to just be sure that the testing was accurate, and I wanted to determine if the tests picked up everything.

Ms. N. Since you trust your subjective opinion more than the correctness of the test results, why go through the time and expense of the testing?

Dr. A. Well, you can't ever be sure enough. I like to be thorough.

Ms. N. If your clinical evaluation contradicted the testing, which would you believe, your opinion or the test results?

Dr. A. Well it depends.

Ms. N. Depends on what? Are you more accurate some days than others with your clinical opinion?

Dr. A. I didn't say that.

Ms. N. You didn't need to. Which is more objective, your clinical opinion from your personal evaluation or the test results?

Dr. A. They are both very objective, very professional. I pride myself on being dispassionate and using only my professional judgment.

Ms. N. Are you saying that it is critical to be objective in making your evaluation of Jen? In other words, is objectivity critical in assessing the truth about Jen?

Dr. A. Yes, objectivity is the gold standard of the scientific process. You don't want the facts tainted by bias or prejudice of any kind.

Ms. N. You have been Jen's observer. How can you not be biased by what you learned in your PhD program, by your experience, and by your own values?

Dr. A. I am a professional. I can stand outside of any biases or prejudices.

Ms. N. What are your biases?

Dr. A. I don't have any that would affect my evaluation.

Ms. N. How do you know?

Dr. A. I just do.

Ms. N. Dr. Allsgood, you have testified that objectivity is a "gold standard" for your work. Objectivity has value to you and guides how you conduct yourself. Has objectivity been proven by the scientific method to be absolutely reliable?

Dr. A. No, it has not. However it comes close.

Ms. N. You developed an objective relationship with Jen. Your need to keep the relationship objective was therefore based on your own "preference", not a scientific fact. Is that correct?

Dr. A. You're trying to put words in my mouth.

Ms. N. My point, Dr. Allsgood, is that you are using a procedure to evaluate Jen that you claim is credible because it is scientific. However, you are saying that the objective purity of the evaluation is what makes your evaluation scientific. Now you tell us that the importance of objectivity is not scientifically-based, but merely common sense. Again, were you telling the truth when you said that your so-called objective evaluation of Jen was actually just common sense?

Dr. A. You can't attack the scientific process. It is an accepted and proven methodology used by clinical psychologists all over the country. It has credibility.

Ms. N. I know it has credibility. I am not sure its credibility comes from its pure objectivity. Common sense has its biases, wouldn't you agree?

Dr. A. Well, I don't like…

Ms. N. Dr. Allsgood, I asked you a yes or no question. Answer it yes or no if you can.

Dr. A. Yes, common sense has its biases.

Ms. N. Dr. Allsgood, would you therefore agree that your evaluation of Jen is biased?

Dr. A. Ummm, I won't go that far. I have the testing to back me up.

Ms. N. Are you saying that the testing is more objective and less biased than your opinion?

Dr. A. I suppose so.

Ms. N. I reviewed the psychometric tests that suggest Jen has a budding "anti-social" disorder. I noticed that the test questions suggested that "aggressive behavior" was frowned upon and viewed as a primary criterion for diagnosing the disorder. Is that correct?

Dr. A. Yes.

Ms. N. Jen's history indicates that someone tried to rape her behind her school building. However, they were not successful because she aggressively defended herself and even struck the assailant with a rock. Is that an indication of anti-social behavior or an attribute of self-protection?

Dr. A. Well in that case, her aggression led to a good result. The testing speaks to her general behavior.

Ms. N. Her school reports that she keeps "bugging" her teachers when they do not answer her questions in class. Is that a sign of a mental disorder or an indication that she takes learning seriously?

Dr. A. Well she is too insistent. That seems anti-social.

Ms. N. Is there scientific evidence that aggressively defending oneself from rape and aggressively pursuing answers to questions are anti-social?

Dr. A. No. That is just part of the testing to get a broad picture of Jen.

Ms. N. People wrote the psychological tests. Is that correct?

Dr. A. Yes, people who are experienced in the field.

Ms. N. Do the test writers decide what behavior demonstrates a disorder, or is there a scientifically proven list that they must follow?

Dr. A. The test writers use their best judgment.

Ms. N. Okay. If that is correct, aren't the test writers left to their own opinions about what demonstrates the disorder and what does not?

Dr. A. Well, it is an educated opinion.

Ms. N. As we have discussed, personal opinions have bias by definition. Since the test writers have biased opinions about what behaviors should be emphasized as anti-social, isn't the test itself biased?

Dr. A. That's blasphemy!

Ms. N. Answer the question.

Dr. A. Well, I don't know if you could call it biased?

Ms. N. Are you disagreeing? Are you saying that the test writers subjective bias does not translate into some bias in the test itself?

Dr. A. No!

Ms. N. Isn't it logical that since your clinical evaluation is biased and your testing is biased, that your evaluation of Jen is also biased?

Dr. A. This isn't fair. I've been doing these evaluations for years. People rely on my opinion.

Ms. N. Dr. Allsgood, when you test and clinically evaluate someone like Jen, how can you ever know if your conclusions and recommendations are correct?

Dr. A. I have my reputation to stand on and other psychologists agree with me.

Ms. N. Isn't it true that other psychologists don't always agree with you?

Dr. A. Yes, that's right.

Ms. N. Are those psychologists any less biased than you?

Dr. A. I resent that question!

Judge. Answer it.

Dr. A. I don't know.

Ms. N. Thank you. I'm not sure you know the *real* Jen either. Do you admit that your so-called objective evaluation of Jen is tainted by bias?

Dr. A. Mr. Gotcha, help me out!

OBJECTIVITY FALLS SHORT

You are like Jen in that there is no purely objective way to define who you are. That means that no scientist can objectively define the "real you" even after "studying" you. They can gather lots of information and develop theories about you. That can be very helpful, even if the results are not conclusively accurate. Your parents and friends are in the same boat, and frankly, so are you. If you can't ever know for sure the objective truth about your identity, how should you view yourself? Try viewing yourself relationally!

The problem is not as difficult as it may seem. You actually don't fit into a box. Give up looking for yourself in a box or assuming that you could ever fit into a box. Strong Relationality can help you elegantly create yourself, not just find yourself. Allow your self-concept to be more of a "becoming" than an objective has-been. To search for the objective self is like taking a visit to Wonderland. There are many trails, but if you don't know *what* you are looking for you probably won't find it. Strong Relationality provides a practical and usable way to build your self-concept with vision and with a template.

I want to reemphasize two Strong Relationality-inspired characteristics that empower you to create yourself and not be a label. I have touched on them in previous chapters, but to fully grasp Strong Relationality's impact on self-concept, we need to revisit them. Many people find that these two concepts are intuitive and even familiar. However, let me stress that they are consistent with Strong Relationality but are inconsistent with the objectivity of Abstractionism/Materialism.

THE RELATIONAL SELF

1. You are not a self-contained thing because your real "self" is *relational,* primarily constituted by your connections to other people, and the world around you.
2. Your immaterial values are an incorporated part of who you are.

You are a relational self. Is this hard to wrap your head around? You may find it easy to think of your identity as self-contained in your body. In thinking of your self, you automatically turn to your five senses. You have a body that you can see, touch, taste, smell, and hear. That appears to be so "real"—so predominantly real. In contrast, relationships are the "spaces in between" you and others. You cannot see, touch, taste, smell, or hear this "space in between". You can see yourself with others, but the relationship itself is not just the "observable" you and them. The relationship is the connection of the "selves" and the resultant meanings that are conceived within the relationship. Within the shared space, parts of yourself are revealed.

Two or more things or people are required to form a relationship. What do you bring to a relationship that is uniquely yours? Well, you bring your material body of course. Many people believe you bring a spirit, energy, or soul—and you also bring your power of choice. However, within this amazing mix of you and them, something else is created that is not *all you* or *all them.* This something is not just the "sum" of the parts. It is something else. Something that is synergetic is something created that is greater than the "sum". Within this, "something" meanings are conceived. Some of the meanings are about you, your roles, your intentions, your values, and your nature. Remember that meanings of self, others, and things are fundamental to human life. The meanings unfold within our relationships, and that is why we can say that we are fundamentally "relational selves". Therefore, we want to anticipate the nature and the quality of our relationships in order to create our desired self-concept.

We live in a world dominated by relationships not isolations, even when we seem to be physically alone. When you look in the mirror, there you are: your eyes, your nose, your head, your chin, and your mouth. Look at your driver's license and you will see the same things (hopefully a little more flattering). What's relational about that? Perhaps you think that no one else needs to be in the picture for you to recognize that that's you. Maybe, but what if you had not previously seen yourself, but only other people? Could you be sure that was really you?

Of course you are an individual! However, when someone looks at you to identify you, what are they doing? They want to ensure that you are not someone else, and as they look at you they are comparing and contrasting your appearance with other people. In the end, they know it's you, but they needed other people's faces to know it. They related you to others. You were connected.

What are you thinking of when you look in the mirror? Most frequently, you are concerned with how you will look to someone else. Even the wicked, narcissistic witch in Snow White was obsessed with how she compared to everyone else. The meaning of how you look (even to yourself) is a function of how you expect others will think of you. You may want to look attractive, unique, similar, tough, ugly, funny, oblivious, or even carefree. Consciously or unconsciously, you use your appearance as a connection that reveals some meaning about yourself.

You may think while looking in the mirror that you just want to admire yourself, scare yourself, or laugh at yourself. However, in doing so, how did you learn *what* was admirable, scary, or laughable? That's right, other people. Your different facial expressions have meaning to you because of your comparison and connection to others.

At the Greenbrier Academy[1] adolescent girls obviously talk about their appearance. In a discussion group one day a student shared how she dressed at home. She was trying to make a point of how difficult it was to just "dress how you feel" without having to worry about other people. Essentially, her dress was more of an undress. She wore the least amount of clothes possible, outer garments, and undergarments. f she could sneak by her parents, her undress was more extreme. Everyone laughed and shook their heads as she told her story. Then, she got serious. "You can't believe the perverts out there. When I was at the mall, I caught 12-year-old boys and older men staring at me, looking at my rear end. Why can't I just be me without perverts getting in the way?"

One of the other girls met her gaze and spoke up. "You're not stupid. If you're putting it out to guys, they're all going to look at you, not just the ones you select. You knew exactly what you were doing and you liked the attention. If you are going to put on a show, don't blame people for paying attention. They were only perverts if you looked really ugly." The meanings of these "visual" connections with others revealed part of her self-concept (among other things).

Look at the context of how and where you connect with someone. You are connected to a cashier as you pay for groceries. You are connected to a violinist in your orchestra as you play the clarinet. You are quietly connected to a stranger sitting by you on the subway. You are connected to Charles Dickens as you read *David Copperfield*. The context of the connection directs how you act in the relationship. In the "here and now", you are always connected, whether intimately or remotely, but still connected. A unique "you" is connected to each context, and always different, even if only in the most subtle ways. Your intentions in a context and the quality of that connection reveal a real part of your perceived identity.

Imagine a person in a hypothetical vacuum where there is not, (never has been, and never will be) anything else. The person is absolutely alone, separated from all living and non-living things. Imagine that no one else knows of the person's existence or even of the vacuum's existence. The person has a body, perhaps a soul, and five senses. However, what is the significance or meaning of the person, or anything about the person if they are absolutely isolated in a vacuum? From a practical perspective, nothing about the person is meaningful or significant to the person in the vacuum. They are also meaningless to everyone else because no one has ever seen them or has related to them in any way. The person may have a name. Is that meaningful, and to whom? Is a name significant if no one else is there? A name has no purpose in a vacuum.

The person has emotional and tactile sensitivity as well as biological functions. Is that meaningful, and to whom? No, those are just the mechanics of "how" the person functions and not the creation of any meaning by themselves. There is nothing that the person can compare them to. They just are. What is the meaning of hunger without food? This organic thing in a vacuum called a "person" does not even have knowledge because knowledge comes from relating to other things.

We can't even call the person an organic thing, because there is nothing inorganic to compare it to. What an incredibly dismal and meaningless existence! Is this really a person? An observer may find something meaningful, but there are no observers. No wonder isolation and rejection are the greatest fears of human beings. Perhaps the fear of death is like the fear of being alone in a vacuum. Non-existence is essentially meaningless existence. A rich self-concept means rich with meaning. We need meaning and purpose to be alive.

LIFE MEANING KEEPS US ALIVE

I know of an old Incan "Elder" who was called to sit with a young woman who was crying out to die. She was weeping and almost delirious as she repeated over and over again, "Let me die, just let me die." He sat quietly until she noticed him and acknowledged his presence with a quick glance. He then said to her, "I have come to show you how to die." Her breath paused, and she could find no words to respond. He asked her what death would give her that she cherished. She said, "I no longer can stand the pain. I don't want to feel the pain." He asked if it was her arm, leg, or stomach that was in pain. She whispered, "No, it's my heart." He responded. "What is this pain in your heart?" "I just don't care any more. Life is not worth living. There are too many disappointments, too much hatred and pain all around me. I can't take it any more." He shook his head. "Ah, there is no good reason for "life"! Why do you wish to kill life when it is you that is in pain?" "Life traps me in its pain. I do not wish to live." "My little one, is it your pain or life's pain?"

She raised her head from the floor. "I can only feel pain. I don't want it."

He wrapped his gnarled, ancient hand around her little wrist. "Does everyone choose pain?" "No, but I didn't choose pain; it chose me. I have nothing else in life but the pain." Holding her wrist gently he said, "It is the life of the excess pain which must die. You must not kill it with anger and revenge. You must put it in the fire and let it die and return to its origin. You must let it turn into heat, flame, and ash. And when it is done, you must gather what it has become and put it back inside of you." I don't understand? Again, in a whisper he told her. "There is only one fire hot enough to burn this pain, and to let it die. It is the giving and receiving of love. The pain cannot cover every place within you. Through whatever place is still open you can allow love to flow in and out. Where is this opening?" She pointed to her solar plexus. He held his hand just above her diaphragm palm down. "Notice the love of this old man enter along with the love of those whose faces will come to your mind, and some that you will not recognize." He held his hand there for a long time. Her breathing slowed. Her tears stopped, Her face relaxed, and she finally looked up into his clear, grey eyes. "Thank you! Thank you!" He smiled as he said, "You die well!"

MEANING AND THE SPACE BETWEEN US

Not all of us will meet a pure, old, wise man to help us in times of crisis. However, as this girl demonstrated, there is a "waning of belonging" that creates incredible pain. Life's choicest meaning flows from our ability to give and receive love. Denying or rebelling against this innate need brings dire consequences. Not all connections are of equal value. In virtuous connections, we thrive and want to stay alive. Life meaning is not just an existential, intellectual idea. It fills the "space between us", and chases away our self-inflicted pain. The "self" outside of quality relationships cannot thrive, and will wither slowly or quickly find its grave. We are always in relationships—that is not an issue. The issue is the *quality* of the relationships.

This relational self could not be captured through Dr. Allsgood's scientific, psychological perspective. The "objective" self was lifeless—like a snapshot with a numeric background. The flowing, moving self is alive in relationships. Certainly, Dr. Allsgood's perspectives were often accurate observations and useful. However, they were not a true and thorough revealing of Jen the person. The clinical explanation of Jen was just too thin.

THE AUTHENTIC SELF AND THE RELATIONAL SELF

The Individual Authentic Self is another theory in vogue proposing the self's separate and isolated nature. We have all heard the saying, "That wasn't the real you." I frequently heard that from my parents. If I did something wrong, my mother would say, "L. Jay., that wasn't you. You're not like that." Then, I would get punished. I always wanted to say, "Mom, that couldn't be the real you that punished the wrong guy. You should have grounded the other L. Jay." However, the real L. Jay. chickened out being a smart aleck with Momma Bear.

It's popular to believe that to be *real,* we have to uncover our authentic selves. That means that what we have been doing is somehow fake. What we need to do is find our authentic self—free it to act without restraint and be who we really are. That means that some authentic entity—our real self—is hidden away or covered up. Who is responsible for all of our actions while the real self is in hiding? How do we recognize the real us? Who is really looking for whom? Is the "self" in hiding, or was it kidnapped? Who else is inside of us, and who can we trust in there? What is the significance of being authentic?

The fixed, authentic self sounds good at first blush, but it doesn't hold up under scrutiny. We need to focus on our here and now actions, and take responsibility for what we say and what we do. Spending time deflecting accountability for our mistakes, using the excuse that we just haven't discovered our authentic self, is a cop out. We are *not* a fixed thing. We are a continuously *becoming.* The authentic self is a complex concept more fully discussed by Charles Taylor[2] and Charles Guignon[3].

Embrace the fact that you are fundamentally relational, and that your body is part of who you are. Of course, recognize the material parts of self. We have a body, but every seven years all of our cells are replaced and our old body is completely replaced. We need to take care of the body. However, our significant and meaningful identity is constantly "re-formed" as our relationships change. You are never the same from one moment to another. Significant meanings within us change and are revised as we constantly relate to others. Of course, some relationships are more meaningful and meaning-filled than others. The Best Life is created by refining the quality of our relationships and by increasing our ability to give and receive love. We are then led to richer and healthier life meanings.

VALUES ARE PART OF OUR IDENTITY

That leads us into Strong Relationality perspective number two, "Our values are part of who we are." We have just verified and emphasized that we are fundamentally relational beings. Our self-concepts are made up of the intentions and consequences of our perceived past, present, and future relationships. The quality of our self-concept is reciprocal to the quality of our relationships. Therefore, our focus should be on *how* to have quality relationships. That is what life is all about. Strong Relationality proposes that the *quality* of a relationship is determined by the *virtue* in the relationship. Let us therefore explore virtues and how to incorporate them into our relationships.

We can be given a variety of labels. These labels refer to a characteristic others prominently see in us. Obviously, we are more than those labels. Fortunately, if the characteristics that we have are dominant we can change them over time. In the meantime, we do not adopt and embrace the labels. We are free to change what people see. This may take time because people see what they are looking for. However, when we see something different in ourselves, others will be led to see something new. When we increase in virtue we change who we are, and old labels are thereby outgrown.

THE SUBSTANCE OF VIRTUE

Virtues are considered values. I am proposing that virtues are not just ideas or thoughts. We can define virtue for our purposes. Consider virtue as a synonym of love. Virtuous character traits such as: integrity, compassion, empathy, patience, forgiveness, and so on, are unique manifestations of love. This love is altruistic—it values others as much as our self (or even more so in some contexts). Abstractionism/Materialism denies this reality and therefore misses the meaning of life. To be virtuous is to do the right thing for the right reason to the best of our ability in a context. A virtuous action in a relationship inures to the emotional, mental, physical and perhaps spiritual well-being of everyone.

Being loving or virtuous is not just an abstract idea. That which is virtuous or loving may manifest in different ways to different people at different times. Nevertheless, when we are inspired by love, our intentions are kinder and our actions are inspired. There are no fixed rules. For example, consider a father and a son. The father can want to have his emotions refined so that he can feel loving and be compassionate toward his son. The father wants to treat him more virtuously. Today, he may have to discipline him, put his foot down, and place the boy in time out. That may be the kindest most beneficial thing for him today. Always being soft and comfortable is not necessarily virtuous or loving. "Tough love" and "soft love" can together be loving, but require different behaviors. However, the intentions of soft and tough love should be the same. In other words, we don't use tough love to exploit others for our selfish gain. To be virtuous, we must act for the non-exploitative, loving interest of others as well as self.

We don't have to feel all happy and excited about someone in order to act lovingly and virtuously towards them. Loving our enemies or being virtuous with enemies is an emotional stretch. If we wait until we feel pleasantly attracted to someone before we act virtuously, we may only get in one or two virtuous acts a day. That is not how it works. We need to *desire to desire* more loving feelings for others. During this interim, we need to act as if we had those better feelings. After a while, our feelings will change and we will become more positive. Our desires and feelings will grow together. We aren't being hypocrites by trying to act differently than we may feel toward someone. That's because our imperfect desires are being intentionally refined as we engage in virtuous acts.

By doing so, our characters are refined and we become a more virtuous and loving person. A virtuous self-concept is not just about virtuously interacting with people that we are easily and naturally attracted to in the moment. It includes *all* relationships, *all* of the time. Life is a refining process, and there are different levels of expressing virtue. Start from where you are now, and whomever you are with. Get on the path of virtue now. A character flaw is anything that stops or inhibits our ability to give or receive love and virtue. Self-improvement is removing those flaws and gaining those abilities.

CREATING A VIRTUOUS CULTURE

Dr. Slife and I have incorporated this Strong Relationality perspective of virtue at the Greenbrier Academy to help our young women develop character and to enhance the quality of all their relationships. Finding a parallel with Aristotle's concept of virtue ethics, Dr. Slife made a presentation at the annual meeting of the American Psychological Association that is now in press to be published in the APA's *Journal of Theoretical and Philosophical Psychology*. The article provides a relational definition of virtue and behavioral examples at the Greenbrier Academy. He refers to Aristotle's virtue ethics in particular. "Aristotle is extremely helpful. Quality relationships concern those virtues and goods that are: 1) worthwhile in themselves, even if we incur pain to get them; 2) constitutive, because they do not separate means from ends, and 3) shared, in that they are best pursued with and for the sake of others."[3] The virtues he speaks of also refer to the Best Life proposed in this book.

CHAPTER SUMMARY

We can all enjoy the freedom from perceiving ourselves as fixed labels. Many of us like to know we are unique. Understanding that we are relational means that we change by the minute. We can be free to enjoy our uniqueness that unfolds in each life relationship. We do not have to accept labels about who we are. Labels are not authentic.

NOTES

1. Taylor, C. (1989). *The Sources of the Self: The Making of the Modern Identity*. Cambridge, MA: Harvard University Press. See also, Charles Taylor, *The Ethics of Authenticity* (Harvard University Press, 1991).

2. Guignon, C. (2004).*On Being Authentic*. New York, NY: Routledge, Taylor and Francis Group.

3. Slife, B. (in press). Virtue ethics in practice: The Greenbrier Academy p.10. *Journal of Theoretical and Philosophical Psychology*.

CHAPTER 7

Standing Up for the Best Life

STRENGTH

The Relational Self and the Best Life are built on virtuous relationships. These relationships require a loving heart, delayed gratification, selfless service, and maturity. These characteristics are developed over time by practice, inspired reasoning, and some trial and error. It's not an easy process. Because of the challenge and the effort involved, some people don't want the Best Life. Some people mistakenly believe that what feels good and what is quick and easy, lead to the Best Life. This so-called Good Life has deceived many people, leading to heartache and waste.

Learning *how* to be a loving person does not seem as difficult as giving one self the *permission* to love and receive love. Children can sometimes set an example for adults. Childlike love can seem almost effortlessly virtuous at times. Perhaps being more childlike (not childish) should be our focus.

VIRTUOUS LOVE

I remember this story from one of my undergraduate classes. A young boy ran into a street and was hit by a car. His injuries were critical, and he was taken by ambulance to the hospital. His parents and family followed. At the hospital, emergency surgery was ordered. However, as preparations were made, the physicians discovered that they had no blood in stock to match his type. Panic ensued. They questioned the family and discovered that the boy's older sister had the needed blood type. The doctor pulled her aside and asked her for help. "Your brother will die unless we operate, but we can't do so without supplying him with the right type of blood. We don't have any here, but we know that your blood is compatible. Would you give your blood to him so we can operate?"

The girl looked down at the floor for a full minute and then looked up. "Okay, I'll do it." The published story indicated that—for the sake of time—a tube carried her blood directly to him. Time passed and the family was frantic. Finally, the physician came out of the operating room and gathered everyone together. "The operation was successful; he will live."

Pandemonium broke out with cheers of joy and gratitude. The doctor was hugged and congratulated by a swarm of family and friends. As he began to walk away, he noticed the sister standing alone, subdued and quiet. He went over to her and put his arm around her. Before he could speak, she looked up at him and said. "Okay, now when will I die?" Tears came to his eyes as the gravity of her sacrifice sank in. "We didn't take all your blood. You will live."

ALTRUISM AND THE BEST LIFE

Altruism (pure love) knows no age limit. This kind of love makes us truly human and raises us to the pinnacle of our humanity. Virtue does not exist without opposition. Courage is meaningless unless one is faced with fear. Giving is often easy, unless it means we go without. Forgiveness is difficult according to the pain we have endured. Compassion is easy unless it will cause us to be late for a good time or a timely harvest. Self-respect often comes by saying "no". Virtue is about making choices—choices to love or not love. Virtue is ultimately a joy that surpasses comfort and satiation. It is innately needed, but must be voluntarily given.

There are many reasons we scoff at becoming virtuous and relational. Perhaps, some of us can't get over ourselves, and we resist even wanting to love others as much as our self. We may believe that a life focused primarily on our best interests and feeling good is more valuable. Unselfish love may seem too high a price to give up the self-serving Good Life. We come up with intellectual justifications for our self-centeredness. We want to justify our desire for a selfish life. We want to give ourselves "comfortable" permission to be self-centered. There are other reasons, but let's not overlook our desires as being primary.

TWO ARGUMENTS AGAINST THE VIRTUOUS BEST LIFE

Most of us choose the Good Life or the Best Life by ultimately following our hearts. However, in doing so we like to be able to explain ourselves. We want reasons that reassure our feelings. Let's briefly touch on two common arguments *against* a virtuous life style. This can assist us in explaining why we choose the Good Life or the Best Life.

The two arguments dispute the universal reality of virtue and altruism. Of course, each argument has different reasoning for undermining the virtuous Relational Self. Our focus will be on whether virtue exists, and whether it can be a stable standard for daily living.

Here are the two statements in opposition of the virtuous Best Life:

- Virtue is relative to whatever we want it to be. Therefore, the love-based virtue of Strong Relationality does not exist. Virtue is merely a construction of our brain.
- Virtue is contrary to natural law, particularly Darwin's "Survival of the fittest" theory, and therefore, it is not a real part of any life context or experience.

IS VIRTUE ONLY A BRAIN FABRICATION?

Let's first consider the argument that virtue is a changeable, relative, brain fabrication. You can see how a personally discretionary definition of virtue would destroy Strong Relationality virtue. Virtue could not be a fixed requirement of a quality relationship. If virtue is only an idea, we can create and change as we wish—it is not a universal, human need. The idea or meaning of virtue would be relative to whatever a person desired. This concept of virtue would create chameleons of us all, changing our "virtue" to whatever we want it to be.

That would be contrary to consistent, relational-based virtue. Relational virtue requires doing the right thing for the right reason. We would virtuously give someone what they need, not what we selfishly want to give them. We give because we care about their best interests as much as our own. A relative or changeable virtue would not have to embrace these requirements.

Let's consider intentions first. For example, a relativist could consider honesty to be a tool for gaining someone's trust to help make a sale. That would be doing the right thing for a selfish reason. It may not necessarily be morally wrong, but it is not relationally virtuous. Or perhaps we act compassionately so others might find us attractive and want our friendship. Again, we are misleading someone to believe we care more about them than is true. We would be putting ourselves first once again.

There are also examples of labeling behaviors as virtuous that are not classically virtuous. Someone might say that stealing a person's wallet is virtuous because that person will learn to take better care of their property. Someone might lie to a spouse about cheating on them to benevolently keep them from being hurt. Perhaps, you have known someone that defines virtue as what is best for them, not for others. In that case, putting someone else's interest over one's own interest would not be virtuous.

VIRTUE AND VALUING OTHERS

My intent is to ensure that "virtue" means valuing other people's interest as much, or in some cases, more than our own. Using relativity arguments to get around the loving, unselfish intent of virtue does not protect the well-being of others. That is the point. Let me give a real life example.

Over 10,000 students graduated from the schools and programs that I co-founded and directed for "at-risk youth". Thousands of other students graduated from schools and programs that were directed by my peers and associates. I learned the following story from my association with one of these programs. No names are mentioned, and a few insignificant facts are changed to protect the anonymity of all parties.

A student diagnosed with depression and a personality disorder arrived at a program. Parents and teachers complained that the student had few friends, was a social outcast, and had no passion for anything. In the course of working with the student, the family, and other treating professionals, important information came to the program's attention. The information was important because the professionals believed that it greatly contributed to the student's present condition.

As a younger child, the student was often ill and bedridden. Outside activities and relationships were limited because of this ongoing illness. Over long stretches of time (two or three continuous months), the mother waited on the child hand-and-foot. She served meals in the bedroom, read stories, combed hair, and brushed the student's teeth. She canceled numerous obligations and discontinued taking care of herself. She ate poorly, and rarely interacted with her friends. All of her focus was on the child.

Neither her husband nor others could dissuade her. Eventually, the child would get better and return to school, only to have a relapse in a few months. This pattern kept playing itself over and over again. The mother continually discussed how important the child was to her, and that she would sacrifice anything for the child's well-being. Her associates commented on how committed and faithful she was in nurturing the child to health.

Finally, a comprehensive blood test revealed that the child's system was full of a particular poison. The professionals agreed that the amount of the poison increased and decreased during specific time periods. This explained the improvements and the relapses. However, the source and method of poisoning could not be conclusively proven.

During the investigation, the mother continually explained how much she loved the child, and would continue to care for him. However, she was prevented from doing so, and within a relatively short time, the child returned to good health without any relapses. Professionals believed that she was poisoning the child in order to care for him. She did not believe that she could fully demonstrate her love unless the child was ill and needed constant care. She made him suffer so she could express her so-called love. Her idea of virtue was certainly unique and relative to her own values. Nevertheless, her overwhelming selfish desire to "love" her child primarily for her own benefit almost killed the child. Love defined outside of the best interests of others is not virtuous no matter how a person defines virtue.

RELATIVE LOVE AND DATE RAPE

Let's review another example of relative virtue/love. Many adolescents acquire their understanding of love from the contemporary media. They listen to music about love, watch movies about love, and read about love online. While learning about love, they get on about "loving one another".

Date rape is a pandemic in the adolescent world. In working with hundreds of adolescents about this issue, I am convinced that most date rapes are never reported. The scenario usually goes as follows. A boy and girl are "together" (nowadays very seldom called a date). They develop a "relationship". The guy often says, "I love you", and the girl reciprocates. They are together somewhere, and he says he wants to "love" her. What does that mean? From a relativity perspective, it means whatever he wants it to mean. Movies, music, and the Internet have reinforced his belief that love is a physical thing. Love is nakedness and intimate touching. It is going "all the way".

He says to her, "I want to love you right now." For whatever reason she says, NO! He gets upset and accuses her of not accepting his sweet love. She says she doesn't care, NO means NO. He tells her he can't help but love her because she is so wonderful and beautiful. She says, NO. He gets upset and says, "I'm going to love you anyway. You can't stop me from loving you!" She says, NO, and then he rapes her.

His justification is that she really loves him, but just wasn't in the mood. "No big deal." He takes no responsibility. He says that rape only happens when you don't love someone. The argument goes on. I've spoken with girls who feel guilty for saying "no", because they also believe that real love is the physical expression of passion. When one can substitute love for rape because love is relative to one's lustful desires, virtue has disappeared. Love is about the well-being of others and not just ourselves. That goes for everybody, everywhere. That commitment to a virtue with boundaries can be found in the Relational Self living the Best Life, not the Low Life. See the chapter note for a further review of relativity.[1]

THE RELATIONAL SELF AND THE DARWINIAN SELF

The second objection to virtue is not necessarily connected to relativity. In fact, this objection rests more with the claims of Darwin and Freud. "Survival of the fittest" means that self interests must and will always be considered first. Natural law requires us to act with absolute self-interest in everything we do. By law, we cannot love unselfishly, give charitably, or share compassionately. Natural law views a life of charitable love as a life of self-deprecation, constant self-denial, and always bringing up the rear. Darwin could even argue that charitable love endangers the loving person and the species. This law says that you can't have virtuous relationships, even if you claim that you want to.

Contrarily, Strong Relationality proposes that this Darwinian interpretation of natural law is wrong. We can consider our own interests *equal* with others interests. Who in a relationship should be primarily attended, you or them? It depends on the comparative needs of you and them. Appropriately putting others first can be painful, but lovingly necessary.

That means at times, single mothers work three exhausting jobs to feed children, players switch positions for the benefit of the team, older brothers give up earnings to send another brother to school, a friend is not easily offended by a socially unaware buddy, and so on. However, our well-being is equally important. Virtue at times may place our personal needs first in a context, and sometimes not.

Let's look at Darwinian interpretations of what could be called acts of love. We are often in awe at the self-sacrifice and service rendered by mothers for their children. Darwinians say that this isn't virtuous love. Mothers are driven by self-interest. Biological, natural law drives mothers to preserve the species no matter what. They have to care for their children—the law makes them do it, not love.

Of course, natural law applies to all mothers with little children. Some behaviors are hard to explain from a Darwinian perspective. What law drives mothers to sell their babies so they can buy drugs or live a carefree lifestyle? What law drives mothers to kill the baby when it won't stop crying? What law causes mothers to prevent their children from marrying or bearing children to perpetuate their seed? Somehow, laws conflict and mothers obey one while disobeying another. However, they cannot morally choose what law to obey because Darwin says that they have no moral choice.

Scientists are carefully observing babies' behaviors. They have noticed infants only a few months old trying to help or assist another infant in need. That seemingly charitable inclination has no reasonable Darwinian explanation that connects their kindness to self-preservation. Could children be born with a propensity to compassionately care about others without self-interest? That can't happen in a Darwinian world.

Have you ever helped a homeless person? Maybe you gave them a meal or clothing. Darwin would argue that you didn't do that because you compassionately and unselfishly cared about that person. You *had* to do it. Have you ever risked your life to save a stranger's life or to protect them from serious injury? Remember that in Darwin's world, we are all competing for scarce resources to survive. If you endangered your life for a stranger, you had to. Why? I can't think of a rational Darwinian reason to explain it. Perhaps helping others and endangering ourselves means we are crazy and in violation of natural law.

While in the military, I talked with many veterans who saw their friends die. Some of them lost limbs trying to save their buddies. I asked them why. Their response was always some sort of description about love, respect, appreciation, and loyalty. These virtues are not recognized in a Darwinian world. Of course I didn't tell these veterans that they didn't really love their friends in arms, and that they were endangering their own lives to somehow ensure their own survival. That takes away the valor and bravery for which we celebrate and adorn our warriors with medals. But Darwin would say that they were just doing what the natural law required.

I could go on, but you get the picture. Life is full of loving sacrifices made to our families, strangers, and even enemies. We have all felt the sweetness that we call "love". It's hard to attribute all of this to law, and not altruistic love. Many of us go out of our way to defend our loving motives to be charitable. We feel hurt to believe that we can't really love others, and that our compassion is unconsciously driven by natural law? Somewhere, there is a Darwinian explanation to rebut our acts of compassion. Nevertheless, Strong Relationalists believe that virtue and the Best Life do exist in spite of relativistic and

Darwinian arguments.

Our responsibility is to determine how to protect the virtue within our relationships. Virtuous altruism includes self-love as part of other-love. Do not be deceived that altruism and virtue require a decision between who is most important—you or them? The altruistic question is: whose needs are most important at the present time? How can they best be attended?

VIRTUE DESERVES PROTECTION

Almost all of the virtues described by Aristotle are "facets" of love. To exercise virtuous behaviors, you must be motivated by an unselfish love. The capability to give and receive love can be considered a barometer of mental and emotional health. All humans innately need love to live and thrive, and we can't self-generate a sufficient amount of love for our own survival. Infants in orphanages that are not touched and handled regularly have a much higher mortality rate than babies that are held. How often do you read that serial killers and mass murderers are "loners"—emotionally embittered in their segregation from healthy, human connection? Love given and received through interactive virtues is life-giving. The individual and the community's needs for virtue are universal.

The Strong Relationality Best Life is a life of virtue. It soothes, fills, heals, and settles the soul. On the other hand, the insatiable hunger of the hedonist to fill the body's (or the ego's) cravings are unfulfilling, and exhausting. Notice that we don't build statues and laud the great hedonists: the famous whoremongers, voracious eaters, conspicuous consumers, addicts, and substance abusers. In movies, we cheer and cry over virtuous characters and their struggles to do the "right" thing. We naturally admire and revere virtuous people. It seems almost innate.

Perhaps you wonder if people agree on what is in fact virtuous, or most virtuous? Are some virtues more important than others? Strong Relationality suggests an answer to these questions. "Virtue conflicts" arise at times requiring you to choose one above another. You are not forced or determined by genetics or environment to choose one or the other. Even in divergent, cultures most people agree that kindness, respect, honor, compassion, integrity, and other virtues are expected and required for the culture to thrive. There may be cultural tweaks about the appropriate behavior of a virtue, but these aberrations are not significant enough to reject virtue as being fundamentally universal.

Even in gangs where members feel threatened by the outside world, virtue among members is expected and required. Honesty, loyalty, courage, sacrifice, and compassion among members keep the gang together. The need for virtue is innate in humans, but choice allows us to reject the path of virtue. Food is a universal need, but nobody forces us to eat. All around us we see the results of virtue deprivation on individual and national levels. How many worldwide problems would be solved if more people embraced virtue? Virtue is good and available, but not easy to choose! Hence, a good self-concept is not easy.

VIRTUE AND THE BEST LIFE

How do we decide which virtue to choose when choosing one means compromising another virtue? These dilemmas, large and small, happen to us all. Your self-concept needs strategies to realize the dilemmas and know how to confidently cope with them. There are no rules of priority to handily tell us what to do. It requires a "moral" choice. The following story illustrates a moral dilemma.

During WWII, a young Jewish mother lived alone in a modest home with her two children. Her husband had died in a bombing of her city. Her life had become her children. She was a faithful, religious woman who was committed to the Ten Commandments, and the principle of integrity. One morning, a knock came to her door. Looking at an angle through the front window, she saw the Gestapo. Electricity ran through her and her hands instantly turned cold and clammy. She opened the door, and they stepped inside. Looking around the room, the leader said, "Are your children here?"

Thoughts raced through her mind. To tell them the truth about the children's whereabouts might save her life, but maybe not. She wasn't sure what they wanted. To lie would be to break a commandment—one of the covenants that she had made with God. To tell them might endanger the children's lives for which she was morally responsible. Maybe they would find out whether she told them or not, so why garnish their wrath with a lie? She said a quiet prayer in her heart. She then looked them in the eye and said, "They are not here. I sent them away." A quick search of the house revealed nothing. They were well hidden, and the Gestapo left.

For most of us, this may appear to be an easy choice. She is responsible to protect the children, and if she must lie, beg, or steal to do so, so what? The children come first. Of course, she wasn't sure that a lie would conceal them and keep them safe. Of course, she had to worry about being killed for lying. Nevertheless, she chose between two virtues. There was no empirical way to make that decision. She relied on prayer, asking for inspiration because she needed knowledge and wisdom beyond her own. After the prayerful appeal, she felt confident and shameless in telling a lie. This does not mean that virtue is relative. It means that in some contexts, one virtue is more important than another. Virtue continues to be the focus, and the question is which virtue.

Let's up the ante. Imagine that the Gestapo came for medicine that she was using for her son who was seriously ill and who would die within 24 hours without the serum. However, her medicine was the last vial available in Germany, and was needed to make more of the serum. An epidemic was ongoing, and without the medicine, 100,000 would die. It would take three days to reproduce the serum, and all of her vile would be required to create more. Does she give the medicine to the Gestapo, or keep it? You may have hypothetically engaged in these dilemmas with your friends. However, imagine the stress of having to make the decision in the real world. At times like these, inspiration from a higher source can be lovingly appreciated. Do I try to save my son or the 100,000? This requires inspiration from a higher source (if it exists), and of course, we can't ignore the billions who believe that it does.

Strong Relationality contemplates the existence of that higher Source, and within this gut-wrenching context, you can make a "right" decision by receiving inspiration into a virtuous heart. What is the most virtuous thing to do considering everyone in this context? Should she save strangers rather than her own child, no matter how many there are? There are no set rules to solve this dilemma, but there is virtuous benevolence available if you know how to access that Source. Call it a Higher Power, the Collective Unconscious, God, the Life Force, or whatever.

I am not promoting any specific religion. However, I am advocating outside-originated inspiration. Stories of inspiration cross all religions and all nationalities. From Beethoven's symphonies written while he was deaf, to the father being unreasonably awakened and inspired to take his family out of a house that would soon catch fire. Inspiration occurs around the world every day.

Whether we seek out the inspiration, or just acknowledge its existence, our self-concept must contemplate this rather unexplainable phenomenon. William James provides a lengthy analysis of inspirational-religious experiences reported from many sources.[4] He does not discuss the dogma of religion, but delves into the religious-spiritual experiences of people from many institutionalized faiths and people unattached. Remember our near-death neurologist friend, Dr. Alexander? There are even psychotherapeutic approaches that are spiritually oriented, but non-denominational, and universal-oriented.

At most, James—the pragmatic psychologist and philosopher—seems to end up a believer in outside inspiration, At the least, he finishes his book, seeming to lean toward belief, while still scratching his head. Inspiration and virtue go hand-in-hand. Strong Relationality allows inspiration to virtuously guide us in contexts where no rule rules.

Relational virtue needs our protection and respect. Why? Because virtue protects real people: you, me, and everyone else. It also is the path to the Best Life, and the most enriching relationships. Life has wonderful meaning when it is full of love and virtue.

NOTES

1. Gergen, K. (2009). *Relational Being: Beyond Self and Community*. New York, NY: Oxford University Press, Inc.

2. For a contrast of strong relationality and relativistic relationality see an article in press that was a presented at the 119th Annual Convention of the American Psychological Association in San Diego. The presentation was part of a symposium entitled "Exploring and Critiquing Ken Gergen's Book *Relational Being*". Brent D. Slife and Frank F. Richardson (in press). Is Gergen's *Relational Being* relational enough? *Journal of Constructivist Psychology.*

3. Mitchell, L.Jay, Slife, B., & Whoolery, M. (2004). A theistic approach to therapeutic community: Non-naturalism and the Alldredge Academy. *Casebook for a Spiritual Strategy in Counseling and Psychotherapy* (Richards, S. & Bergin, A. (Eds.). Washington, D.C: APA Books.

4. James, W. (2008). *Varieties of Religious Experience: A Study in Human Nature*. Charleston, SC: Forgotten Books.

CHAPTER 8

I Think I Believe In Myself: Overcoming Doubt About Our Self-Concept

Have you ever doubted yourself? This doubt is not about whether you could do something, or if you could reach a goal. I am referring to doubt about your self-concept—who you think you are. The symptoms may include not feeling motivated about life, or not being fully committed to a life purpose. You may question yourself often, or you may frequently wonder if what you are doing is worth the effort. For some reason, you may feel tentative or hesitant about your life direction. You question whether you can be *sure* about yourself, and who you hold yourself out to be. Commitment is difficult without certainty. Can we commit to ourselves, if we are not sure who we *think* we are? How do we obtain enough certainty to fully commit ourselves?

Have you ever defended a belief that you were not sure was true? You strongly believed it was true, but you were not certain. Have you wondered how in the world you could put energy and passion into protecting a belief that you were not certain was true? That is risky! You had conviction without certainty.

We previously reviewed why scientific, objective analysis alone cannot give us certainty about who we are, or even who we *think* we are. If objective certainty is required to commit ourselves to a self-concept, we will never be committed. We are left with the task of committing ourselves to a self-concept without knowing for sure that it's "me". Some of us hold back in life because we are paralyzed by our doubts. We are afraid of making mistakes about being a *specific someone,* and so we morph our way through life like a chameleon—trying to safely blend in. By doing so, we miss the real joy of living, of being somebody. We need to calm the fears from doubting ourselves so that we can live a life of purpose and conviction. We make mistakes, but they can be our road signs, not our failures. I learned this at a young age.

SUPERMAN TAKES A FALL

When I was in kindergarten, my buddies and I would play superheroes at recess. My favorite was Superman. We had a great time, and we saved the world from destruction at least once a week. There was a large barn in an open field with a cavernous hayloft that I passed on my walk home from school. Sometimes, my little friends and I stopped and played in the loft. I would stand and look out over the field at the large door that served as an entrance and exit for hay bales. I imagined myself flying like Superman out of the door and around the neighborhood. One day, my friends suggested that I really was becoming Superman, and that I should try to fly. I wanted to with all my heart, but I was afraid. Finally, a buddy (or really a protégé of Lex Luther) convinced me that all I needed was a cape. Yeah, Superman wears a cape, and that empowered him to fly. We made a cape out of—I don't even remember what—and I tried it on. All of the guys said, "Wow". It looked good. With the cape on, I went up into the loft and straight to that big door. Without any hesitation, I held my hands above my head and jumped. To my surprise—and to the terror of my friends—I fell to the ground at what seemed super speed. Thankfully, the high grass saved me from serious injury, but my breath was knocked out and my mouth and nose bled.

I was confused. I felt like my life was ruined—not by the fall, but because I couldn't be a flying Superman. Even my buddy's suggestion that I needed a red cape gave me no hope. I was committed, and I chose wrong, but I was only *partially* wrong. On that day, I learned more about who I could be. Yes, I couldn't fly, but I did not give up adopting Superman's **purpose** to make the world a safer place. I was simply wrong in believing I had superpowers. (You actually don't turn into Superman until age 16.)

We want to minimize our mistakes, but we don't want to minimize our purpose or our potential to make this world a better place. We need to live a life of courage and also have good judgment. When we care enough about ourselves and other people, we can embrace our doubts and take inspired risks. Our virtuous intentions can protect us along the way. Let me share a quotation that passionately advocates living life courageously without certainty. This is a quote from Fitz James Stephen, also frequently quoted by William James.

"What do you think of yourself? What do you think of the world? These are questions that we all must deal with. They are riddles of the Sphinx, and in some way or another, we all must deal with them. In all important transactions of life, we have to take a leap in the dark. If we decide to leave the riddles unanswered, that is a choice; but whatever choice we make, we make that choice at our peril. If a man chooses to altogether turn his back on God and the future, no one can prevent him; no one can show beyond reasonable doubt that he is mistaken. If a man thinks otherwise and acts as he thinks, no one can prove that he is mistaken. Each person must act as he thinks best; and if he is wrong, so much the worse for him. We stand on a mountain pass in the midst of whirling snow and blinding mist, through which we get glimpses now and then of paths which may be deceptive. If we stand still, we will be frozen to death. If we take the wrong road, we will be dashed to pieces. We certainly do not know whether there is any right one. What must we do? 'Be strong and of a good courage.' Act for the best, hope for the best, and take what comes [...] if death ends all, we cannot meet death better."[1]

A LIFE OF DISCOVERY OR AVOIDANCE

We can have one of two attitudes towards life. We can live to ensure that we are never deceived. In doing so, we must be extremely critical, observant, careful, hesitant, and objective about who we are, and how we fit into the world. Or, we can live to discover our life purpose, and to commit to something bigger and more important than ourselves. That means that we must be careful and observant, but also courageous, committed and in love with our life purpose. Certainly, we try to minimize risks, but we take them.

Too many of us are afraid of a commitment because it may not be the right one. We hold back, looking for more certainty, as opportunities pass us by. We find a certain comfort inside our safe little bunker that we believe is our protection. We are unaware that we are insulating ourselves from the joys and fulfillment of quality relationships. We avoid standing shoulder-to-shoulder with others who really care about something more than comfort, or never making a mistake. Sometimes in life, our solutions to a perceived problem create bigger problems than the original problem. Passively retreating from the risks of life is one of those paradoxical solutions. Our protection becomes our demise. We end up not really living at all.

OBLOMOV

Oblomov is a classic Russian novel written by Ivan Goncharov. Oblomov, the main character, is the quintessential risk-avoider.[2] The author painstakingly takes he reader through Oblomov's thoughts and emotions, as he safely watches life drift by from his couch. Opportunities come his way. His friends invite him to social functions and gatherings that he politely avoids. A close friend visits him often and cajoles him about doing something with his life. The friend is persuasive, but ultimately unsuccessful. Financial opportunities come his way, but he ignores them. Finally, a beautiful woman somehow falls in love with him. He ends up having to choose between her or his safe and comfortable couch. The couch wins. Later, his good friend ends up marrying this beautiful woman. Oblomov dismisses his feelings and retreats to the couch. He tried to avoid possible rejections, failures, disappointments, and complications, by staying safely on the sidelines. However, he completely misses out on life.

My son read this novel and was depressed for a week. A life of doubting, retreating, and fearing mistakes can be as crippling as a disease. Hopefully, we will never be an Oblomov, but how often do we retreat to the couch and resign ourselves to stay there? The fear of the unknown can paralyze us, and the shame of making mistakes can keep us on the sidelines. Commitment is not just about certainty. It is also about purpose, love, relationships, and devotion. What is a mistake-free life without those things?

CAN WE REALLY AVOID LIFE DECISIONS?

We may mistakenly believe that we can avoid making decisions without certainty. That may be the biggest deception of all. We can think that when we have doubts about a decision, that we can avoid risk by not making the decision.

We falsely believe that being passive is the path to safety. Let me briefly review how William James views decision-making. Sometimes, there is no place to hide. James observes that we have to make some decisions, whether we want to or not. They are a special category. Additionally, there are decisions that are so pressing and important that we almost *have* to make them. They are so compelling that we are drawn to them like a moth to a flame.

THE FORCED OPTION TO MAKE A DECISION

Sometimes, we have to make a decision. We can't avoid it. William James calls this a "Forced Option".[3] This is what is technically known as a "logical disjunction". We usually think about it as an "either-or" proposition. "You can either accept my apology or go without it." Can you avoid making a decision about this proposition? No! The circumstances require an acceptance or a rejection. There is no in between. We are frequently confronted with forced options.

Here are a few obvious examples. An employee demands a raise or they will leave your company. They will not be dissuaded. You are forced to either give or not give the raise. A college offers you a scholarship for the fall. You must accept it or go without the scholarship. Someone offers you a calorie-laden dessert and says, "Take it, or I'll eat it." Your child says, "Come to my game, or don't come." You find someone hurt from an accident, and you either help them or you don't. These examples are typical scenarios. They may or may not be significant or life-changing.

Let's consider Oblomov's life. Ignoring decisions did not eliminate having to make decisions. Passively demurring and pretending not to be committed one way or another was his response to forced options. His decisions were no, no, and no. Whether he liked it or not, he made decisions that he could not avoid.

Those who try to avoid forced options are often trying to minimize the risks from making a decision. They hope to avoid the consequences of decision-making. However, that doesn't work. In Oblomov's case, he was left with the consequences of passively staying on the couch. He decided to forego love, relationships, business opportunities, and social interactions. Consequences follow forced options, no matter how the decision is made, or what is ultimately decided. The same goes for many decisions about our self-concept and life purpose. You can't avoid many decisions about choosing the path of the Good Life or the Best Life.

THE LIVING OPTION

A living option is not a forced decision, but it is compelling. The degree of interest in the subject matter makes it compelling. You may decide to become a more interesting person because you want to be more attractive to another person. You decide because you care. If you didn't care for the person, you wouldn't care to make the decision. If someone asked you to choose between being a duck or a goose, you may not be interested. You could just walk away without making a decision. Being a duck or a goose may not be important to you, and therefore you don't decide either way. The same can be said about living options that are within your self-concept. Options that are not attractive to you may simply be ignored. However, the more attractive the options, the more they become living options.

MOMENTUS CHOICES

Once-in-a-lifetime situation are momentous choices. You can't postpone the choice, and the option may or may not be available in the future. Let's assume that you want to visit Europe. You are unable to afford the trip right now, but another family invites you to go with them. You have another opportunity to learn how to break cement with a sledgehammer. You can't do both, but you don't have to do either one. You really want to go to Europe and you may not have another opportunity to do so. Of course, you love breaking up concrete, but it doesn't feel momentous. Going to Europe is momentous for you, so you decide to accept your friend's offer. We may have once-in-a-lifetime choices to make about our self-concept. We may have short windows of opportunity to claim a mentor, have a unique training, or pursue a life-changing experience in a foreign country.

Normally, we have to make forced, living, or momentous, decisions without all of the information. We can't make a totally objective decision because we lack knowledge. Even with lots of information, we don't know the end result. We are taking risks no matter which option we take. We can't completely avoid the risks. We can become as informed as possible about our decisions, but in the end, there will always be room for doubt. Therefore, we need to make decisions that include risks, and commit ourselves to those decisions. This is particularly true in making decisions about who we are creating ourselves to be.

Assume that we are asked to choose between the Good Life or the Best Life. Is this a forced option? We might think that there are more than two life styles. Maybe we want to choose some combination of the Good Life and the Best Life. We may see these other options as an avenue to avoid choosing the Good Life or the Best Life. That won't work. The Good Life and Best are specifically defined to create a forced option. In each life context, the options are to care about others as much as yourself (the Best Life) or to care more about yourself than others (the Good Life). You have no choice but to choose one or the other when a context arrives.

From a *long-range* perspective, we can *desire* to choose one or the other as our life path. However, our desires can change over time. In reality, we choose the Good Life or the Best Life one context at a time. This cannot be avoided. Therefore, we all choose the Good Life or the Best Life on a daily basis. We can't escape choosing between the Good and the Best as we have defined them. Frequently renewing a long-term preference to live the Best Life will make it easier to choose Best Life options in Life contexts. We are forced to decide between the Good and the Best Life continually, and we usually have to do so with limited information.

Before leaving this reality of being forced or pressured to make a choice without absolute certainty, relate it to your self-concept and worldview. Can you remember some of the forced, living, and momentous decisions in your life? Think of one or two. What were the circumstances that forced you or pressured you to make a decision without absolute certainty? Now reflect on how you made the decision. Think about how much objective certainty and thoroughly objective thinking went into the final decision. What was the clincher?

HOW WE REALLY MAKE LIFE DECISIONS

Don't doubt your decisions because you doubt your objectivity or your lack of information. Most of our life decisions, such as our life-concept, are not finally decided because of objective analysis. Worrying about a lack of objectivity is useless. I am advocating that we be as rational and objective as possible in our decision-making. However in doing so, I realize that even if we have a perfectly objective and rational basis for making a decision, we are rarely motivated to choose that option. What else is there?

William James made an incredibly profound observation. I view it as a Jamesean Maxim. "As a rule we disbelieve all facts and theories for which we have no use."[4] Stated in the positive, we all have personal preferences, biases, and hopes in which we are invested. They are deep within us and often haven't been consciously put into words. Protecting those interests is what is "useful" to us. In all of our decisions, we want to protect and promote those interests. Understanding this rule of thumb can help us recognize how we can try to objectively view life, but are helplessly subjective in doing so. That applies to what we believe will give us the Best Life. We have a strong tendency to believe what we *prefer* to believe.

Realize that we are moved to disregard or disbelieve information that undermines our deep-level beliefs or desires. These are our conscious or unconscious beliefs and biases. They affect how we receive and code information. We welcome and seek validation for our deepest biases. Once we understand and own-up to this phenomenon, we can live with it and work with it. This tendency is a part of our nature.

I remember being at a basketball game and sitting by a mother of one of the players. She pointed out which player was her son, and we watched the game together. Her son turned the ball over several times, missed most of his shots, and fouled out of the game. I didn't know what to say because I didn't want to hurt her feelings. It turned out that I didn't need to worry. She turned to me and said, "Didn't he play a wonderful game? I loved the way he blocked that shot." I just stared at her. She wanted him to have a good game, and she wanted it so badly, that she just focused on one good play and ignored all of the mistakes. She *chose* to believe what was useful to her. It wasn't objective at all.

We do this all the time. I remember during a political campaign hearing the candidates debate one another. Lots of issues and reasons were discussed for each person's political position. I thought it was a good debate. Afterwards, I left the auditorium with my friends to eat pizza. At the restaurant, one friend said, "I'm going to vote for [Candidate A], because he wants to cut taxes." Other friends made insightful and sometimes critical comments about Candidate A. My friend simply said, "I don't care. He wants to cut taxes." What was most useful to my friend was tax cutting, and he essentially ignored the rest of the discussion. Another friend wanted to vote for Candidate B because she was the best dressed person on stage, and much easier to look at. "If they are going to be in office for four years, and we have to look at them, then we might as well enjoy it."

Analytical scholars also choose to believe what is useful to them. William James recounted attending a lecture in which the speaker proposed ideas that were new, but not supported by conclusive evidence. A group of renowned scholars ridiculed the proposal, because it was not based on enough objective evidence. James pointed out that the evidence was actually rather substantial. He confronted this group with the proposition that they were simply choosing to believe what was useful to them. Many of their beliefs were supported by objective evidence not any more substantial than the speaker's evidence. James claimed that what was useful to them was protecting their reputations among their constituents. They were making useful decisions based on ego and not pure objective analysis.[5]

James is not advocating that we throw reason out the window and mindlessly follow our emotions. He did not like making analytical errors or being duped. However, he recognized that after all of our objective thinking and reasoning, we will choose to protect what is useful to us whenever possible. In other words, the driving force behind our decisions is linked to our desires and values not our objectivity. We can even be emotionally committed to objectivity. We look at the objective evidence through the lens of self-interest. That is what it's like to be human. We are left with the charge to carefully uncover and understand our deepest desires and values. We can actually be more reasonable by openly revealing our most treasured values and interests. With awareness and disclosure, we and others can consciously evaluate how our decisions are useful to us. That may eliminate some of the times when we say, "Why did I do that?"

This honest soul-searching can help us understand why we embrace elements within our self-concept. We are going to choose to be what is most useful to us. Let us be careful to consciously know what we value most. What are our primary desires and preferences? We are bound to choose a self-concept that expresses and manifests those desires. Creating a self-concept is another way to obtain what we most desire. Let's not kid ourselves. When we understand this human tendency, we can understand that to change our self-concept we must change our values. This may range from clarifying or re-prioritizing our values, to adding some and dropping others. Of course, changing what we love and value is not a cognitive function. Changing requires more than just using our brain.

THE BRAIN SELF AND THE HEART SELF

Emotional "thinking" can lead us to comfortably choose without certainty. We are not Dr. Spock creatures who only function as logical machines. We have emotions that express thoughts differently than our brain. We are consciously thinking with our brain when we are creating language, sounds, and pictures inside our mind. We also think with our emotions. Recently published books have been written about emotional intelligence.[6]

Research has suggested that the brain may not think alone. Some scientists are uncovering evidence supporting that the heart may have a mind of its own. New technology has revealed that neural pathways carry information from the brain to the heart, and that separate neural pathways carry information from the heart to the brain. Results show that the heart has ten times more pathways to the brain than from the brain to the heart. In other words, it seems as if the heart gives information to the brain that originates in the heart.[7]

These heart "thoughts" may be expressed as emotions instead of cognitive ideas. They interact with the brain to help create our "thinking/feeling" experience. If so, the "click" of emotion you sense in thinking about your self-concept may very well be the emotional thoughts from your heart. The age-old maxim, to "think with your heart" may be more real than previously imagined. If the heart is the center of desires, passions, and preferences, it can communicate these to the brain in hopes that they will be honored.

When the heart and the brain disagree, we have internal conflict and stress that can actually create heart disease and stroke. Brain and heart disagreement tell us that there are at least two sides or opinions about a thought. This can be useful if acknowledged. For example, we may experience conflict about our self-concept. That is a red flag alerting us to clarify what is happening between the brain and the heart. What are the specific bones of contention?

Just listening to the heart or just the brain disrupts the full thinking process. When their inputs are combined, we gain a more realistic knowledge base for making choices. Nevertheless, their combined efforts rarely produce certainty. However, unity of mind helps us deal with the ambiguities of life. Their continued disagreement indicates that a serious conflict needs to be resolved. These internal disagreements are often at the center of our dysfunction. They create a lack of confidence in our decision-making. This is not a bad thing. We are alerted by these feelings that a priority needs attention. Without a reconciliation of some sort, we are not really "together". Our self-concept can be fractured. Our commitment to one choice or another is diluted. However, the heart and mind can come together if we help them interface with one another. We need them working together to fulfill our deepest desires.

Unfortunately, some people only believe in the brain's rational input or on in the heart's emotional input. They want to exclude from thought, one or the other. For example, objectivists are all about reason and scientific proof. Some pure objectivists argue that emotions should not be allowed to interfere with logical thinking. They posit that to be accurate and correct, judgments need to be without emotional bias. Of course, there are those who want to be exclusively intuitive and listen only to their hearts.

DECISION-MAKING WITH INTUITION AND INSPIRATION

We often hear people talk about, "going with their gut" as well as listening to their heart. In both instances, they are referring to flashes of intuition or inspiration. We often wait for that "feeling" before making a decision. Many of us place considerable trust in these feelings. What are they really? We are talking about more than indigestion or a heart flutter.

For our purposes, we will consider them as originating from two separate places. Intuition originates in the unconscious mind. Inspiration originates from an outside source such as a Higher Power or Jung's "collective unconscious". Since many of us consider them as part of our decision-making strategies, let's summarize how they operate.

In his best-selling book, *Blink,* Malcom Gladwell compares conscious reasoning with "blinks" or intuition from the unconscious mind.[8] As we will discuss later in more detail, the unconscious mind contains vast amounts of information that it categorizes and processes out of our awareness. On occasion, the unconscious is prompted to communicate information or its opinions to the conscious mind. Apparently, the unconscious mind not only stores information, but also analyzes it and comes to its own conclusions. The communication is often called a flash of intuition, a blink, or a flash of insight. It just pops up, seemingly out of nowhere.

Gladwell points out that these blinks are not just impulsive thoughts. The unconscious has done a lot of work putting the thoughts together, and we are just unaware of this processing. However, we often find these blinks to be accurate, and we often follow their direction. Intuition can be very useful, and it can save our conscious mind both time and effort. We do have to remember that our unconscious is not infallible. It can make mistakes just like our conscious mind makes mistakes. The integrity of our intuition comes from the correctness of the information stored in our unconscious. Additionally, we must trust the reasoning faculties of our unconscious mind to give us reliable intuition. As Gladwell points out, it can make mistakes and has limitations. The unconscious mind is not magic.

Inspiration falls in a different category. Not everyone believes we can receive inspiration from an outside source. Most biological determinists do not believe in sources outside the body that are immaterial or beyond capture by the five senses. However, many people believe in a higher power, a life force, life after death, or a collective unconscious, and so on. As William James points out people all over the world report experiences or connections with these outside sources.[9] They may receive comfort, knowledge, verification, insight, or creative vision. Beethoven claimed that his Ninth Symphony was given to him by inspiration. He heard it played in his mind, and wrote out the music of what he heard. Some people refer to prayers being answered and warnings given to avoid harm. In any event, inspiration comes from a source outside the person, but the person must perceive and interpret the inspiration.

People who trust inspiration have usually had a series of similar experiences. These experiences have common characteristics such as a feeling of love that attends the inspiration. Experience over time can create a sense of familiarity and trust in receiving inspiration. Sometimes, a unique and powerful experience like a Near Death Experience, creates a sense of trust because of its vividness and intensity. We would be prudent to review our experiences with inspiration to build trust in what we feel is inspired.

Obviously, we can be confused about whether we are experiencing intuition from our unconscious, or inspiration from an outside source. The flashes and mental impressions from each source may seem to be similar. The only way we can distinguish them is experience. I have heard that inspiration is usually attended by a sense of peace and certainty. Without that peace attending an impression or an experience, we may have reason to pause.

Intuition or inspiration may attend an objective analysis. Perhaps, a feeling of confirmation or a sense of doubt may attend a well thought out conclusion. For some people, that provides credibility to their decision or conclusion. For others, intuition or inspiration has not been part of their life. Let us be mindful how we recognize intuition and inspiration. Many people claim they can't imagine living without it. Others cannot imagine ever having it.

Creating a self-concept and choosing a life purpose are the types of experiences where people often sense intuition and inspiration. Because the subject is so important and far-reaching, we can understand how the unconscious would be active in the process. Additionally, for sources that may be outside of ourselves, they may also have a connection to our life that we don't understand. Receiving inspiration is a very personal matter and impossible to evaluate with pure objectivity.

REDUCE THE RISK OF SELF-CONCEPT CHOICES

You can have a self-concept and worldview without certainty and still feel safe. I am not recommending "blind faith" and impulsivity as the answer. Understand that you have a responsibility to gain knowledge from every reliable source, and that includes fact-finding, rational thinking, and worthy opinions. You are also responsible to understand thoughts coming from you heart. Finally, intuition and inspiration must be carefully evaluated and experienced to determine their reliability. All of these influences go into your decision-making. They exercise roles in choosing the Best Life and your self-concept. However, skillfully using them all together will not eliminate risk in making important, life decisions.

Safety is not found in objectivity, subjectivity, or a combination of both. They can lead us astray. We need to be passionately committed to an honorable life purpose! This purpose can almost spontaneously prioritize our biases and preferences. It determines what are useful and desirable actions. It also automatically categorizes destructive actions.

We are protected from making hurtful mistakes by following a virtuous, honorable purpose. How does it work? We make decisions that are most *useful* to us. We look for ways to validate and manifest what we most value. In doing so, we are not easily distracted or dissuaded from what is most useful. When we accept an honorable purpose as our life treasure, we create a path for living. That path protects us from whatever would hurt or limit our purpose. We make decisions that further our purpose, and we are skeptical of decisions that would harm it.

We all do this to some extent. However, our purposes are often divided or ill defined. That dilutes our commitment to our purpose, because it isn't clear and vivid in our mind. We can't focus on what is blurry. Mixed up or cloudy purposes are not powerful and compelling. Much of our fear and uncertainty about life decisions arise because we aren't committed to a direction or purpose. Some days we may be drawn in one direction, and on another day we are drawn somewhere else. A clear, honorable life purpose allows us to focus on a desirable destination. You can illustrate this concept by taking a piece of paper and drawing a circle. Mark a spot in the middle of the circle (that's you). Your objective is to go "somewhere" in the circle. How many paths can you take to get "somewhere". That's right, you have thousands of paths, even if you don't know when you actually get to "somewhere". Who knows where you might end up? You don't even know. Now mark a point on the edge of the circle. That is your life purpose. Your new task is to get from the middle to the point on the edge. How does that affect focus and decision-making? It helps to clearly know where you're going.

However, we need more than a clear objective to be safe. We need a virtuous, honorable objective. That means that our objective includes loving and caring about people as much as ourselves. A Best Life purpose also certifies that the means we follow to get the objective are virtuous. We now have a loving objective, and we have a well-defined means to get there. The ends and means are consistent.

How does this reduce the risk in daily decision-making? We have already decided that our purpose and objectives are safe and honorable. We have a safe destination. We also know that acts of virtue are safe and honorable. By putting them together, we have a safe destination and a safe means to get there. We are not just safeguarding ourselves, but others as well. If we are constantly seeking the well-being of our self and others, and if our means of accomplishment are courage, compassion, integrity, forgiveness and so on, then we have minimized the consequences of our possible mistakes. What does minimize consequences mean? If we are sincerely trying to be honest, compassionate and so forth, what kind of errors would we logically make? We might miss the mark of being honest or compassionate. However, we are still in the virtuous ballpark. Our intentions and our virtuous means to obtain them are barriers to destructive options. That is our safety net. The consequences of our mistakes can be minimized if our intentions are honorable and purpose driven.

I have a plaque on my wall that says, "The Purpose of Life Is a Life of Purpose." That is what will allow us to use rational thinking, heart thinking, intuition, and inspiration to make life decisions safely. Our life purpose and our values are reflected in our self-concept and our commitment to the Best Life. The Best Life not only gives us joy and fulfillment, it is the safest life course.

Much of life is like that. **Creating and defending your self-concept is an act of hope and desire mixed with the facts**. In spite of objective analysis, you can't comprehensively know who you are or whether your self-concept is absolutely "true". How can we cope with life and death beliefs always shaded with ambiguity? What would the Volkswagen from the Introduction say?

NOTES

1. James, W. (1956). *The Will to Believe and Other Essays in Popular Philosophy*. Mineola, NY: Dover Publications, Inc.

2. Goncharov, I. (2005). *Oblomov*. (D. Magarshack, Trans.). London, UK: Penguin Books, Ltd.

3. (James, 1956).

4. (James, 1956).

5. (James, 1956).

6. Goleman, D. (1995). *Emotional Intelligence: Why It Can Matter More than IQ*. New York, NY: Bantam Books, Inc.

7. McCraty R (2003). Heart-Brain Neurodynamics: The Making of Emotions. HeartMath Research Center, Institute of HeartMath, Boulder Creek, CA, Publication No. 03-015.

8. Gladwell, M. (2005). *Blink: The Power of Thinking Without Thinking*. New York, NY: Little, Brown and Company.

9. James, W. (2008). *Varieties of Religious Experience: A Study in Human Nature*. Charleston, SC: Forgotten Books.

CHAPTER 9

The Morality and Ethics of Self-Concept

THE GOOD, THE BAD, OR THE NEITHER

Do you consider yourself a good person, a bad person, or neither one? Maybe, you think you are a combination—an "in-betweener" of good and bad. Then again, you may not believe that people should be classified as "good" or "bad". Good and bad mean different things to different people. Because of these differences, you may think that "good" and "bad", are terms too ambiguous to be useful in distinguishing one self. However, can you actually stop thinking about yourself as good or bad? You have learned well, how to *feel* good or feel bad about yourself. You are not just evaluating what you can do, but who you are. For example, we are not referring to whether you are a good or bad hockey player or even a good or bad cook. You are judging your essence—the quality of your being.

However, without some calibration tool, how do you know if you are becoming a better person? As we create our self-concept, we unconsciously set up criteria of whether we are going in a favorable or unfavorable direction. Some of us may have given up trying to improve ourselves. We have just thrown in the towel. Perhaps, we don't *think* we can be better than we *think* we are. That may mean that we have judged ourselves unrealistically. We've trapped ourselves needlessly. We've lost hope in ourselves. This chapter is about renewing our hope in who are and who we are becoming.

Rather than judge yourself by whether you have reached a destination, focus instead on your direction. If you choose a road and consistently stay on it, you are constantly getting closer to a destination. No one in this life has arrived at their final destination. The key to a positive self-concept is to stay focused on the direction, not on whether you have arrived there. By living one day at a time, you can control the direction in which you are traveling. You can start over one day at a time. You can feel relieved and encouraged every day by just turning to face in the most favorable direction. Then, you begin moving in that direction, step-by-step. At the end of the day, you can calibrate how well you have maintained your direction. Tomorrow is a new day.

Without beating ourselves up or berating ourselves for not being at a destination, we can enjoy the satisfaction and confidence of moving in our chosen direction. We can know that we are becoming a better person. The key is picking a quality road to a desired destination. That is where the Best Life enters the picture. When we are focused on building quality, virtuous relationships, we are on the best road. Giving and receiving love in virtuous ways affords us the Best Life of joy and peace. We personally benefit, because we improve ourselves to achieve better relationships. It's a win-win proposition. We never fail as long as we can turn in a favorable direction and start moving.

Let's not stigmatize ourselves by thinking that we are good or bad, or that we are a final product. We can judge whether we are going in a good or bad direction. Sometimes, a moral judgment of our self turns into a permanent, deterministic judgment . We think, "I'm either good or bad, and that's the way I am." However, we are not a piece of steak that is judged permanently as Grade A or Grade B. We are not deterministic meat. We are alive and always changing. What is important is that we are moving in the right direction. Sometimes, we may get turned around in the wrong direction. In that case, we need to refocus and reorient ourselves to get back on course. When we are moving in the right direction, we are a good person no matter where we are on the road.

We are tempted to only judge ourselves by our past. That can be misleading and stifling. We view the past as the past, unchanging, never to be revisited. We see the past as a "fact". We look at our past and judge ourselves. This may be helpful in knowing the direction and the momentum in which we have been traveling. But what about today? Today is also meaningful. Our past may be full of mistakes and failures. If so, we are tempted to judge ourselves as not being very good. We are not motivated to change our direction, because we have arrived at being a good or bad person. The same can be said for those who view the past as a history of successes and good decisions. If so, we are tempted to judge our selves as being good. We think we have established ourselves as good because of our past. We may not be motivated to stay on course. We have been stamped as Grade A so we don't have to worry very much about what happens in our life today. These are crippling attitudes, because they focus on the past and make final judgments. They neglect the present and the responsibility to be a quality person in the here-and-now.

Sometimes we are not aware of needing a course correction. We are unconsciously moving off course while we think we are on course. This requires us to have random moments of introspection and self-honesty. Our challenges and trials in life also afford us rare opportunities for honest self-evaluation. Because of these opportunities to correct our course direction, trials can be beneficial. I learned this to be true.

SELF-SCRUTINY—THE FAST BURNER

On one occasion, I was forced to scrutinize myself for quality in an excruciating way. In my early thirties, I viewed myself as a fast-burner, having experienced a bit of success on my way into life. My family life was wonderful. I loved my wife and four children, for whom I felt an undying commitment to their well-being. My wife was devoted to creating a loving and secure foundation for our four young children. She chose to give them all of herself during their crucial, developmental years. I had graduated from law school and was well into my career. We had a good life.

One evening, while sitting in a serene place, my heart began to do indescribable things inside my chest. I almost passed out several times. I felt sharp, piercing pains, mini-explosions, dizziness and disorientation. I finally got home and into bed but could not sleep. It was a long night for me, full of reflection and incredulity. The next morning the ambulance arrived and it was finally determined that I had not suffered a classic heart attack. However, the symptoms continued and worsened. I could not work and traveling in a car was a certain brand of torture for me. Weeks passed, and then months, and even years with little change. Something was wrong with the electrical stimulation of my heart. However, medicine was not advanced enough at the time to help me very much. After a year, we had gone through our savings, and I still could not work. I remember losing our home and our cars.

That's enough reflection. You get the picture—tough times for a young husband and family. In the midst of this I had a "coming to truth" meeting with myself. I had always perceived myself as a worker, a helper, and a producer. *I* was the one who helped other people. I thought that I did so because I cared about them in a pure, nonjudgmental way. Don't get me wrong, I wasn't intentionally insincere or hypocritical. However, I discovered that my deepest unconscious beliefs were inconsistent with my conscious beliefs. All of a sudden, I was on the other side of the table. I was weak, sick, and unproductive. I wasn't a fast burner any more, I was just burned out ashes.

With this new realization, how could I value myself? I had once helped the downtrodden and the weak. And I thought that I did so without judgment and with total compassion. If this was true, then I should also value myself without being judgmental or full of pity. I couldn't do it. I loathed myself, and I fought hard to just find enough self-esteem to stay alive. I valued competency and productiveness more than almost anything. I understood that I had always cared about others, and I helped them because of sincere compassion. However, to my painful surprise, I realized that deep inside of me I prided myself in being stronger and more capable. That realization disgusted me. I wanted to believe that the love and compassion that I had for others was more sincere than it really was. I also wanted to value myself not just for my productivity and utility. I was now in the camp of the weak and the downtrodden.

I could not have made it through all this without the love of someone purer than me. My incredibly gifted and loyal wife nursed my body and my soul. My body took years to recover, but I made it. My soul healed faster. Her pure love of me in spite of my weaknesses allowed me to respect myself and to understand that humans have inherent worth not based on their utility. It also gave me the startling conviction that I would live and that I would have an opportunity to bring her every joy in my power. I could never repay her. Unfortunately, she died in an automobile accident before I could give her all that she deserved.

I learned that quality of self was not tied to self-worth. As a human being, I could not earn or change my inherent worth. However, that did not mean I could not become a better person. I struggled with what that meant. I had to change my criteria about whether I was a good person or not. I was able to make a course correction and to be more centered on the road toward a Best Life destination. I could improve the quality of my self. For me, this consisted of removing a sense of superiority that I felt put me somehow above those less fortunate. In other words, I had to refine understanding of what was most valuable. My quality as a person improved because I gained more love and compassion for other people.

THE ETHICAL AND MORAL SELF

Morality and ethics can be rather obtuse subjects. I will define them in a general way for our purposes. Ethics relates to societal rules of conduct. Morality relates more to individually chosen rules of conduct. Ethical rules are set by a society. Moral rules originate in an individual person's mind or from a Deity. A person's conscience may be thought to be sensitive to the person's sense of morality, whether adopted from Deity or from one's own perceptions. The general focus is on the rules of conduct.

We all have our own rules of conduct, and they define our morality. Some people have very specific and well-defined rules, while others have more general rules. To lead a moral life is to be true to one's moral code of conduct. Our personal code of conduct is a part of our self-concept. That code also determines whether we can live the Best Life or the Good Life.

There are those who deny that we make moral decisions, or that we are even moral beings. Some people want to distinguish what is right from what is moral. They do so by making what is right as merely a personal preference. Some people find morality not "useful" to them. They don't want to be constrained by specific rules. Being branded "right" or "wrong" is offensive to them. They define freedom as being free of rules, especially moral rules. They argue within themselves that they can avoid morality; that they are "above" it. Difficulty arises when the consequences of free actions are evaluated. It is logical and even intuitive to look at consequences as good, bad, indeterminate, hurtful, helpful, etc. These types of measurements are laden with morals, especially when connected to human relationships. Let's take a look at rules and consequences. We will discover that intentions are as important as the rules. Morality consists of rules and intentions.

FOUR STRATEGIES FOR DEALING WITH RULES

Let's consider four strategies of dealing with rules in relationships. Perhaps, you can find the one that most matches your style.

- *My rules for me and my rules for you*—I don't believe in stealing and neither should you.
- *My rules for me and your rules for you*—I don't believe in stealing, but you follow your own rules about stealing.
- *No rules for me and my rules for you*—I can steal if I want to but you can't. (A favorite of some adolescents.)
- *My rules for me and I don't care if you have rules*—I have my own set of rules, but you can live without rules if you want.

Notice that strategies *can* be altruistic or totally self-serving depending on the context. Which type of person would you want as a business partner? Which type would you want as a best friend or an intimate associate? Which type would you prefer partying with? Which type would make the best CIA agent? Notice how the context plays into your choice.

You can be altruistic in wanting someone not to steal because you believe it is in their and your best interest. However, what about wanting someone to follow your rules so they will be more predictable and easier to take advantage of? That's not altruistic. Would it be altruistic to restrict yourself from stealing but tolerate someone else's stealing? Where does the victim fit in to altruism? Is it altruistic to stay away from people who have different rules than you? What if they are stealing from you? Whose best interest, if anyone's, would be served in each of the above scenarios?

You can see how intention in many cases is as important as the rule? Rules are helpful guidelines, but intention in following them determines if we are altruistic or selfishly utilitarian. However, rules cannot be avoided. Even the anarchist has a rule: "I will do whatever I want". "No rules for me" is a rule. Our moral intentions in complying with the rules affect the quality of our identity, who we are.

Ethical rules represent the values of a society, and moral rules represent the values of an individual. The rules are the manifestations of the values. We can therefore think of moral intentions. When we are considering a moral direction, we are not just referring to following all the rules. We are talking about our hearts. We are touching on our values and motivations. To change direction on our life road, we not only change behavior, but we also change our priorities, our desires. We can be moving in a quality direction without living all the moral rules. We stay on the road by focusing and refocusing our desires. By staying on the road and moving in the desired direction, we find ourselves living more and more of the rules. Our hearts point us in the directions we travel, not just our minds.

We can feel good about ourselves if our hearts are focused on a quality direction such as the Best Life. We don't have to feel like a failure if we don't abide by all the rules. We can keep trying. We are required to point ourselves in the right direction and desire our quality destination. In simple terms, we are good if we are moving in a quality direction, and we are not so good if we are moving away from it. Changing directions is easier to accomplish than immediately reaching a destination. Being good is within our reach.

MORAL OBJECTIVES

Consequently, in considering the moral self, I have chosen to focus on personal motives rather than rules or philosophical positions. Let's focus on the moral issue of whether we primarily act out of contrived self-interest or altruistic interests? That is a predominant issue in creating a moral self-concept. Much of self-improvement is mastering our desires. Perhaps you have read some of the novels written by the Russian author, Dostoyevsky, that plumb the depths of moral desires. Determinism even addresses our tendency to act selfishly or altruistically. The answer to the question of where our deepest desires originate, distinguish choice from determinism.

We know that not all religious beliefs are altruistic. The cause of religion has been exploited to justify genocide as a virtue (the Nazis seeking to "morally" cleanse the human race of corruptible Jewish blood). Any belief system can be spun for exclusively selfish and exploitive interests even if it is caste as altruistic. We are left with bottom-line questions. What are our motives? Who do we really want to be? What direction do we wish to travel?

THE BEST LIFE AS A MORAL CHOICE

There are many roads and lifestyles to choose from. I am promoting the Best Life of loving relationships and altruistic motives. This choice proposes that relationships connected through virtue and mutual interest lead us to a joyful life with healthy emotional and physical well-being. A life of selfishness and narcissism exploits people and leads to a life without fulfilling meaning. However, the Best Life can have times of sensually feeling good. Choosing between the two requires making an important decision. Are other people really important enough to care about as much as self or sometimes even more so? Can we really value other human beings that much? Biological determinists say no. Some people cannot find that much value in someone else's life compared to their own.

Our moral self—the motives and rules we choose—are determined by how much we value our self and others. There are those who have moral rules based on pure selfishness. Charles Taylor, a contemporary philosopher and politician describes a "morality of purely egoistic gratification"[1] which he believes is sponsored by radical materialism. This brand of morality is compatible with selfish instrumentalism. That means that we approve of using other people as instruments to our selfish gratification. Taylor quotes a French philosopher, Pierre Naville, who takes issue with this brand of living. "We are assured that there have been philosophers and atheists who have denied the distinction between virtue and vice, and who have preached debauchery and license in their morals."[2]

We choose our quality of life by facing in an altruistic direction or a self-serving direction. Which is the favorable direction? Which will lead us to the most joyful and fulfilling life? How important is love?

THE DILEMMA OF HUMAN WORTH

Taylor points out what he considers a truly difficult hurdle for determinists or materialists to surmount. *Can we find reason to believe that humans have inherent worth*? We've touched on inherent worth, and we will review it again later on. Unless inherent worth exists, taking care of the infirm elderly, the psychotic, the criminal, the non-producer in society, can make little sense. He restates Nietzsche's thought, that if we are only motivated by "self-interest" which powers a "negative morality, then recipients of kindness don't deserve it. "[...] pity is destructive to the giver and degrading to the receiver, and the ethic of benevolence may indeed be indefensible."[3] We can consider "indefensible" to mean irrational or without good reason. In other words, a morality based exclusively on self-interest would not value kindness to others. No one would deserve pity, and there would be no reason to be benevolent. This selfishness would require moral rules of conduct that only favor the individual self and not others.

At first, when I became ill, I actually believed that my kind friends pitied me in a condescending way, and that receiving help from them belittled me. I experienced what Nietzsche was saying, because I was not convinced of my inherent worth. Fortunately for me, I got over it.

Taylor's hurdle is a significant problem for the materialistic determinist. If we are born with an exclusive self-interest, how can we sacrifice self for another? How can we be truly benevolent? That's a tough question. Following this logic, we just can't have benevolent motives. We may seem to act benevolently. Remember that Dr. Gazzniga's emergent theory proposes that our benevolent actions are actually driven by self-centered desires created by genetic mutations. In other words, our apparent benevolence is fake. We only act benevolent when it will primarily promote our best interests. How does that fit into your world of experience?

People make incredibly unselfish sacrifices for others every day. I am not just talking about mothers caring for babies, or fathers sacrificing for their children. Strangers make compassionate sacrifices for people that they don't know. Are they acting selfishly rather than being unselfishly compassionate? Imagine someone diving into a frigid river to save an elderly woman whose car slipped off the road into the swirling water. After fighting hypothermia, exhausting every bodily muscle, and filling up lungs and stomach with filthy water, the rescuer pulls the woman to safety. While the rescuer is lying on the beach, sucking air and trying to recover, a reporter runs over and asks a question. "Why did you save that old lady that you didn't even know?" The rescuer looks up and says, "WHAT?" Without hesitation the reporter asks, "What benefit did you get from saving her? Are you looking for a reward or just publicity? What's your angle?"

The presumption is that even a rescuer risking life and limb to save someone else's life *must* have a selfish motive. The reporter assumes the rescuer wouldn't risk their life because they were more concerned about the person in danger. Do you think the rescuer was offended when asked that question? Would you be offended? (We won't discuss why the rescuer threw that reporter in the river.)

Many people from all sorts of belief systems feel intuitively that humans have inherent worth. This emotion is so strong, that some people knowingly sacrifice some self-interest to benefit another person. As mentioned earlier, even babies are observed to act empathically and compassionately.

Taylor resolves the dilemma of inherent human worth in the love called *agape.* This refers to the equal love of all humans given by a Higher Power. Agape assumes that if this superior presence recognizes inherent worth in humans, we can trust to do likewise. However, this belief steps outside the world of materialism, and is therefore unavailable to those who are true materialists.

For those readers who are pure materialists, but feel a desire to believe that other humans have equal, inherent worth, carefully consider how this can be justified materialistically. If you have reasons that are logical and rational, share them with others. There are many people who are still struggling with this dilemma. In the meantime, for everyone's benefit, let's nurture our benevolence in the best way we can.

My bias is toward a moral self-concept that includes loving and benevolent motives. We are moral beings. The question is, "What are our morals?" Sincere compassion, integrity, and appropriate sacrifice in our relationships lead us to the unselfishly moral Best Life. However, sincere desire for immediate gratification, selfishly motivated decisions, and artfully exploiting others, lead us to a selfishly moral Good Life.

We can never reach the *ideal of altruism* in this life. However, it can be our ultimate destination. We need to be pointed in that direction. We can feel good about our self if we are moving in an altruistic direction. We can't afford to pass final judgment on ourselves because of past mistakes. We live in the present. We are moving in one direction or another right now. We aren't trapped into following the path of the past. Let us judge ourselves by the direction we are traveling today. We may not be able to change the past, but we can change our present orientation. We can focus on moving in the right direction.

We deviate from our benevolent path periodically, and we wonder why. If we choose to move toward loving relationships, why should we lose our way? Why do we turn ourselves around and move away from the Best Life? Often, we simply lose our desire for the Best Life of unselfish love. Our desires fluctuate. Parts of our self get disoriented and focused on just feeling good. This can be frustrating and discouraging. What we need is a stronger, more consistent desire to point ourselves in an altruistic direction. We need to work on our desires.

DESIRING TO DESIRE

One of the obstacles or vehicles to the Best Life and unselfish love is our fluctuating desires. We are not born to be altruistic or relentlessly selfish. In each life experience, we *choose* our motives. Life is about refining our moral choices. As of today, we are not totally altruistic or totally selfish. Our desires fluctuate. We can be pulled in either direction. Therefore, we need to consciously decide which desire we will feed and nourish. Do we choose to value altruism or exclusive self-interest? By choosing to value one over the other, we demonstrate an even higher desire. We can desire to increase our desire for altruism. By doing so, we aren't allowing our moment-by-moment feelings or desires to dictate our actions. We are honoring a *higher desire* to refine our moment-by-moment desires. As a result, our in the moment desires will become more consistent. We can thereby become more spontaneously altruistic day by day.

We can learn to discipline our desires. That is the heart and soul of morality.

We don't have to choose to act how we feel in the moment. We can protect ourselves from believing that if we feel attracted to something in the moment that that is what is best for us. Feelings come and go. Fleeting feelings do not always express our complete desires. We can make moral commitments to ourselves about what we want to consistently desire. These commitments are made after soul searching and contemplation. However, once made, we need to honor them. They are the heart of our self-concept and determine if we are choosing the Best Life.

Once we make the commitment what do we do? You may be familiar with a famous Native American story about a father, his son and their dogs. Their two dogs were always fighting. One day the son asked his father which dog would ultimately win. The father looked at the dogs and asked, "Which one do you want to win?" He paused, and then said, "When you decide, then feed that dog the most, and he will win." That is true of our inevitable conflicting desires. We can choose one and feed it the most. Over time, that desire will become the most predominant desire.

It is natural to have conflicting desires. Everyone feels kind and compassionate at times, but we also feel self-centered at other times. We need not judge ourselves for having conflicting desires. It is part of human nature. However, we can judge ourselves on what we "desire to desire". Why is that logical? As the Native American father said, we will feed the one we want to win. We will feed the desire we want to win. Either the desire to be selfish or the desire to be altruistic will be fed and nourished the most. That is a conscious decision for which we will be accountable to ourselves and to others. How do we feed our desires? How do we guide which desire will win?

We can learn to *desire to desire.* Our lifestyles feed one or the other. We can choose a Best Life lifestyle. In the choosing, we are deciding to increase our desire to live and acquire the Best Life. We commit to not making decisions based on moment-by-moment feelings. We make decisions based on what will support the Best Life. We have Best Life criteria that include taking good care of ourselves and others.

BEST LIFE LIFESTYLE

We can organize our life to increase our desire for the Best Life. This may include the following decisions:

- Associate with people who share the desire for the Best Life.
- Take good care of your health and emotional well-being.
- Look for opportunities to help and express appreciation to others.
- Read good books and engage in discussions about the qualities of the Best Life.
- Learn from others how to overcome the challenges of living the Best Life.
- Set up a daily regimen that may include reading, meditating, praying, focusing, and planning to live the Best Life that day.
- Avoid feeding self-centered desires of pity, immediate gratification, anger, jealousy, and resentment.
- "Wallow" in the gratitude of what you have rather than being consumed by what you don't have.
- Honor and respect the differences in other people.
- Avoid discriminating who you love in spite of their choices and beliefs.
- Feel the love that comes your way.
- Avoid the activities or contexts that feed your desire for the selfish Good Life. Be wise and mindful.

HONOR YOUR MORAL CODE AND EMBRACE BEING A GOOD PERSON

In doing these things, our desire for the Best Life increases. Our *desire to desire* more of the Best Life is paying off. It becomes our moral compass. By adopting the above recommendations, we will develop a firmer grip on the direction we have chosen.

Choosing our moral direction in life allows us to feel good about who we are. We can know that in spite of our mistakes we are making progress. We are moving down the road and we can feel proud of ourselves. By carefully choosing our direction we are led to be a morally good person. The chosen direction becomes a part of our self-concept, and our plans to improve ourselves. We can prevent past mistakes from taking away the Good Life.

NOTES

1. Taylor, C. (1989). *Sources of the Self: The Making of the Modern Identity*. New York, NY: Cambridge University Press.
2. (Taylor, 1989).
3. (Taylor, 1989).

CHAPTER 10

The Self—Real or an Illusion: Consciously Influencing Our Unconscious Novel

WHAT'S INCLUDED IN THE SELF

Grasping the reality of the self or a self-concept can be elusive. What were the developers of the English language thinking when they created the words: me, you, them, I, and us? Were they just referring to a human body that seemed to be intact and distinct from other human bodies? Or were they also thinking of personalities, past experiences, talents, roles, patterns, accomplishments, and more when they considered an "I", "you", or "they"?

Scientists and others seem to have trouble putting the "whole self" together. Acknowledging the material part of "self" is easy to do, even for a child. However, what else goes into the reality of self? We can get confused deciding where to draw the line about the self when we consider the intangibles, the talents, roles, accomplishments, personalities, and so on. The self assimilates much of the world around it to become part of its identity. For example, some people think of their awards, jobs, homes, and even their pets as part of themselves. With all of this ambiguity surrounding the limits of a self, science gets unsettled. This can be a headache. As we have discovered, science demands certainty and predictability.

You may have noticed how kids with rich and accomplished parents sometimes take on their parents' accomplishments as part of their own identity. As they move through social circles, these youths may look down their noses at others or speak condescendingly to the "have-nots". Where do they get these haughty attitudes? Most of them haven't done anything noteworthy themselves. They are running around on their parents' coattails—usurping their parents' successes as part of themselves.

Nevertheless, they honestly believe that they are what their parents have become. In fact, in some cultures, parents have to pay for their children's indiscretions, or are found criminally accountable for their child's crime. In court, the parent assumes the identity of the child. Again, where should we draw the line about what constitutes our self?

BOUNDARIES OF THE SELF

I remember a young man who was committed to a disturbing internal image of himself. When asked to envision a picture of what he looked like, the imaginary picture always included his mother by his side—or at least in the background. He couldn't imagine himself without her in the picture. This enmeshment was very much alive in his real life. He was struggling between being his "own" man or his "momma's boy". She desperately wanted to take care of him, and she made him feel safe and secure. However, he also wanted to "man-up" and be responsible for his own well-being. I can't describe the near-psychiatric break he experienced getting his mother out of that identity picture. We wonder who he was before and after she was taken out of the picture? Did his real self change, or did he simply see what was always there?

THE SELF AS A DETERMINISTIC ILLUSION

Let's take a quick look at a scientific theory that attempts to keep the self within the bounds of material reality, but also tries to explain away the immaterial nuances of the self as an illusion. This theory demonstrates the difficulty of limiting the "self" to just the material body. The attempt is futile. However, in redemption, it also gives us a metaphor that we can use in crafting our self-concept as both a material and an immaterial entity. Please note that this theory itself is a metaphorical description of how the self came into being and how it functions. The theory should not be mistaken as a fact.

Bruce Hood says that the brain creates the "self' as an illusion to enable the biological body to function in the world.[1] In other words, he believes in biological determinism, but he also understands the human need to have a sense of "self" and the need to have a rational strategy to interact and survive in the world. How can this "sense of self and a rational strategy" be exclusively attributed to a genetically determined body of flesh and bone?

His theory merges with the philosopher David Hume's Bundle Theory. He says of Hume, "He tried to describe his inner self and thought as no single entity, but rather bundles of sensations, perceptions, and thoughts piled on top of each other. He concluded that the self emerged out of the bundling together of these experiences."[2] In other words, a human is a bundle of nerves and cells that create sensations, perceptions, and thoughts that combine together. As they combine together, they cause the human to act or behave accordingly. There is no central self that exists autonomously as a human entity. Instead, he views us as a bundle of deterministic sensations. (Perhaps that is why we like to think of ourselves as "sensational".)

ILLUSION OF SELF TO ORGANIZE BIOLOGICAL SENSATIONS

Hood identified a big problem in coming up with his theory. *What gives these sensations a rational way to act and survive in a social world?* In other words, how can an amalgamation of sensations combine together in a rational manner? His answer is that the brain creates an illusion, a story of what the human is experiencing. The brain then places the illusion of a self within the story. The brain can then make rational decisions according to the flow of the story. Hood describes this as the "center of a narrative gravity".

Essentially, the brain creates an outline to follow, and that outline is the story. The human's behavior is a "reaction" to what is happening within the story. The brain has no choice but to react in the most self-interested manner as each experience unfolds.

Hood believes that social influences like peer pressure are what the illusory-self primarily responds to. The theory asserts that this reactionary process fosters rational decision-making and allows the illusory self to survive in the world. Voila! He solves the "chaos of sensations" problem by creating an illusory self to unite the sensations in order to perpetuate the theme of a fictitious story.

REJECTING THE DETERMINISTIC ILLUSION OF SELF

Please note that not all scientists agree about brain theories. In fact, Hood specifically rejects the Ego Theory or the Pearl View Theory set forth by Galen Strawson. The Pearl View says that the self is "an essential entity at the core of our existence that holds steady throughout our life."[3] Apparently, Hood viewed the Ego or Pearl View of a core self as inconsistent or inadequate to explain his material and deterministic view of humans. This is another example of scientists having critical differences of opinion about human nature. We are not constrained to believe either one.

If the self is determined and without choice, why bother with a self-concept that is based on choice? This would be futile whether or not the self is considered a pearl, ego, or illusion, because all three are determined. They all preclude creating a moral choice empowered self-concept.

Deterministic explanations of the "self" make a pretense of creating a self-concept. The illusory-self eliminates real choice or moral preferences as we have defined them. We just are, and even what we desire, just is. We can't help but think and act as our biologically generated "sensations" or ego directs us.

What's it like to think of yourself as an illusion? Webster defines illusion as a "misleading or false representation of reality".[4] What's it like wondering who creates your illusion if the self is the illusion? How can a nothing create a something? Who or what decides what is an illusion?

Stephen King should write a novel about someone who discovers they are an illusion, but they try to naively live life as if it were real. Finally, they discover their freedom from moral accountability, and they try to eliminate their moral conscience. He could have us wringing our hands when this person's life falls apart as the illusion of freedom from moral conscience takes over. They act however they want in the moment. Imagine believing that guilt is conquered. Now, you can feel okay about doing whatever you can get away with. However, in the end, conscience can't be cast aside as an illusion, and the person ends up being a psychological wreck. This could even be another sequel in the movie world of the *Matrix*. (Please note that Hood cleverly argues that people should still be held criminally accountable in spite of their actions being determined.)

THE CONFUSION OF AN ILLUSION

How can we really value anything that we know is an illusion? Would you treat someone differently if you believed that they were just an illusion? If our dominant belief was that we are illusions, we could not rationally give ourselves permission to engage in the seriousness of life. Why get all worked up about something that is "not"? Hood sees us as reactionary victims of society. One of his messages is that each brain exists in an ocean of other brains that affect how it works. In one sense that is quite relationally true. However, he takes a fatal deterministic step by saying that the brain has no choice but to deterministically react to the other brains (people) around it.

However, a relational belief in choice recognizes that other people certainly influence us, but we have a value-laden choice in how we behave in most contexts. Our lives are not just reactions to the stimulus around us. We can act and not just react. That is the heart and brain of the real self.

The illusion theory doesn't adequately explain how we can honestly and sincerely engage in life's passions and intensities while knowing that our "self" is a figment of the brain's imagination. The theory somehow allows us to ignorantly go on experiencing life as if it was real even after we learn it's a fiction, a brain trick. Hood goes so far as to claim that the material brain is essentially the self. That of course is not what I am proposing.

A NARRATIVE VIEW OF THE SELF

However, the illusion theory gives us a useful metaphor in creating our self-concept. Leaving the deterministic perspective, we return to a relational or choice perspective. Let's consider how viewing life as a narrative story can actually help us make moral choices and live the Best Life. Our narrative story can help us craft our self-concept and even give us a convenient structure in changing how we live.

Our story or narrative is not derived from a bundle of sensations. Instead, our mind can choose to use the "idea" of a novel or a biography to clarify our identity and our values and to create our self-concept. Examining life as a story unveils some of our deepest desires and unconscious patterns. Viewing ourselves as the primary character in a story may shock us or enamor us when we see ourselves as the protagonist in the story. We are able to see ourselves from a different perceptual position. We may be able to see patterns, perspectives, and angles that we wouldn't normally see.

YOUR IDENTITY IN YOUR LIFE STORY

Imagine that you could review a biography of your life to this date. Assume it's well written. Notice that the author is insightful and a good wordsmith. Perhaps, there are photos and illustrations to emphasize events, experiences, and significant relationships. As we read any biography, we look for a theme, and we want to identify the roles of various characters. To make the story interesting, there must be conflicts and struggles so the protagonist can overcome them. Of course, in this story "you" are the protagonist. Think about your life so far and identify the theme, conflicts, challenges, significant relationships and events, as well as the role you play in your story. Do this as a third-party reader, someone who wants to understand and know more about you. What do you learn?

Let me suggest a structure for evaluating your life narrative. Most significant characters in a novel fit loosely into the identities of predator, victim, or rescuer. Before asking yourself, which one fits you, let me explain these identities.

THE PREDATOR

We see a **predator** as someone who uses others for their own benefit without giving much consideration for the other's well-being. We easily identify murderers, rapists, burglars, and tax scammers as predators. They prey on other people to fulfill their own physical or egoistical desires. They leave broken hearts, broken banks, broken bodies and psyches, and a wave of broken hearts... behind them. We're generally on the lookout for these obvious predators.

However, there are predators in camouflage who are difficult to identify. For example, an enabler is also a predator. Although one can enable unintentionally, a selfish enabler wants to keep someone dependent in order to control that person. This may be done by preventing a child from ever "falling down", or by putting "golden handcuffs" on an adult to keep them economically dependent.

Making another person emotionally, physically, or financially dependent satisfies some need or desire within the enabler. Of course, the other person is weakened even as they are cared for. Enablers can be motivated by monetary greed (like a pimp), by a psychological weakness, or even just a need to dominate. Enablers dishonestly and selfishly prey or feed off someone else's life energy. Obviously, there are various levels of enabling.

There are also predatory friendships. Some predatory friendships are obvious like in the movie, *Mean Girls.* Other examples are subtler. We all have seen a social climber, someone who insincerely cultivates friendships in order to climb a social or financial ladder. They get other people to care about them and trust them. However, it's a scam. When the predator gets what they want, the friendship is ignored, leaving the person emotionally hurt (or maybe worse).

VICTIMS

We usually refer to those who are preyed upon as **victims**. We feel responsible to help them. Therefore, we solicit family, government, charitable organizations and others to take care of them. We can mistakenly assume that the choices of all victims are severely limited. Forces outside and beyond their control often overpower them.

On the other hand, some people learn how to use victim status for their own selfish benefit. In other words, some victims actually have greater access to choices than what is apparent. Let's focus on them, because they add interesting "juice" to a good story. We also need to check out how victims play a role in our life.

VICTIM POWER

What do I mean about a victim who has control? Let me give you an example. In one of my wilderness programs, a student purposely played the victim role. Prior to coming to the program, the student made little effort to do anything but entertain himself. Hey quit almost every endeavor for one reason or another. They quit guitar lessons, swimming lessons, school assignments, and even stopped cleaning their room. What happened? Someone always rescued him by pulling him out of a responsibility or doing it for him. That's power and control! His strategy became, "be helpless if you want someone to do something for you." It worked wonders. (You probably guessed that an enabler was mixed into this salad. And you're right.)

This student was in a group of six other wilderness students. During the beginning of their training, they arose one morning and geared up for a hike to another waterhole. The victim hid in his sleeping bag, complaining of a stomachache. The ache lasted all day, and the group couldn't hike. The next morning, the student said he wasn't going to hike, and that he had to go home. As a result, everyone was glued to the campsite, because the team had to stick together.

Peer pressured ensued, and everyone pleaded with this student to at least try. They offered to help in every way to make the hike easier for him. Nothing worked. They spent another night in the same place. Everyone was getting edgy and anxious. Note that the stomach pain was acknowledged, evaluated, and treated by the staff. Once the student announced that he was going home, the stomach pain miraculously went away.

The next morning I visited the group, already knowing what was happening with this student. I wanted to know if the issue was "victim control". I gathered the group in a circle around the student. I told the student to stay in his sleeping bag and to not participate in the discussion. We discussed the group's training to become a search and rescue team. I explained how difficult it is to give aid and treatment to someone who is resistant. The injured person may be groggy, in pain, or even in shock. Training to work with a resistant person is normally difficult to make real.

At this point I patted the foot of the victim. I explained how fortunate the group was to have him with them. I embellished how similar the student was to an injured search and rescue victim. I explained that it wasn't the student's fault. He didn't know how to do anything else. I compared the student to a young child, and I emphasized he was too immature to have mature and respectful relationships. We discussed the danger of giving the victim any responsibility. I thanked the student for being that way and admonished him to not change, at least not while the group needed a victim. The group needed an uncooperative victim to prepare for search and rescue, and I assured the victim that he was doing a great job. I remarked how it might get boring, and that he might be tempted to change and act stronger and more mature than he really was. However, I expressed confidence that he could use a victim's stubbornness to hold out and remain helpless.

Of course he was listening to everything that was said from inside his sleeping bag. I asked each member of the group to thank the student for being a victim and for playing such an important training role for the group. Everyone could see how the victim identity was now playing an active, non-victim role in assisting the group. The meaning of being a victim changed in this context.

Pretty soon the student sat up and wiggled out of his sleeping bag. He looked at me with squinting eyes and said, "I'm not your bitch. Let's hike." When he saw that the victim role was "not" giving him control, he abandoned the strategy.

I was concerned what would happen when I left, so I gave specific instructions. I demanded that the student not abandon the victim role, and that the group needed to continue training for uncooperative search and rescue subjects. I directed the student to periodically just give up and try to make everyone else take care of him or to manipulate the group to do what he wanted. This disempowered the student from actually controlling the group with victim behavior. The "victim gig" was out in the open.

In the end, he wasn't forced or blamed for quitting or not trying. He tried to quit a few more times to no avail. However, the meaning and pay off for being a victim changed in the student's mind. He began to adopt a new strategy for meeting his needs: try harder and take some responsibility. Obviously, this was a process, but a new story began to unfold with him playing a completely different role than being a victim.

LEGITIMATE VICTIMS

We can be legitimate victims, like when our house burns down or we get struck by lightening. These are circumstances that we don't consciously or unconsciously set up. During those times we do need help, compassion, and encouragement. However, we need to periodically look at ourselves, and notice if we are gaining control by merely playing the victim. If we seem to attract rescuers in our life, that's usually a sign that we are sending out victim signals. As compassionate helpers, we need to know "how" and "when" to give people what they need, not necessarily what they want.

RESCUER

What does it mean to be a **rescuer**? I have revealed that my favorite rescuer was Superman. I was not only enamored by his super powers, but I liked to believe that his rescuing motives were unselfish. In other words he wasn't helping out to get paid. There are wonderful rescuers who jump into raging rivers, loan money, listen compassionately, and give their time to those in need just because the need is there. Rarely do these unselfish rescuers ask themselves if people deserve their help. They just care about people and show it unselfishly.

MOTIVES FOR RESCUING

However, rescuers can also be fake. How so? It comes down to motives. I had a friend that went around looking for bullies who picked on weaker kids. Why? It was because he "liked" to beat up bullies, and rescuing others allowed him to do so without getting in trouble. In other words, he was a bully in disguise. (I was glad he liked me.) Rescuers can say things, do things, destroy things, hit things, and even steal things without getting in trouble. As long as their actions seem reasonably connected to rescuing a poor victim, the mayhem may be excused.

There are other rescuers who like to create debts. I tried this when I was 12 years old. I would mow someone's lawn and then knock on the door expecting to get paid. "Hey, I just mowed your overgrown lawn; don't you think you owe me ten bucks?" Sadly, it worked sometimes. We often set up debts unconsciously.

Perhaps, we work a shift for a fellow worker at our employment saying, "Oh, think nothing of it." However, at some future time we want a day off and hit up our fellow worker. "Hey man, you owe me. Remember that one day I worked for you?" It's okay to incur an obligation from someone, but they need to know it's an obligation up front before you do them a supposed favor.

A fake rescuer may also be motivated to control someone else. They like being needed, wanted, or just feeling powerful. These rescuers sniff out fake victims. Again, enabling is an easy example. The victim wants someone to "do for him or her" and is willing to give up some control over life decisions in order to be rescued. The rescuer wants recognition, affection, redemption, or sex. The victim uses the rescuer and the rescuer uses the victim. It's a negative symbiotic and even parasitic relationship.

ARE YOU A PREDATOR, VICTIM, OR RESCUER?

As we review our life histories, notice if there is a predator, victim, or rescuer theme. Our narratives help us recognize our unconscious motives. Do we selfishly use other people while disregarding their well-being? Some people even learn how to play all three roles.

Living the Best Life requires us to clean up these roles and tendencies if they exist. These selfish roles are more closely connected to the proverbial, self-consumed Good Life. The only safe way to eliminate these motives and roles from our self-concept is sincerely loving other people and ourselves.

Virtuous caring creates a different life theme for our stories. Our personal stories can be joyful, honorable, and have happy endings when we love others and serve unselfishly. There will be pain, and there will be conflict. We may even get used or abused. We can deal with that if we can disable our vulnerable pride and selfishness.

THEMES IN OUR LIFE NARRATIVES

The past only lives in our present minds. The most powerful effects of the past are the present beliefs from our interpretation of what happened. We can misinterpret events like a violent abusive assault as *meaning* that we are somehow defective. That belief is a lie. We didn't make someone abuse us. To get rid of this destructive lie we need to update our interpretation of what those old experiences really meant. Reliving the experiences as vividly as possible with the virtue of love allows us to change the meanings we attached to the experiences.

You can help change false beliefs and patterns that are perpetuated by themes of the predator, victim, or rescuer. Certainly, if we want to change past themes for our future book, then loving, serving, forgiving, and sharing need to be our new themes.

Perhaps you remember novels or biographies where these roles were played by various characters. Have you noticed while reading a story (or even watching a movie), that you start giving advice to the characters? "Can't you see what is happening?" "Stand up for yourself." "Stop being such a selfish punk!" Seeing these roles played out in other people's lives is easier than noticing that we often do the same things, and can play the same roles. We should notice how we feel about these characters and their roles, because they can be self-revealing.

PROJECTIONS

What I mean is that we have emotional reactions to some people and the roles that they play. This is sometimes called projection. In particular, we feel deep rejection, dislike, or disgust when we think about or interact with certain people. Often, we can't even pinpoint "why" we feel that way, but other times it seems pretty clear. In any event, this can mean that the offending person mirrors or "projects" what we believe is inside of us. I heard that Mother Teresa received motivation to be a better person when she saw Hitler one day in the mirror while looking at herself. That may be a bit of folklore, but it demonstrates the point. Recognizing a potential weakness within herself helped motivate her to become a saint.

We may realize unconsciously that we have a weakness that we don't want to admit or address. We don't want to be reminded of this weakness, but when we are faced with someone who personifies that weakness, our fear or belief that we have that weakness ignites our rejection of that person. In doing so, we are actually rejecting that part of us that we are ashamed or afraid of.

I've seen this idea of projection played out through group exercises. In almost every group, there are people who throw an absolute fit even thinking about whether they are reacting to their own weakness recognized in another person. Why don't they just laugh it off or give it serious thought? Instead, their elevated emotional response validates the projection.

We all need to be sensitive to how we respond to others, and to be especially thoughtful about those people we seem to abhor. They can give us insight into our own self-concept and what needs to improve. Honest feedback and insight is needed to create a Best Life self-concept.

AWARENESS OF OUR LIFE STORY

A self-concept is not a simple, one-sided cartoon character. We are complex beings, and making conscious choices about our identity requires noticing how we treat others and *why* we do what we do. A necessary skill in creating a self-concept is *awareness*, being consciously aware of how and why we are relating to others. We also need to be aware of the themes in our ongoing story, and the roles we are playing. Viewing life as a narrative story gives us this useful outside perception of ourselves. Getting stuck in a specific type of awareness can cause anxiety, depression, and other problems.

Developing conscious awareness is a skill. Like breathing, we all think we know how to do it. In fact, most of us feel that we just do it, and that it doesn't require any skill. Of course, that isn't necessarily true. Yoga and similar practices teach people how to breathe more purposefully and effectively. Teaching people how to breathe is actually big business. Conscious awareness is another skill that we are learning more about with advances in neuroscience. Because creating self-concept depends heavily on conscious awareness, let's take a brief look at what this entails and how to improve our awareness skills.

THE MIND AS A TOOL

Let's first take a look at how our mind functions from an operator's standpoint. We can assume that the mind is a tool in how we interact and function in the world. The self uses the mind in perceiving the meaning of what is happening around us and within us. Like any other tool, irrespective of its quality and make up, *how* it is used determines its effectiveness. We can wake up to the reality that the mind can go feral, operating without much guidance or direction like a wild thing. Some of us just let our minds wander and operate as if it had a life of its own. We can't have the Best Life without learning to skillfully use our minds. That includes knowing how and in what ways we pay attention to the world around us.

THE IMPORTANCE OF FOCUS

The Open-Focus Brain: Harnessing the Power of Attention to Heal Mind and Body by Les Fehmi and Jim Robbins, explains different ways that we pay attention in everyday life, and it provides us with exercises to expand our attention skill sets[4]. The fundamental concepts that they explain are driving new breakthroughs in the field of biofeedback and brain stimulation.

NARROW FOCUS

They observe that our culture has us fixated in "narrow-focus attention", characterized by intensity and stressful readiness to cope with danger and difficulty. Being stuck day after day in this intense way of paying attention stresses out our brain, nervous system, and organs. This causes all sorts of physical and emotional ailments. Additionally, this narrow focus prejudices our perspectives of self-concept and the world around us. We are led to ignore much of what is outside this narrow focus to our detriment. It limits the usefulness of our mind as well as clouding our vision of what we are and what we can be.

Let me share a story from their book. Kyle is a boy who grew up in a home where life was unpredictable. He never knew when he would be hugged or smacked around. His dad drank excessively, and Kyle was on constant alert to avoid a "whipping" if he could. You can imagine how this affected the boy. On his bus rides home from school, other kids laughed and joked while Kyle sat quietly focused on what was going to happen at home. He hardly noticed the other kids.

At school he developed a reading problem. At first his teachers suspected that he needed glasses to improve his eyesight. Finally, they learned that he was so tense and focused he could only see one word at a time. He stumbled and stuttered, not knowing what the next word was. By helping his eye muscles relax his visual scope broadened, and he eventually could see two or three words together, and then finally phrases. His limitations were linked to the narrow focus from which he viewed life and even words in a book. Humans with chronic stress develop a chronically narrowed visual view of the world. They are conditioned to have a narrow focus.

STRESSFUL NARROW FOCUS

In our fast paced world, we feel compelled to get as much accomplished as possible and eliminate all mistakes in our work and even our play. Many of us suffer from information overload. Fehmi and Robbins point out that there is more information in one Sunday issue of the *New York Times* than all of the written material that was available to readers in the fifteenth century. There are two billion web pages on the Internet. Our brains get fatigued trying to keep up with it all, and that especially happens when we feel compelled to keep current about our interests. We do so through a narrow, rigid attention that fatigues our mind and our nervous system. We are wired and tired. You can imagine how this affects our self-concepts and the Best Life.

ATTENTION FOCUS AND BRAIN WAVES

The intensity of our focus can be accurately measured. Our attention focus correlates to four types of brain waves. The brain produces alpha waves at 0.5-4 hertz during sleep. Theta waves at 4-8 hertz are produced during twilight consciousness like when we are deeply relaxed, daydreaming or falling asleep. Alpha waves at 8-12 hertz are produced when we are relaxed but still alert to our surroundings.

The last type, beta waves are divided into 3 categories. Low-beta at 13-15 hertz happens when we are relaxed but are attentively interested. That could be a person taking a test for which they are well prepared and feel confident in doing well. Mid-range beta at 16-22 hertz is characterized by focused external attention. High-beta at 22 hertz or higher, correlates with tense muscles and emotions like anger and anxiety. This could be a person taking a test without knowing the subject, or it could be someone cut off in traffic and reacting angrily. The beta levels, especially high-beta, arouses heart rate and respiration along with other stress related physiological responses.

A beta state is not necessarily bad. In fact, it protects us from harm and helps us precisely focus on a task that really needs to get done well and on time. However, when we become conditioned or even addicted to living every day life in a high beta state we are racing through life missing much of what is happening around us.

Obviously, this narrow focus impacts how we pay attention and relate to other people. Relationships are the most important parts of our life, and how we pay attention affects the quality of our relationships. For our own health and to cultivate quality relationships, we need to control our brain pattern wavelengths.

CUTTING BACK ON NARROW FOCUS

Fehmi and Robbins offer a number of exercises enabling us to consciously control the intensity of our attention focus. We want to learn to live more in an Open-Focus state in order to enjoy what is around us and to care for our relationships. We can visit narrow-focus, higher beta-type attention when really necessary. In the meantime, we can slow down our minds and learn to interact with life. Not everything is about life or death, and we can learn to live that way. However, we need knowledge and practice to do so, because most of us have been conditioned to function at a hyper-attentive level. That is not the Best Life.

CHAPTER SUMMARY

We can view life as an ongoing story, and in doing so; we can craft that story and our role to be about living the Best Life. We can learn much about ourselves from the perceptual position of a reader learning about a story. We have also learned how important it is to honestly recognize patterns in our life that help us identify our motives. Relating to the predator, victim, and rescuer can give us helpful insights into how we actually connect with others and why. That insight can help us move and stay in a Best Life direction.

Additionally, we have access to resources that help us learn how to pay attention. All our life we have heard parents, teachers, and others tell us to pay attention. Normally, that meant to pay high beta focused-attention on what they wanted us to do. We're probably pretty good at focused attention. We now have a reason and a methodology to develop other levels of attention that can enrich our lives and our relationships. We can consciously make the brain a better tool. In short, we can slow down. (I wonder if ADD or ADHD is an unconscious attempt to decrease the intensity level of our focus by frequently changing the object of our focus.)

There are no hard and fast rules in defining the self. We are significantly made up of our experiences and our relationships, as well as our brains and bodies. We do not have to believe that our moral decision-making self is an illusion. We can honestly and sincerely choose to be morally responsible to others and even to God, a Higher Power. Personal, moral accountability can inspire us to be better and to not beat ourselves up with excessive guilt. Guilt is like pain; it gives us helpful feedback. Excessive guilt like excessive pain can cripple us. Usefully receive the message from a pang of guilt and move on. We can be primarily motivated through creating our *real* self and a joyful Best Life.

NOTES

1. Hood, B. (2012). *How the Social Brain Creates Identity*. New York, NY: Oxford University Press.

2. (Hood, 2012).

3. (Hood, 2012).

4. 2014. In *Merriam-Webster.com*. Retrieved May 27, 2014, from http://www.merriam-webster.com/dictionary/illusion

5. Fehmi, L. & Robbins, J. (2007). *The Open-Focus Brain: Harnessing the Power of Attention to Heal Mind and Body*. Boston, MA: Trumpeter Books.

CHAPTER 11

Self-Concept Trickery: Brain Biases

As we consciously craft our self-concept, we need to know if our whole mind is cooperating. To do so, we need to get a handle on our biases. We are biased beings. We can't help it. It's easy to fool ourselves. This chapter unveils some of our most common biases and how they work. In doing so, I hope to engage your biases by bringing them to your awareness. If we wish to make unbiased choices, we need to understand what we're up against. However, be aware that biases have positive intentions and aren't necessarily bad. Let's just hope we can consciously mediate their influence on how we make decisions, especially about who we think we are.

We have an innate tendency to form biases. However, remember that we have choices about the biases that we embrace both consciously and unconsciously. Of course, those choices are limited by the experiences and information that we acquire. We don't have access to all of the choices that we could be free to choose from. However, as we honor our ability to choose and expand our access to choices, we can change our biases. We will touch on several types of bias including: Confirmation Bias, Certainty Bias, Happy Brain Bias, Social Isolation Bias, Cultural Bias, Availability Bias, and Heart Bias. As we do so, we can see how they can affect our self-concept. Let's first look at how influential biases can be.

BIAS AND CONSPIRACY THEORIES

Conspiracy theories are alive and well. Many are classic examples of bias. The WWII Holocaust conspiracy continues to gain notoriety and followers. Essentially, this conspiracy asserts that Jews falsely contrived the story of the Holocaust and the murder of six million Jews to gain post-WWII money from the U.S. as compensation for the atrocities. The conspiracy denies that the Nazis targeted the Jews for murder or extermination. It denies that concentration camps were death camps with gas chambers, although it admits that Jews died in refuge camps from disease and malnutrition. It suggests that rather than six million, only about 300,000 Jews died during the war. Of course, no historical organization or society from any country has accepted this conspiracy theory or its accusations. The Holocaust is a well-documented, settled, and established historical fact.

As previously mentioned, the Greenbrier Academy for Girls is a college preparatory and therapeutic boarding school for adolescent young women. GBA periodically sponsors trips for its students to the Holocaust Museum in Washington, D. C. They return and write essays on the evidence, geography, pictures, and testimonials of survivors and perpetrators that they study at the museum. They also write their feelings and thoughts of what such a holocaust means to them about the world. Some students have said that the experience was the biggest "wake-up call" of their lives. When they read that some believed that the Holocaust was fake, I can't print the venom of their responses. For some of them, denying the Holocaust was tantamount to denying reality or common sense. For the students, seeing was believing.

BIAS CAN BE SINCERE

Nevertheless, in spite of all the evidence, many of the "non-believers" appear to be sincere and adamant that the atrocities never took place. Except for a few of these conspiracy theorists, the rest of the world is convinced that there was a Holocaust, and that the Nazis sought out and murdered millions of Jews, including those in the gas chambers. So how can the facts be so ignored or denied? British journalist, Will Storr, recently published a book about the confusion of believing. His book, *The Heretics: Adventures with the Enemies of Science,* explores the reasons why facts don't always work.[1] The Holocaust conspiracy theory is among the extraordinary examples used to make his point.

He took one of these conspiracy theorists to a concentration camp in Majdanek, Poland. Among other things, they inspected one of the grotesque gas chambers that had been historically preserved. The non-believer insisted that it was a "mock-up" and ignored or rejected other tangible, visible facts at the site. He ignored the fact that doors inside the gas chamber could only be opened from the outside, and he insisted that the Jews could have gotten out if they wanted to. He creatively came up with reasons why no killings could have been performed there. Seeing all of the evidence did not lead to believing. Instead, his beliefs led him to see what he *wanted* to see.

Intrigued by a person's ability to deny the facts, Storr traveled with an avowed Creationist to a dinosaur "dig site". The more bones that he saw, the less he believed in dinosaurs. For him, the existence of dinosaurs meant that God did not exist. (He wasn't as reconciling as Dr. Alexander after his near-death experience.) Again, believing was seeing.

Later, Storr met with a UFO-spotter. In this case, the spotter wasn't denying a plethora of evidence. Instead, he was trying to *create* evidence. Rather than postulating, guessing, or surmising that UFO's existed, he was passionately adamant that they existed. However, he had woefully inadequate evidence to support UFO's. Most of it was not credible enough to be admitted in a courtroom, or seriously considered by a physicist. Much of it was simply second, third, or fourth degree hearsay. Nevertheless, he believed he had seen a UFO.

I must share with you a personal experience that may be more about schizophrenia than "believing is seeing". You be the judge. At one time, I was a JAG (Judge Advocate General)—a lawyer, in the US Air Force. One of my responsibilities early on was to investigate claims for money damages filed by civilians. One day, someone who lived in the desert came into my office to file a claim. He said that Air Force planes were flying too fast over his home in the desert, and that their sonic booms had ruined his innate receptors inside his head. These receptors allowed him to communicate with aliens from other worlds. He was very sincere. The claim was a substantial amount—over five trillion dollars. Thankfully, it was above my settlement authority, so I got out of the investigation. True story! This was either believing is seeing or, shall we say, something else entirely. I could have heard him wrong, (believing is hearing), but I had the written claim to back me up.

CONFIRMATION BIAS

The examples that I have shared are rather extreme examples of Confirmation Biases. This kind of bias refers to believing "in the absence of the facts", or "in spite of the facts". This rather natural human tendency can affect your self-concept and your worldview. You want to be "real", but your perception of reality (including yourself) can be tainted with Confirmation Bias. Your mind plays games with you. This does not mean that you lack integrity. It means that the perceptions of your five senses are unconsciously influenced to perceive what will support your biases. You normally don't even know that it's happening because most biases operate at an unconscious level. Once brought to your awareness, you can decide how to manage or change biased beliefs, especially those regarding your perceived identity. These biases can be positive or negative. Just know that they are contrived by your unconscious mind to give you what you want.

Confirmation Biases prevent us from taking in some facts and discounting others. This kind of bias "shields" us from reality that is not useful to us". Therefore, we can give ourselves permission to do what we want to do in spite of the facts. At first this may feel frightening, undesirable, or even dishonest in most contexts. So how should we view and accommodate our bias tendencies? A bias can lead us to believe that the means (seeing only what we want to see) justifies the ends (protecting our biased interests). As a hypothetical example, suppose that we unconsciously want girls to be more productive than boys. Assume that we unconsciously give the boys less opportunities and attention than we give the girls. The boys are therefore less productive. The means (giving the boys less opportunities) is justified by the ends (girls end up being more productive than boys). In this example, our bias allows us to give more opportunities to girls than boys. As a result, our bias has been confirmed.

Confirmation Bias is so pervasive that it can infiltrate scientific process or methods. How could there be inherent bias in a process designed and promoted to avoid bias? Remember how Dr. Allsgood's bias was revealed on the witness stand? The empirical or scientific method begins with a hypothesis that represents a proposition or hope that the scientist has reason to believe may be true or valid. Thereafter, a careful, objective procedure tests the hypothesis with safeguards to protect the results from any bias.

However, if Confirmation Bias is a psychological factor and a common feature of human nature, then a dilemma is created. In spite of the objective nature of the procedure, somebody has to implement them. If a human scientist unconsciously influenced by Confirmation Bias implements the procedures, we can reasonably assume that bias could affect the outcome. The potential bias may innocently sneak in because much of it derives from our unconscious nature. Nevertheless, there are conscious biases in the sciences like everything else. William James notes this in a conversation he reported and commented on.

"Why do so few 'scientists' even look at the evidence for telepathy, so called? Because they think as a leading biologist, now dead, once said to me, that even if such a thing were true, scientists ought to band together to keep it suppressed and concealed. It would undo the uniformity of Nature and all sorts of other things without which scientists cannot carry on their pursuits. But if this very man had been shown something which as a scientist he might *do* with telepathy, he might not only have examined the evidence, but even have found it good enough. This very law which the logicians would impose upon us—if I may give the name of logicians to those who would rule out our willing nature here—is based on nothing but their own natural wish to exclude all elements for which they, in their professional quality of logicians, can find no use."[2]

We can wonder what James would say today about the politics and economics of science with its myriads of institutional interests. Scientific investigation costs money and sponsors of scientific investigation have their own biased interests. Credible and honest scientists are often left having to pursue projects that can get funded, not their most passionate projects. To make matters more difficult, the sponsors often consciously or unconsciously exert pressure to attain their hoped-for results.

To minimize this type of bias, other scientists must duplicate the scientist's results before the results are accepted in the scientific community. This requirement helps minimize perpetuating bias. However, unconscious bias may creep into the duplication experiments. All scientists are human, and are therefore subject to Confirmation Bias even if they don't "have a dog in the fight". Whether they are promoting a result or checking the validity of a result, unconscious bias can creep in. Bruce Lipton said, "There is no doubt that human beings have a great capacity for sticking to false *beliefs* with great passion and tenacity, and hyper-rational scientists are not immune[...]When our human minds get involved, we can choose to perceive the environment in different ways"[2]

We see this all the time in nutritional science. I am always confused about what is "healthy" to eat. Scientific "breakthroughs" promote products that other scientists have "proven". Do we eat the whole egg or not? Do supplements work? Is saturated fat healthy or not? Is raw food healthier than cooked food? Is red meat bad for us? Is it safe to eat genetically engineered plants and animals? We can find scientists to support both sides of these questions. We wonder if conscious and unconscious bias plays a part in these nutritional controversies. The relevant point is that if the most objectively structured mental processes (like the Scientific Method) can be affected by Confirmation Bias, our self-concept and how we view the world can also be affected.

HAPPY BRAIN BIAS

You probably already know that you have a "tricky" brain. It not only can trick others, but it also does a good job tricking you. Most of this trickiness is motivated by brain bias. David DiSalvo proposes a theory in his recently published book, *What Makes Your Brain Happy and Why You Should Do the Opposite.*

What I wish to communicate with the metaphor of a happy brain is simply that under various conditions, our brains will tend toward a default position that places greatest value on *avoiding loss, lessening risk, and averting harm.* Our brains have evolved to do exactly that, and much of the time we can be thankful they did. However, these same protective tendencies (what I am calling the tendencies of a 'happy brain') can go too far and become obstacles instead of virtues. Our challenge is to know when to think and act contrary to our brain's native leanings."[3]

For example, the conspiracy theorist may believe that the world is *endangered* by a "conspiracy" that must be disclosed. And the Creationist may have been *protecting* his "belief" in a higher being. These types of beliefs can act as biases that cloud all contrary evidence, no matter how persuasive. Do you have a self-concept that is so beguiling that you ignore or rationalize evidence to the contrary? How many people are mouthy, aggressive, intimidating, or even violent because they are biased in their belief the world is a dangerous place? They act that way because they feel that they need to protect themselves. These "tough guys" and "tough gals" are actually biased, and acting out of fear.

How much of your self-concept is based on your brain bias to avoid loss, lessen risk and avert harm? Those are basic, sound, common sense objectives. However, a Best Life of quality relationships, developing interests and abilities, and a passionate dedication to your life purpose may require some risk taking. Realize that creating a self-concept requires dealing with internal conflict. It's okay. It's normal. It's important to accommodate both our ambitions and our brain biases for safety. We are constantly mediating both interests as we move from context to context in life. We endanger ourselves when we try to ignore or shut down our ambition or our bias. Brain biases must be disclosed and compromised.

BIAS AND SOCIAL PRESSURE

Long ago, my wife and I had to work through some brain biases. We were newly married, and we wondered whether I could go to law school while we started a family at the same time. Our brain biases wanted to minimize risk, avoid loss, and avert any harm. Our finances were limited, and we were comfortable being a part of the crowd. The Social Bias (which was easy to adopt) said, "Don't be stupid. Postpone a family, or don't even have one." She was committed to personally nurturing the children, especially in their early years. That precluded her from full-time employment. We were sobered by the responsibility of caring for a vulnerable child who depended on us completely for their health and well-being. We also wanted to be a part of the social scene.

I could go on, but you get the picture.

We also wanted to have our family early so that we could actively participate in our children's teenage years. We wanted to actively engage our grandchildren, and be a significant influence in their lives. Without knowing anything about happy brain biases, we carefully and even prayerfully considered what we should do. We were anxious. The specific fears and risks were slowly identified. We researched how to minimize the risks within our control, and we started our family while I was in school. That wasn't a popular or even a politically correct decision. Some family and friends looked askew at us. Our bias to take an easier, less risky direction was strong. However, our life purpose and ambitions also motivated us, and we tried to accommodate the risks within our control. Our brains somehow survived, although I am still trying to catch up on my sleep. It wasn't easy. In the meantime, our children have made the world a better place. They are appreciative of the time they spent with their mother, especially since she died before her fortieth year.

To fulfill our passions and our life purposes, we can learn to acknowledge Happy Brain Biases without fighting them. In acknowledging those biases we can satisfy them to some extent. Thank heavens our brain is biased to keep us safe, and that it's normal to feel anxious about the unknown. Nevertheless, we need to break down the general anxiety into specific risks and deal with them one at a time. Often, we just feel anxiously biased and stop there without understanding our feelings. Building a self-concept will require reconciling specific, perceived risks communicated to us through our brain biases. Otherwise, our brain may stifle us, limiting our access to attaining the Best Life and quality relationships.

CERTAINTY BIAS

Certainty Bias is similar to the Happy Brain Bias. In fact, it describes another component of keeping the brain happy. DiSalvo calls it our attention to the brain's craving for certainty. "One of the most perilous gene-meme double whammies that humans possess is the notion of certainty. Our natures and our learned biases lead us to believe that we are right whether or not we really are[…] Neuroscience research is revealing that the state of not being certain is an extremely uncomfortable place for our brains to live: The greater the uncertainty, the worse the discomfort."[4]

After discussing research on this subject, he states. "What this tells us is that the brain doesn't merely prefer certainty over ambiguity—it craves it. Our need to be right is actually a need to 'feel' right. Neurobiologist Robert Burton coined the term "Certainty Bias" to describe this feeling and how it skews our thinking."[5] The Volkswagen in my dream suffered from Certainty Bias by adamantly believing that it was a tractor in spite of the evidence otherwise. Once the Volkswagen was convinced that it was a tractor, its desire for certainty made it blind to change.

Do you know someone that has to be right about everything, even things they obviously know nothing about? Have you experienced passionately arguing for a belief that you don't actually understand? For example, the implications of quantum mechanics to explain all sorts of things seem to be in vogue. I hear people using quantum mechanics phenomena to explain "stuff" without being able to clearly distinguish how it differs from Einstein's Theory of Relativity. We like to feel certain, whether we are or not. Few people understand the math behind either theory. Burton describes how a "well-established schema" like a self-concept is called into question by a brain that is biologically-biased against change and gets defensive when considering new information. He believes that your brain has a few automatic strategies to protect its craving for "certainty". Each strategy deals with new information as a threat to already existing beliefs.

Here's how they work when considering a self-concept change:

- New insight may look encouraging until the brain realizes the threat to its already-settled self-concept. At this point, consideration ends, and the information is set aside.
- New information threatens the comfort of the self-concept's status quo and is disregarded quickly.
- The new information looks good, but why suffer discomfort now? Store it away for future reconsideration.

When do we get beyond the discomfort from overruling our certainty and make a change anyway? This usually happens in one of three ways. First, we can become consciously aware of our bias and after honest reflection we deconstruct the beliefs supporting the bias. In other words, we discover the bias is not worth keeping and we replace it with something more palpable. Let's refer to our previous example. Discovering how the bias was created could deconstruct the bias towards girls' productivity over boys' productivity.

Again this is just a hypothetical. Assume that the biased person is male. The deconstruction may reveal a sibling rivalry with a sister who constantly got better grades in school or achieved higher athletic awards. The brother might have assumed that the reason was gender related. He believed that she performed better because she was a girl, and therefore he didn't have to take second place personally. As time passed, he became "certain" that this was the case. And there you have it. The bias was created. In deconstructing the bias, he understands his illogic in creating the bias and gives himself permission to give up its "certainty".

Another approach was demonstrated in my wife and I's decision to have children in spite of financial and social risks while attending law school. At first my wife and I just felt anxious and uneasy about starting a family. Rather naively and slowly we identified specific risks and dangers supporting the emotionally-driven bias to postpone our family. Creating a plan to minimize the risks helped overcome our certainty bias to follow the "accepted course". In this case, the bias was not removed, but its underlying concerns were cushioned through recognition and planning. We came to grips with prioritizing what was really important to us.

Dr. Alexander's near death experience demonstrates the last approach. Essentially, his experience in the "other world" blew out his scientific bias. What I mean is that his near death experience was so compelling, so real and significant to him, that it created a new Certainty Bias that replaced the old one. Perhaps you have read about enemy soldiers of different races and nationalities whose biases against one another were embedded and inflamed through their home cultures. Nevertheless, in the heat of battle one enemy soldier rescues or saves another enemy soldier from death. The intensity of battle, exhaustion, pain, and yet compassion combine together and "blow out" the old certainty biases that all Nazis are bad, all white people are superior, or all believers in *whatever* are evil. A new bias of tolerance and appreciation replaces the old one. The significance and intensity of experiences allow new meanings to crystallize and override old biases.

Imagine the comfort we feel in believing who we are and how we connect with the world. No wonder we are emotionally threatened when considering a major change in our self-concept. This kind of self-concept bias about our present identity may constitute what psychologists sometimes call "denial", or an unconsciously driven inability to see and confront the need to change.

We protect our biases all the time. Perhaps you have noticed tendencies in yourself or others during a conversation. How often do you find yourself searching for a response justifying, rationalizing, or proving your own thoughts before someone has even finished their statement? You are "protecting" your beliefs by not engaging in open dialogue. Other people may do the same thing to you.

You can intuit when someone is listening to you, when listening includes "openly" considering your thoughts. Their quick and sometimes emotion-laden responses to you often mean that your ideas cannot be comfortably considered. You are not being heard. This often happens in families or among intimate associates when yelling becomes the "tool of persuasion" as one person tries to protect their beliefs rather than reason or empathize with the other. This is a fear-laden response.

Recognizing certainty biases in our self and others paves the way to better relationships. Understanding that we are all biased with bias-induced fears can help us not be easily offended. We have reason to give people a break instead of harshly judging their seeming irrationality. Our empathy deepens. We can learn to understand people's fears and appropriately help them deconstruct their beliefs about the risks feeding their biases. We can better deal with our own biases about who we think we are or have to be.

SOCIAL ISOLATION BIAS

DiSalvo theorizes about another influence that creates bias. "In short, people with an acute sense of social isolation appear to have a reduced response to things that make most people happy, and a heightened response to human conflict."[6] If you recognize this tendency in you, discover and deconstruct the biases that isolate you from others. Somehow, you have created a dangerous bias about the risks and dangers of human relationships. However, the biases themselves may be more dangerous than interacting with others.

We are relational beings that need relational nourishment. Pushing people away can not only make you emotionally ill, but also stupid. You are isolating yourself from important knowledge about life and the joys of living that only comes from relational connections. You may, for whatever reason, believe that few if any safe relational choices exist. Okay, our self-concept needs to emotionally protect us when necessary, but not at the expense of loving and receiving love. If overcoming this fear is too difficult to do alone, seek help. You're worth it!

CULTURAL BIAS

Our biases can be created by the power of cultural influences. We feel resistance to changing our self-concept if that change violates the cultural beliefs that repetitively bombard our conscious and unconscious minds. These cultural beliefs and values are constantly ingested and digested by our brains. This is true whether we daily tap into the worldview of parents, siblings, Fox News, CNBC, Lil' Wayne, and so on. DiSalvo says, "You didn't realize that years of ingesting these labels framed your self-perception. Without ever really challenging the point, you simply expected to be less athletic than your brother, and that influenced you to not participate in sports, but rather spend time being the smart kid who gets all A's [...] Thinking differently of yourself just doesn't feel right; in fact, it makes you anxious and uncomfortable. Breaking a deeply internalized frame like that is extremely difficult—just becoming aware that it exists is a major step."[7]

Cultures promote biases that are often referred to as "politically correct". There is tremendous social pressure on members to embrace the biases that are in vogue at a particular time. Early Twentieth Century Russia maintained a social/political bias that all citizens should share property equally, and therefore personal ownership became forbidden. This bias was coercively implemented in communist regimes that outlawed private ownership. Imagine the suffocating influence of these cultural beliefs on Russians' self-concepts, whether you consider the influence good or bad.

The United States maintained a contrary bias, particularly during the Nineteenth Century. Individualism and self-reliance were emphasized and promoted socially and politically. This led to entrepreneurship, economic growth, and vast disparity between the rich and poor. Imagine the implications of emphasizing individualism on American self-concepts and its impact on the quality of human relationships.

The Russian bias thwarted rewarding individual effort while the American bias excused the collateral damages to others from getting to the top. Both biases have positive objectives, but the fears and perceived dangers driving them created different, but real societal consequences. These biases literally created cultures. Social and societal biases are powerful forces to be respected and understood developing one's own self-concept.

We are unconsciously biased by the majority bias of the subcultures that we embrace, and they affect our individual perception of who we think we are. Cultural Bias seems to be an inescapable human phenomenon. We can be careful to examine the source of our own biases, and we can consider if we adopt them because they are popular or for some other reason. Our self-concepts must take cultural biases into consideration to know how we fit into our world.

Nonconformists often resist conforming to a culture that they reject. However, all the while they work hard to conform to the subculture of their choice. This may be a subculture of non-conformity, a group they enjoy being a part of. As you can see, bias is inescapable.

We can carefully evaluate how much our overall self-concept is a reflection of the biases within our chosen culture or subculture. Do we basically view our self-concept to predominantly include the biases attached to societal classes like "old people", gangs, professions, females, heterosexuals, atheists, Peruvians, and so on. We are much more! We are part of the complete human family. We can relate to others by recognizing that they are also much more than a classification with stigmatized biases. Virtuous love looks far beyond a subgroup that we may fit into. (Have you ever wondered about the biases of, "elderly, Peruvian women who practice orthopedic medicine, carry rosaries and chase stinky biker men"? Now, that's a bias-ridden classification!)

AVAILABILITY BIAS

We also have to deal with Availability Bias. This is a logical way that biases are created. DiSalvo says that, "When you expose yourself to one perspective and ignore others; the availability of that perspective (about politics, for instance) leads to a bias that the chosen perspective is the right one."[8] In other words, the more you expose yourself to one perspective and ignore other perspectives, you are more likely to create a bias. Your original bias is reinforced not just because it is rational, but also because your brain likes the comfort of *familiarity.*

He uses the media as an example. Most people think crime is increasing and is much higher than statistics show it to be. This is because the news media focuses on crime, and they constantly show crimes, criminals, and trials. We have unlimited access to evidence that crime is all around us, even if it is actually decreasing. This type of bias requires a lot of self- discipline to counteract. You may not like exposing yourself to options that you may disagree with. However, by doing so, you can balance out some of your biases.

We create biases in our own children without even realizing it. Some of their biases are kind of wild. My daughter spent considerable time with her mother in the kitchen. They created gourmet meals together to the delight of everyone sitting at our table. She watched and heard over and over again how to combine ingredients and cook certain dishes. As a teenager, she spent the night at another girl's home. The girls and the mother prepared dinner together. My daughter drove them crazy by correcting them on how to combine the ingredients and how to cook. *"You should do it ' this way' or you're going to ruin good food."* I don't think she got invited to another sleepover at that home. She really was unconsciously biased that things had to be done a certain way.

How many times have you been corrected by someone, or you have corrected someone else because they weren't doing something the way you were taught? Familiarity breeds comfort, and also bias. Well-chosen conscious biases are part of the normal creation of life preferences. However, holding on to a belief just because it's comfortable makes little sense, especially for those who want to progress and learn. Bringing unconscious bias to consciousness empowers more intentional decision-making.

WORLDVIEW BIAS

Worldview Bias is akin to cultural bias. Frequently, changing self-perception requires changing important worldviews or even worldview filters like AM (Abstractionism/Materialism) or SR (Strong Relationality). This domino effect happens because beliefs are interrelated, and the efficacy of one belief depends on the efficacy of another belief. If one interconnected belief changes, a chain reaction begins. A simple bias is connected to a web of beliefs. You must avoid the simplistic naïveté that you can just target one belief at a time to change your worldview or identity. Think more of "clusters" of beliefs that interrelate than isolated beliefs. Again, Dr. Alexander is a good example. To change his self-concept and his purpose for living, he had to change his worldview of biological science and the scientific process.

Assume that we've developed a worldview bias that "winners win and losers lose". In other words, winners and losers are born that way. In this example, we have put ourselves into the loser's category. Somehow we have learned to cope with being a loser, and then we fall in love. We desperately want this relationship to work, but of course we're just stuck being a loser. However, this relationship drives us to challenge our biases. What might have to change for us to have a good chance at making the relationship work?

Let me suggest a few possibilities. Perhaps we can believe that our lover loves losers. But, that may mean that our lover is a loser themselves, and what can we expect when two losers get together? What if we can change our self-concept to believe that we are a winner? We have to come up with new understandings about how we became a loser and kept on losing. What new beliefs and strategies are required to be a winner?

Do we really know how to act differently than losing? Wanting to act differently doesn't mean we know how. Maybe we could give up the bias that losers lose and winners win. That means we have to come up with a whole new set of beliefs to understand what it means to win or lose, and whether it even makes a difference. Then we have to determine if the change would give us a better chance to make the relationship work.

I hope that the message is clear. Changing a worldview core bias can be complicated. However, these dominos of change are our real challenge if we are serious about letting go of a core bias. Fortunately, people do it all the time, and so can we. Understanding the process can help us gear up and not get discouraged as we work through change. A real problem exists if we are biased to believe that we only live for immediate gratification.

Lest we get overwhelmed by complexity, please know that much of the change process happens at an unconscious level. Readjusting beliefs can happen quickly, and then we can move on. Changing our self-concept requires engaging our unconscious mind—that part of us that handles complexity much more quickly than our conscious mind. However, consciously knowing what we are going through and why gives us patience and insight when we get stuck. We will learn some conscious processes to cope with biases in the next chapters.

NOTES

1. Storr, W. (2013). *The Heretics: Adventures with the Enemies of Science*. London, UK: Picador.

2. James, W. (2010). *The Will to Believe and Other Essays in Popular Philosophy, and Human Immortality*. New York, NY: Digireads Publishing.

3. DiSalvo, D. (2011). *What Makes Your Brain Happy and Why You Should Do the Opposite*. Amherst, NY: Prometheus Books.

4. (DiSalvo, 2011).

5. (DiSalvo, 2011).

6. (DiSalvo, 2011).

7. (DiSalvo, 2011).

8. (DiSalvo, 2011).

CHAPTER 12

Managing Multiple Selves: The Lawyer, The Scientist, and the Spirit Within Us

A BRIEF EXPLANATION

Allow me to introduce the next three chapters. We are going to conduct an abbreviated psychological autopsy of the self. Don't worry, this kind of autopsy is not messy. We will metaphorically open up the self and check out its parts. In doing so, we will gain useful insights about our self-concept and the Best Life. We will focus on two important questions: What are the components of the self? And how do they interact and function? We will gain insight into how we can better organize the individual parts within ourselves. There are many differing opinions about the components of the self. I will share current views from various scientists as well as some observations of my own.

We will divide the components of the self into two categories. The first category manages the operational parts of the self. Scientists have identified universal patterns of thinking that they equate with these parts of self. Thinking about operational patterns as separate parts of the self is useful in understanding how we think and behave. Comparing the self to a machine is inaccurate in many ways. However, for our purposes, it is helpful to compare the operational parts of the self to parts of a machine. Machines have parts that give it strength, timing, direction, protection, and so on. Likewise, we will examine the operational parts of ourselves that help us make decisions, perceive reality, and create emotions. We'll label some of these parts: the rational and emotional self, the heart and mind self, the fast and slow self, the remembering and experiencing self, and so on.

The second category handles the personality parts of the self. These parts are more like "mini-selves". They seem to have their own values, personalities, preferences, and opinions. Their interactions together help create a person's ultimate values, preferences, and personalities. As we will see, the relationships among these personality parts create mental and emotional strength or weakness. Creating a healthy self-concept requires recognizing and mediating these relationships among the mini-selves. We will give them names like Protector, Connector, Mission, and Equalizer.

SELF-PARTS AND MINI-SELVES

Opening up the self means that we uncover behaviors, thought patterns, emotions, and beliefs. We need to discover what they really mean. We are curious about how they interrelate. We want to know how these aspects of ourselves affect the Best Life.

What do we first notice as we open up the self? We are probably surprised that there are so many individual parts. We have all felt divided, as if there were two or more of us vying for attention. We are not talking about the psychological diagnosis of "Dissociative Identity Disorder" formerly known as "Multiple Personality Disorder", but something common to us all. How many times has a part of you wanted one thing and another part wanted something else? "I want to get in shape, but I also want to relax and be comfortable." "I want to get married, but I also want independence." A new discipline called Social Neuroscience views the mind as a relational world in which unique parts of the self live together.

Creating and nurturing a self-concept requires managing the individual parts within us. We are truly relational beings with both internal and external relationships. In order to build a self-concept from multiple parts, you must have an understanding of what we call the "self". Thinking of the self as multiple parts or mini-selves stimulates creativity in building our own self-concept. Let's explore how this works.

Interesting, we intuitively treat each other as if there were more than one of us. In the course of a day, we often speak as if there was more than one of us. The following phrases demonstrate how we treat the self as multiple parts. "I'm not myself today. You didn't show up while you were in the meeting. I'm sorry, that wasn't the real me. Do you love me for who I am or just part of me? I'm going to get myself together. That was the feminine me. Which of you will show up for the game today? I want that, but give me this. My unconscious did that. When the good you shows up, we can talk. My spirit is restless. I'm an addict, but I have a sober side. The animal in me just can't say no."

The list could go on. We even talk to ourselves, sometimes out loud. It makes you wonder who is talking and who is listening? These every day occurrences cause a lot of confusion. In this chapter, we will consider current theories about how to conceptualize these multiple selves in useful ways. We will also consider practical suggestions of how to incorporate these theories into creating and managing our self-concept.

Please remember that these theories are simply metaphors to explain how the brain and the self operate. Notice that I use the words "brain" and "self" together. I do so for simplicity in presenting these ideas. I am not implying that the self is exclusively the brain, or that the brain is exclusively the mind. The names and descriptions of the metaphors help us make sense of our behaviors. This is not an exact science.

Self-parts can work together for the benefit of the whole self and not just the individual parts. The key is creating team-building parts that care about each other, but care about the whole self even more. We are truly relational beings with relationships that are cultivated internally as well as externally. Here are some benefits of functioning as a team of operational parts or mini-selves:

- We already acknowledge that the self has multiple components. Why not take it a step further?
- Effective decision-making means developing an internal consensus.
- Knowing how decisions are made within us helps us understand how we hold ourselves accountable.
- We can develop more confidence in our decision-making if we understand the dynamics involved.
- We can consciously facilitate internal negotiations among the separate parts of ourselves.

- We can create internal collaborations that lead to greater creativity and better problem solving.
- We can better understand and reduce internal stress and conflict.
- We can develop empathy and learn to love all part of ourselves (not just our favorite parts).

THE CONSCIOUS AND UNCONSCIOUS MIND

We've all heard of the conscious and unconscious mind. We probably have different understandings about what they are, how they function, and how they interact. Let's point out features of both that we can agree upon. Our mini-selves are more active in the unconscious mind.

We'll keep it brief for our purposes. Our mind (including our brain) runs almost all of our bodily systems. These systems interact in a precise, organized manner to keep us alive and functioning. Literally, billions of physiological functions happen every second. Somehow, the unconscious mind coordinates these operations. We also have millions and millions of memories. The unconscious mind seems to be their repository. Additionally, our operational parts and mini-selves reside within the immense expanse of our unconscious.

Our conscious mind is unaware of all these operations happening simultaneously. Consequently, it seems inferior to the unconscious mind. However, the conscious mind is able to delegate responsibilities to the unconscious. For example, once we consciously learn to ride a bike, we are able to do so with little conscious thought. The unconscious takes over, and these behaviors become automatic. We consciously speak, listen, focus, and move around. We picture our unconscious and conscious sides doing different things. Both sides are critical to our self-concept. We can simply think of the unconscious as that part of the mind that functions without conscious awareness.

While the unconscious mind handles billions of information bits at one time, the conscious mind can manage only a handful. Nevertheless, we normally consider the thoughts of the conscious mind as representative of who we are. We also consider our moral choices to be products of our conscious mind. Accountability for our actions is generally attributed to the conscious mind. However, the unconscious and the conscious minds interact in some way. The conscious can even intentionally affect what are normally unconscious body functions. For example, meditation can manipulate body temperature, heart rate, and blood pressure. On the other hand, the conscious mind relies on the unconscious for information processing, flashes of insight, memory retrieval, and decision-making.

We still do not understand exactly how the conscious and unconscious minds interact. When the conscious and the unconscious minds disagree, the unconscious typically wins over time. The story about my daughter being afraid of the invisible witch is an example of this. To assertively create and maintain a congruent self-concept, we must understand how the conscious and unconscious interact. We want to find ways for them to operate cooperatively, rather than being in constant conflict.

THE LAWYER AND THE SCIENTIST

Many of our operational parts are connected to the unconscious. Let's take a look at two of these. One metaphor to describe how the self operates is the Lawyer and the Scientist. This metaphor describes operational parts involved in our decision-making. A major proponent of this metaphor is Leonard Mlodinow, a noted scientist who embraced Social Neuroscience at its first meeting of organizers in 2001. He states the importance of answering some of the perplexing issues we have raised in this chapter.

"If you really want to understand the social world, if you really want to understand yourself and others, and, beyond that, if you really want to overcome many of the obstacles that prevent you from living your fullest, richest life, you need to understand the influence of the subliminal world that is hidden within each of us."[1]

The Lawyer and the Scientist inside of us reside in that subliminal world. (Many people want to perform autopsies on lawyers while they're still breathing, so here's your chance.) Mlodinow proposes that these two parts of the self are in opposition to one another. Research has isolated two opposing ways that our minds seem to operate. He calls these the Lawyer and the Scientist. These are operational parts of the self that work for our mini-selves. The Lawyer was described by William James as that part of us that substantiates and rationalizes what is desirable or useful. The Lawyer Self searches for evidence and justifications to support our already chosen belief.

On the other hand, the Scientist comes up with an idea or hypothesis, gathers evidence, looks for regularities, forms theories explains their observations, and tests them. Of course, the Scientist has the more rational and logical approach. You would think that all of us would instinctively prefer the Scientist within to make our decisions. Wrong! Research indicates that what we really want is to fulfill our desires. Getting what we want makes us feel right. In other words, we tend to go from belief to evidence, not vice versa. Our essential desires are the prominent forces in decision-making, and they are not just wistful dreams.

Psychologists sometimes call this process "motivated reasoning".[2] You may wonder how the Scientist lets the Lawyer get away with this? As discussed earlier, the philosopher, Kant (and many others) believe that we only experience the world through our senses. They propose that our eyes and ears take in information, and our brain then arranges and interprets that information. As a result, we are never aware of what the real world is like beyond our sensory interpretations. Accurate or not, the interpretation is what we call our experience. This means that our emotions, memories, and even our perception of reality are constructs created by the brain from incomplete and sometimes even conflicting data. They assume that this applies to our self-concept.

"We use the same kind of creative process to generate our self-image. When we paint our picture of self, our attorney-like unconscious blends fact and illusion, exaggerating our strengths, minimizing our weaknesses creating a virtually Picassoesque series of distortions in which some parts have been blown up to enormous size (the parts we like) and others shrunk to near invisibility. The rational scientists of our conscious minds then innocently admire the self-portrait, believing it to be a work of photographic accuracy."[3]

Mlodinow is essentially saying that the Lawyer self manipulates our perceptions, thereby controlling the evidence presented to the Scientist. From a Kantian perspective, the evidence or memories are "crafted and shaped" together by the Lawyer to support whatever is desired. And the Scientist is left to work with tampered evidence. In this regard, the Lawyer exerts control over the Scientist. As William James argues, our desires cast a powerful shadow over our decisions by tainting, coloring, and justifying the desires to be fulfilled. Our deepest desires tell the Lawyer what to do. If this is even partially true, we want to know where our desires come from. Our fundamental desires are part of our moral choices.

Clients hire lawyers to help them get what they want. Similarly, our internal Lawyer is like a tool of our desires. On the other hand, our internal Scientist acts like a security guard, patrolling the boundaries of our biases. This perspective helps us understand how we make some decisions. However, neither the Lawyer nor the Scientist seems to be the ultimate decision-maker. They are simply on the payroll.

Think for a moment about who you want to be, and how your internal Lawyer and Scientist have worked to create this desired self-perception. Are you unsure or unclear about who you are and want to be? That's fine. The purpose of this book is to motivate us to get clear about our self-concept. It is part of the process. If we have sincere, conflicting desires about our self-concept, we probably have multiple lawyers and scientists representing each partisan desire. That sounds rather chaotic and confusing. It doesn't feel good either! In fact, these conflicting desires are at the heart of self-conflict. Life is a continual resolution of internal and external conflicts. It's called growth. Accept this as an exciting challenge. Resenting this ongoing process undermines successful resolutions.

You would think that our desires only support positive beliefs, because that seems to be logically what is most useful. However, that is not always the case. What about those people who think "ill" of themselves, those who feel unworthy or incompetent? Why aren't they "puffing up their strengths"? A mini-self in them may be doing so, but another mini-self has fully committed to a negative or contrary belief.

Imagine someone who sabotages success when it is right in front of them. These poor souls may have a mini-self that concluded from intense relational experiences that they're unlovable. This is not a fact, but a perceptual conclusion, that explains the meaning of various relational experiences. Their internal Lawyer for whatever reason was unable to spin the experiences into something positive. For example, as time passes, when they wonder why they are rejected by someone, they return to the perceptual conclusion that they are unlovable.

Once this type of belief gains traction, it's tough to change.

Remember that parts of self cannot be *forced* to believe that what they think is untrue. This can cause some mini-selves to believe one thing and other mini-selves to believe something opposite. These mini-self conclusions can be adopted as truth, and in this example, it creates self-loathing, hopelessness, and helplessness. The person may try all kinds of strategies to overcome the pain, or to mask it. Unfortunately, this often leads to substance abuse, anxiety, depression, and withdrawal from life. We have all heard the metaphor of the "divided self". This is it in a nutshell.

Here's what can happen when another mini-self disagrees with being a loser and wants to prove the person's worth. This mini-self may try to force the person to be successful, but when success is near, the mini-self with the "unworthy belief" steps in and sabotages the success. (Remember the "loser" home run hitter in Chapter One?)

What we learn is that mini-selves can have their own lawyer and scientist. Mini-selves try to do what is most useful for them. Each is honestly promoting the quality of self that they believe to be real. However, the harder they try, the more internal contention ensues. Sometimes, one mini-self will suffer exhaustion or exasperation and quit for a while. The winner doesn't necessarily have the best lawyer and scientist, but it has the most dominant desire. Can you see the importance of aligning our desires to the Best Life? If there is a core within us, perhaps it is our desires.

THE RATIONAL AND THE EMOTIONAL SELF

Some people view the brain as a computer with millions of little units combining together and creating artificial intelligence.[8] This metaphor certainly minimizes the emotional aspect of being human. This metaphor also assumes that the mind works by myriads of little mindless parts that somehow operate in *complex cooperation* with one another. Surprisingly, they fall in line through some external means and combine to create thinking and bodily functioning.

On the other hand, David Eagleman proposes that we have a rational self and an emotional self.[4] Eagleman believes that the mind has parts that are *individually intelligent*, and that they interact in the spirit of competition. These are more like the mini-selves that I previously described. Eagleman says that our minds effectively work on principles of conflict. (Conflict can exist without contention.) Much of this competition involves the rational versus the emotional mind.

Theoretically, the competition is beneficial because it forces us to consider all of our options. We assume that having more choices is useful, thereby improving the quality of our thinking. In addition, we hope that this conflict ultimately leads to cooperation. This equates to a democracy where individuals have various opinions and influence. To get anything done, one needs to at least to get a majority to agree.

"In contrast, parties in a democracy hold differing opinions about the same issues—and the important part of the process is the battle for steering the ship of state. Brains are like representative democracies. They are built of multiple, overlapping experts who weigh in and compete over different choices. As Walt Whitman correctly surmised, we are large and we harbor multitudes within us. And those multitudes are locked in chronic battle. There is an ongoing conversation among the different functions in your brain, each competing to control the single output channel of your behavior. As a result, you can accomplish the strange feats of arguing with yourself, cursing at yourself, and cajoling yourself to do something—feats that modern computers simply do not do."[5]

His study of the mind would include identifying the parties, discerning how they compete, and observing how the brain regroups if everything falls apart. He describes the unconscious as: under the surface, automatic, implicit, heuristic, intuitive, holistic, reactive, and impulsive. The conscious faction is: cognitive, systematic, explicit, analytic, rule-based, and reflective. He sees these two always battling for control.

Two subsets of these two factions are what he calls the "rational and the emotional" minds. In the democratic U.S. political system, we could analogize these two identities to our political parties, the Republicans and the Democrats, but let's not go there. However, let's hope that our mental democracy is more efficient than our government, and not inclined towards mediocrity.

Can you think of a time when you seemed to operate like a democracy of rational or emotional selves? Did you eat the chocolate cake or not? Rational and emotional parts can be on each side, advocating to "eat up" or to "push away". They all have their unique opinions, and those opinions are all stirred in the pot or baked in the pan. One emotional part may say, "You'll *feel* so good as you taste each bite." Another emotional part may say, "Sure, but you'll *feel* like a slug in half an hour for the rest of the day." A logical part may say, "It's only 360 calories and you can cut out two items at dinner to end up with the right amount of calories for the day." Of course, another logical part counters with, "How many times have you decided to cut back on dinner and followed through? That's right, none!"

Some people want to believe that human nature has only one genuine aim. The result is that we are either true to our self by following that aim, or we are capitulating to a deviant "false" self. To be true is not to deviate from the one true aim. It is clumsy believing that at any one time we have only one genuine aim. This simplistic perspective awkwardly explains that we fluctuate back and forth in our actions because we are either genuine or disingenuous. The resolution is to get genuine, or as we often hear, "get real". The problem in following the true aim is knowing what's "real" and then knowing how to get there. Eagleman proposes another approach. He proposes that we have multiple aims. We can therefore view our incongruence as a "conflict or competition" between the rational and emotional parts of these aims. In doing so, he recognizes that we have rational aims and emotional aims.

In fact, an emotional aim and a rational aim represent two different desires. We could roughly say that immediate gratification is the emotional self and delayed gratification is the rational self. They are conflicting desires.

He is a determinist and views mankind as having instinctive desires for immediate gratification. For example, if we are hungry we want to eat *now*. However, he also recognizes that a person can have deterministic, but delayed actions as well. He sees people as conditioned by past experiences to respond rationally or emotionally to an environmental event. Conditioned here means environmentally "determined". We are conditioned to act emotionally or rationally.

Choosing who dies in a railway accident is his classic example. Five people are on a track, and the train is barreling toward them. The trainman can switch tracks to cause the train to miss the five, but one person on the new track will die. Will they switch tracks? Eagleman states that most people will rationally choose to give up one life for five unless the one is somehow related to the trainman. That would make the decision more emotional than rational.

He changes the scenario to a train again barreling down on five people. This time, the decision-maker is on a bridge looking down at the train track and at the five people below. Besides, the decision-maker is a "large" person who could lay down on the track and stop the train, saving the lives of the five people. Should the decision-maker push the large person to the track below to save five lives?

The result would be the same as in the previous scenario, giving one life for five. However, because physical contact is required to push the large person to their death, most people would do nothing and let the five die. He proposes that the emotional mind is triggered by the intimacy of physical contact with the large person, thus preventing the logical choice. We can imagine the rational and emotional mind being persuaded to make these types of decisions even, if they were not deterministically conditioned.

You don't want the rational or the emotional part to dominate all of your decisions. Eagleman proposes that you are determined to act as one self-part or the other depending on past experiences, and it appears you have little or no choice. However, we can recognize the rational and the emotional differences of mind and assume that we have choice. What we value at the time will guide our efforts.

For example, most people enjoy controlling their own bank accounts and financial resources. However, some people opt for employers to withhold money for savings or other purposes. Why? Through personal experience, these people have learned that they will not save, but will spend. Their logical solution is to have it put in a safe place. This is a rational decision to avoid a context where the emotional self normally takes control. Many decisions can be anticipated and made well in advance through internal negotiations. This negotiating process can be incorporated into the self-concept and enhanced with practice. We can all benefit from this strategy if we want to act more rationally.

Another example of being rational is deciding which desire to focus on prior to beginning a task. This is especially helpful when having to complete tasks that may be boring or a hassle in the moment. Think of mopping a floor and how tedious and boring that can be. We don't do it, or we try to get out of it.

However, what happens if ahead of time we agree to focus on the long-term results of mopping. We do this by staying focused on how pretty and clean the floor will be, and how good the room will smell when the job is done. We also imagine and focus on how good it feels to have the job done. We're focusing on the *results* and not the process of mopping. When you do this, even mopping the floor can become a tolerable thing to do. (You're not rational if you can actually get excited about mopping the floor unless you get a Gatorade at the end.)

REFRAMING

When we enjoy a job well done, it motivates us. People can actually get excited to do menial tasks when they focus on the end benefit rather than the process. We can call this a reframe. Not only do we reframe our focus, but we also reframe what is a desirable, short-term objective. With practice, we can change our sense of desired gratification into a feeling of completion rather than a feeling of physical comfort. The criteria for gratification shifts from avoiding tedium and boredom to enjoying a clean floor. The key here is for the emotional and rational parts to agree in advance of starting the project. The emotional part can then be motivated to work fast so that the enjoyment of a clean floor can happen as quickly as possible. This process can give us access to flexible choices about what motivates us.

This ability may help explain why an otherwise impulsive, impatient drug-user can stand in the cold rain for hours waiting for their dealer. Learning how to recognize and consciously initiate these simple strategies can improve our abilities to get things done while having more enjoyment in life. That's a useful step to the Best Life.

WHAT IS SELF-DISCIPLINE

Rational and emotional interactions bring to mind questions about self-discipline. Have you ever thought about what self-discipline means? It's certainly a virtue when used with virtuous intent. But, how does it work? Let's think about it as interactions among operating parts or mini-selves. Self-discipline keeps one part from getting what it wants while another part is satisfied.

A mini-self may want more work, to get mad, to eat three pizzas or to have more fun. Discipline refers to somehow controlling or restraining that part or mini-self from doing those things. The amount of discipline may range from not ever or not now, to no more. Who disciplines whom? I don't know! It seems that our other mini-selves and our ultimate desires certainly have a voice in self-discipline. However, I don't think we experience *coups* of one mini-self taking over the government of self. Somehow, our sovereign self is ultimately responsible for our moral decisions. However, our various parts and mini-selves are strongly influential throughout this process.

ADMINISTERING SELF-DISCIPLINE

How is the discipline administered? Self-discipline means that we somehow discipline ourselves. Somehow a part or mini-self is prevented from getting what it wants. This may be coercive restraint of some kind or it may be a successful negotiation and a mutual agreement. I believe that the parts and mini-selves can develop ways to discipline one another without being coercive. Developing empathy with inner negotiation skills can lead to the best kind of self-discipline. That can bring about agreement and mutual assistance. Keeping mini-selves focused on the Best Life encourages them to discipline themselves for the end result. This can lead to better overall results than throwing exaggerated guilt trips, blaming, badgering, or bullying our internal parts and mini-selves. Self-discipline of the whole self may be better accomplished through self-discipline of parts and mini-selves.

Let's leave our democracies and turn our attention now to how our minds gather information for decision-making. We know that the Scientist relies on the Five Senses and nothing else. Those senses may be enhanced with telescopes, microscopes, earphones, and other instruments. However, in the end, the scientist is able to ultimately see, hear, touch, taste or smell something. Because the senses reveal a "something", they conclude that it must be real.

Our parts and mini-selves need information to act upon. We can usually rely on our Five Senses. (This reliance gets tested in Las Vegas at magic shows.)

However, we seem to also gather information about values, preferences, morals, ethics, and what some call "spiritual sensations" or inspiration. Is there a way to gather information beyond relying exclusively on our Five Senses? Let's take a brief look at a possible addition.

THE HERMENEUTIC SENSE

William James argues that a desire to believe, supported by facts and reason, can give us rational permission to believe something. In fact, that seems to be the way of all believers including scientists. That doesn't ensure we will believe the truth of something. It will help us "experience" believing. Let's consider a process that some academicians and others use to gather knowledge in the search for truth. The process is called *hermeneutics.*

Hermeneutics describes our *experiences and their meanings as the focal point of reality*. The hermeneutic inquiry focuses on how we experience something.[6] Hermeneutics assumes that reality is revealed in the experience. Therefore, we want to broaden and deepen our understanding of any experience. Sensing material things may be part of the experience but they are not the total basis for making the experience real. All elements of an experience are required to make it real or a true experience.

Hermeneutics assumes that we have another sense of awareness in addition to our Five Senses. This sense recognizes our compelling connections to other humans as well as other unseen things like love and virtue. This sense is somehow a part of our self. James describes it thusly.

"It is as if there were in the human consciousness a sense of reality, a feeling of objective presence, a perception of what we may call 'something there,' more deep and more general than any of the special and particular 'senses' by which psychology supposes existent realities to be originally revealed."[7]

Our experiences can include a sense of connectedness to the seen and the unseen. The functions of the mind and this sense of awareness or connectedness to other things is part of any experience. Our sensory awareness, the meanings, and the materials in a context combine to create the reality of the experience. Our hermeneutic sense may be the *ability to perceive* that "feeling of objective presence" or that "something there" which is part of so many life experiences. We don't have an objective way to evaluate or measure this sense, and therefore scientists may eschew it. However, hermeneutics speaks to the parts of our experiences we all seem to recognize that are usually ignored or explained away.

This hermeneutic sense has been organized into what is called the "hermeneutic circle"[8] to help us understand our experiences more completely.

CONTEMPLATING A SPIRIT SELF

Viewing ourselves as a combination of mini-selves also accommodates religious perspectives. We can't ignore "spirit" because much of the world believes that some form of spirit interacts with the material body. Many of us believe that our self includes spirit, and that the spirit and body together constitute our mortal self (and even our eternal self). Remember the Cartesian Duality that says that the body and the mind are separate but united entities? The spirit/mind duality is based on similar reasoning.

Science has yet to discover material proof of spirit, and therefore those resting their faith in science look askance at the notion of spirits. However, our worldview based on the assumptions of Strong Relationality allows us to rationally believe in a spirit-self. In doing so, science is not rejected by Strong Relationality, but we recognize that scientific theories are forever evolving and changing. For example, we no longer believe in scientific theories like, "The earth is flat", or "Atoms are like little raisins". Therefore, additional approaches to empiricism (like Hermeneutics) are important, viable tools for investigating truth. You could say that Strong Relationality allows us to have an expanded picture of reality and alternative ways to experience it.

The spirit-self is considered by many people to be immaterial. Others view it as refined matter not yet discovered by scientists. Beliefs about the self pre-existing this life and surviving beyond mortality rely on acknowledging a spirit-self. Higher Power or Deity is believed to interact with us in a "spiritual" manner. Consequently, we must have a spirit-self for spiritual relationships and to discern spiritual communications.

People universally describe spiritual experiences as unique from all other experiences. We hear people refer to recognizing or sensing someone else's spirit. We previously reviewed William James inquiry into this uniqueness. Some of us also believe that Source or a Deity gives humans (by spiritual means) knowledge, comfort, discernment, virtue, and other qualities. In other words, a higher power assists us in developing our self.

Consequently, believers logically view the spirit-self as directly interacting with other self-parts including our mini-selves. In fact, these believers see the spirit-self as the ultimate decision-maker.

Moral accountability is often equated with spirit accountability. In other words, we are spiritually accountable to this Source or Deity and to other people for how we interact with them. More precisely, our relationships have spiritual consequences in the present and far beyond.

Some minds have difficulty justifying the existence of morality without acknowledging the existence of spirit, Source or Deity. For them morality without a spirit source is simply human-made ethics, subject to fashionable change.

As you can see, there are many factors that encourage people to believe or disbelieve in a spirit self. Those who end up believing or having faith in spirit usually do so because of their personal experiences. They view their experiences similar to the perception characteristic of Hermeneutics. They think that the explanations of the Five Senses are insufficient to describe the sense of an "objective other" and its presence in life experiences. They find many rational and useful reasons to believe in a spirit self. Like believing in a non-spirit self, belief in a spirit self is not compelled. Both beliefs are choices, acts of faith. Perhaps we choose not only what is useful to us, but also what speaks to us.

THE BEST LIFE COLLABORATION

The Best Life requires a group effort within us as well as with those outside of us. We obtain the Best Life by leading our parts and mini-selves to work together. We want them to care about each other, to have empathy and collaborate in mutual endeavors. We bring them together by helping them feel and think unselfishly. As the parts within us work for our overall Best Life well-being, they become united. When they immaturely go off in their own directions, we get distressed. We know that conflict helps the parts to grow as long as conflict doesn't turn into contention. Resolving conflict means growth of the self.

NOTES

1. Mlodinow, L. (2012). *Subliminal: How your Unconscious Mind Rules Your Behavior.* New York, NY. Vintage Books.

2. (Mlodinow, 2012).

3. (Mlodinow, 2012).

4. Eagleman, D. (2011). *Incognito: The Secret Lives of the Brain.* New York, NY: Pantheon Books.

5. (Eagleman, 2011).

6. Ricoeur, P. (1981). *Hermeneutics & the Human Sciences* John B. Thompson, (Ed.). (John B. Thompson, Trans.). Cambridge, UK: Cambridge University Press.

7. James, W. (2008). *Varieties of Religious Experience: A Study in Human Nature.* Charleston, SC: Forgotten Books.

8. (Ricoeur, 1981).

CHAPTER 13

Scientists' Metaphors of The Multiple Self

SELF-PARTS AND SELF-CONCEPT

Let's continue our psychological autopsy. In the previous chapter, we explored the multiple self and how relationships affect our overall self-concept. We examined the benefits of treating ourselves empathically and virtuously in order to reconcile internal dissonance and confusion. We touched upon the pervasive influence of both the conscious and unconscious. We gained insight into our decision-making through the Lawyer and Scientist metaphor. We learned strategies of choosing when to be rational or emotional. We also carved out space for a spirit-self.

In this chapter, we'll look at a few more patterns of human thinking and behavior proposed by scientists. In doing so, we will gain practical insights and identify strategies to build our self-concept and help us learn to get along with ourselves. We want to combine our self-parts to better accomplish our desires. Most importantly, we will continue to "get ourselves together". Here are the parts we will explore:

- The Heart and the Mind
- The Fast Brain and the Slow Brain
- The Remembering Self and the Experiencing Self

UNITING SELF-PARTS

As we continue to uncover self-parts in our autopsy, let's keep in mind how they can collectively work together. We have discussed how the mind creates a life narrative as an ongoing story. Eagleman suggests that this story unites our operational parts and our mini-selves. Why is this necessary? The internal self-parts experience conflict when they disagree. As a result, our actions are weakened because these internal parts resist, or even sabotage. However, all parts want to perpetuate the general theme of the life story. Therefore, when a decision or event occurs, the parts may disagree on how to integrate them into the ongoing story. Consequently, a negotiation ensues.

The parts recognize the ambiguity in perceptions and memories, and the ambiguity becomes the focus of the negotiation. The parts argue over the perceptional gaps, and create (and even fabricate) meanings and memories to continue the flow of the story. A successful internal negotiation of these ambiguities can unite the self- parts.

Remember the story of the two young women who endured violent rapes? They gleaned different meanings from very similar experiences. One viewed the rape as a validation of her worthlessness while the other viewed it as validation of her attractiveness. Prior to the horrible incident, both had different life stories.

The life theme of one young woman's story was her worthlessness. In spite of its negativity, these parts of her found validation in the rape experience. It reaffirmed the idea, "I am garbage". The other young woman's life theme was her attractiveness and desirability. As a result, the parts interpreted the violent rape as a radical confirmation of this theme. Both of these young women interpreted her experience as a continuation of her life theme. Their ongoing life themes, as well as the physical experience itself, influenced the *meaning* of what happened. Of course, life themes can change as we will discuss in another chapter. Keep this idea of life stories in mind as we dissect more self-parts.

PATTERNICITY

Eagleman proposes another mind dynamic for understanding the interactions of self-parts. This works with the same principles as a continuing narrative. Patternicity (identifying and using patterns) is sought by self-parts in order to reduce the energy required to fulfill their duties. In other words, self-parts look for patterns in what they perceive. When they identify an event occurring a few times, they respond automatically. They don't have to analyze or think it through. It's repetition. They've been there, done that. Even groups of parts can agree on these patterns. Agreeing that a pattern exists eliminates the need for the parts to discuss how to respond to the event. This conserves energy and eliminates a committee meeting.

However, there are times when events occur that fit no pattern. How is that handled? Eagleman explains that there is a CEO in our mind that shows up when patternicity is interrupted. Now, the CEO does not have the answers, but like a mediator or arbitrator, it organizes the parties of the mind to facilitate a new agreement. It knows the specialties among the mind parts and contacts them to find the best way to solve the problem. The CEO generates interaction among the parts to create a majority solution. In this model, the mind flies on automatic pilot until a pattern is broken, or new issues arise. At that point, energy is expended among the parts to find a solution.

Our self-concepts are too often flying along on automatic pilot. It's easy to for our parts to configure themselves accordingly and get comfortable. They lead us to respond automatically to the familiar elements of our life. However, when something breaks the pattern, the mind is forced to go to work. We resist changing our self-concept, because it breaks a huge system of patterns, and requires a great amount of energy. When we consider changing our self-perception and feel resistance, understand that the resistance comes from self-parts wanting to maintain patterns. It's just easier. We need to carefully consider the costs and benefits of change. In doing so, don't succumb to some parts of yourself that prefer to be lazy.

THE HEART SELF AND THE MIND SELF

People often tell us to listen to our "head" or to our "heart". What's the difference? These two sub-selves remind us of Eagleman's rational/emotional distinction. However, in addition to describing a process of thinking, the heart/mind distinction has biological origins.

Over the last two decades, the Institute of HeartMath has researched the neurological connections between the brain and the heart. This research has inspired the creation of biofeedback instruments that evaluate stress-related ailments. The research found that the mind is biologically and energetically located *throughout* the body, not just in the brain. The findings suggest that the heart sends more neurological messages to the brain than it receives from the brain. The messages that the heart sends to the brain actually seem to guide and change brain functions. The conclusion is that the heart has a "mind" or an intelligence of its own. The desires of the heart interact with the logic of the brain. If so, the age-old saying "listen to your heart" may be truer than we ever supposed.

Therefore, the "self" may be considered to include at least two relatively independent mini-selves: one biologically located in the heart, the other in the brain. They interdependently influence decision-making. However, this research has not established either one as the primary decision-maker. Biofeedback technology seems to facilitate congruence and cooperation between the brain and the heart, which again, is a relational objective.

Research also suggests that the neurological input from the heart to the brain is necessary for its normal logic-based functioning. Antonio Damasio suggests that the emotion-based messages to the "thought centers" in the brain are absolutely required for rational decision-making.[2] This contradicts the long accepted belief that emotions are enemies of rationality. Personal experience and scientific research tells us that our most pervasive and intractable thoughts are accompanied by the most intense emotions. Neutral rational beliefs and memories are much easier to change than emotion-laden thoughts of an intense experience.

This explains why visual and auditory affirmations that attempt to change beliefs or behaviors usually do not work. Mini-selves that are emotionally committed to a belief can disagree with an affirmation, and then reject it. The same explanation may apply to the persuasiveness of rational explanations. Rational explanations are sometimes ignored by various self-parts. Intense beliefs influenced by the heart typically resist bare logical explanations. Therefore, rationality alone can fail to effectively change beliefs or behaviors.

The emotional heart often overrides the rational brain. If this is true, our changing self-concept requires agreement by our heart and our brain. We can't force acceptance of this by sheer will power. We need mutual agreement. Like other metaphors we've discussed, the heart and the mind require internal empathy and negotiation. We need effective methods to achieve this congruence.

THE FAST BRAIN AND THE SLOW BRAIN

Psychology offers us another metaphor to help us understand how our mind operates. Daniel Kahneman researched how the brain is separated into two distinct parts. In his book, *Thinking Fast and Slow,* he discusses some of his findings. He clearly states his purpose. "My main aim here is to present a view of how the mind works that draws on recent developments in cognitive and social psychology. One of the more important developments is that we now understand the marvels as well as the flaws of intuitive thought."[3]

Quick, intuitive thinking relates to the Fast Brain. Deliberate thinking relates to the Slow Brain. Fast and slow thinking correlate to the unconscious and conscious mind. Have you ever encountered someone with a wrinkled face, squinted eyes, and a snarling, half-open mouth? Did you automatically assume that the person is angry and ready to "let it rip"? You had no plan to assess this particular person's mood; you just automatically and involuntarily did it. That is fast thinking: intuitive and automatic. It's an unconscious process.

When presented with a complex multiplication problem, you slow down and go through steps. Maybe you refer to memorized multiplication tables, and then apply the strategy several times in order to obtain the final result. That is slow thinking with the conscious mind. Your whole body was engaged in this slow process demonstrated by changes in blood pressure, heart rate, muscle tension, and so on More energy is required for slow thinking than fast thinking.

The concept of fast, unconscious thinking is similar to Gladwell's description in his best-selling book, *Blink.* Fast thinking is the result of the unconscious mind having access to your memories, experiences, thoughts, and beliefs at extraordinary speed.

In any given context, the unconscious automatically matches present circumstances against these extensive memory files. The result is a lightning-fast communication to the conscious mind in the form of an intuition or conclusion. I say "intuition" because the unconscious does not reveal the information or processing that led to the conclusion. There is no explanation or justification for the conclusion.

The communication is often a feeling or an impression. Often, these impressions are very accurate, but they depend on the quality of the information and the processing skills of the unconscious. They are not infallible. However, the conscious mind normally accepts the intuition when the impression feels strong and reassuring. Some readers may believe in spiritual impressions or communications. These communications may also seem like intuitions.

For those of you that believe in spiritual communication, be mindful in distinguishing intuitions from spiritual impressions. Doing so will help you identify your self-thoughts from spiritual communication. Often we ask ourselves, "Was that just, me or was it God?" The experiences should somehow be notably different from one another.

The conscious mind needs additional energy and time to think. Just like working on a math problem, when the conscious engages, energy is drained and time is consumed. Of course, the unconscious mind may contribute while the conscious mind is operating, but the heavy lifting is done by the conscious mind. To conserve time and energy, it is tempting to rely on fast thinking for everything. However, we need to learn to use both wisely in order to function intelligently.

Paradoxically, we generally refer to the slow thinking or conscious mind as the "self". We do so without knowing what is happening in the unconscious mind. Interestingly, that is where most of the action happens. This obviously raises questions about agency and responsibility as we have discussed[6]. When possible, slowing down our decision-making process enhances the interplay between the conscious and unconscious minds. In spite of the speed and immediate access to information, we still make a lot of intuitive errors and mistakes.

When time permits, make decisions using both the conscious and unconscious mind. However, we need to be careful how we evaluate an intuition or unconscious thought. We may have experienced changing an intuitive answer on a true and false exam without having a good reason to do so. We are just second-guessing our intuition without being conscious of any information to justify the change. We are usually better off to go with our first intuition. If a decision must be made in the moment, and your conscious has little to contribute, go with your intuition. Overanalyzing can be paralyzing and can even create false information.

Why is this? You are not an expert or a genius about everything, even at an unconscious level. Our intuition depends on what we have experienced, the facts we have recorded, the conclusions we have drawn, and how our biases are functioning unconsciously. Remember that intuition is different than perceiving knowledge from an "outside" intelligence source like revelation, inspiration, or Jung's collective unconscious[7].

Fast thinking would be even more reliable if we were expert about everything or had immediate access to all relevant information. (Only my wife fits into that category.) In the meantime, let's slow down and evaluate our intuition, impressions, and biases from the unconscious. Astoundingly, we may discover that some of our unconscious beliefs and perceptions are not accurate. However, when our conscious mind can't confirm information uploaded from the unconscious, that doesn't mean the intuition from the unconscious is faulty. Be sure that the conscious has credible resources before overriding the unconscious.

If you deny a "blink" or an intuition, you create a dilemma. You must now reconcile the conscious and the unconscious. Changing unconscious perceptions and beliefs are more difficult than changing the conscious mind. This can be at the heart of people's frustration, particularly when the conscious mind wants to change an unconscious part of the self-concept. How can the unconscious be persuaded otherwise when it holds most of the cards? Conscious awareness of the dynamics is the beginning of the journey. We will discuss specific strategies to do this later on.

THE REMEMBERING SELF AND THE EXPERIENCING SELF

The Remembering Self and the Experiencing Self have two very different perspectives of our life experiences. These two parts play off of one another in order to affect our permission and motivation for any given action. They are illuminating metaphors of human nature. Kahneman explains. "I find it helpful to think of this dilemma as a conflict of interests between two selves (which do not correspond to the two familiar systems) [*By systems, he means the fast and slow systems discussed above*]. The experiencing self is the one that answers the question: 'Does it hurt now?' The remembering self is the one that answers the question: 'How was it, on the whole?' Memories are all we get to keep from our experience of living, and the only perspective that we can adopt as we think about our lives is therefore that of the remembering self"[4]

A research experiment found important distinctions between remembering or experiencing. Individuals undergoing painful colonoscopies were asked to rate the extent of their pain from 0 (no pain) to 10 (unbearable). Two evaluations were made. First, they rated their pain while they were experiencing it. In other words, during the colonoscopy, the patient was asked at one minute intervals to rate their pain. This was recorded until the end of the medical procedure.

Second, *after* the procedure was completed, the patient was asked to evaluate their overall pain level from the colonoscopy. Patient 1's procedure lasted only 8 minutes, but the intensity of the pain at the beginning and the end of the procedure was very high. During the 8 minutes, the pain rating went from 2 to 8 at different times. The peak-end pain average was 7.5. Patient 2's procedure lasted 24 minutes, but started out with minor pain and ended with minor pain. This person's range of pain at different times during the procedure went from 0 to 8. However, the peak-end average was 4.5.

From a minute-by-minute quantitative evaluation, the 24-minute patient endured more overall pain because it took longer to complete the procedure. However, when the patients evaluated their experience from a more detached memory perspective, the 8-minute patient rated the procedure overall more painful (7.5) than the 24-minute patient (4.5).

At first glance, the results do not appear to be reasonable. Over time, Patient 2 actually suffered more pain than Patient 1. However, in hindsight, Patient 1 evaluated the entire procedure more painful than Patient 2. In other words, suffering more overall pain did not make the person describe the most overall pain experience as the "worst" or most "uncomfortable" experience.[5] The Remembering Self and the Experiencing Self had different criteria for pain and comfort. Both sides experienced the pain differently. The duration of the pain had no effect on the ratings of total pain.

Interestingly, the experiment suggests that longer procedures minimizing peak pain lead to the best overall patient satisfaction. However, during a procedure, the patient's Experiencing Self will probably demand a quick ending to the intense pain. That means that the experience would end with the pain at a high level. That is not what the remembering self wants. These findings create a dilemma for physicians and psychotherapists. How do you satisfy a patient's desires to *minimize* pain? The question is "which" pain--the pain that is being experienced or the pain that is remembered after the experience? Peak pain at the end of an experience may persuade the person not to come back.

How does this affect creating a self-concept? As we plan ahead for who we want to be, we refer to our memories. Present remembrance of past events is the only way we have to evaluate who we are and what we want to experience in the future. However, can we rely on the Remembering Self alone to guide our self-concept? The Remembering Self can lead us into experiences that the Experiencing Self finds too painful in the moment and quit. Our self-concept can be sabotaged. Was it a good decision to repeat the experience? We can carefully decide in advance of a decision to carefully consider the perspectives of the Remembering Self and Experiencing Self. The Remembering Self may not be dismayed by reflections of painful peak experiences if the ending of the experience was low intensity. However, we must consider if the Experiencing Self will quit or continue when peak pain is reached during the experience. In doing so we can better weigh the cost/benefit of saying yes or no to a self-concept proposition. Understanding how these two selves operate can help us make better decisions. In particular, we don't want the Remembering Self getting us into situations that we can't handle at some intense moment. We don't want the Experiencing Self to prematurely quit a situation that is going to get better if we can hang on.

With this assurance, we may be willing to commit to that workout regimen, new job, new relationship, physical disability, and so on. Then again, more accurately anticipating the intensity of pain during an experience or series of experiences may keep us from getting into circumstances over our head.

In any case, we realize that the Experiencing Self and the Remembering Self are often at odds with each other. In making decisions, we should consider both sides. We can conduct a more informed cost-benefit analysis before deciding how to act in any given context.

Understanding the nature of both sides encourages internal negotiations among these parts. Knowing how they function eliminates frustration and confusion when they are in conflict. We can recognize the cause of our discomfort and slow down to resolve our internal differences. Understanding the dynamics of these two selves can help us decide how we will experience the Best Life. We obviously have two choices: we can live to maximize the moment (Experiencing Self) or live to create important, meaningful memories (Remembering Self). Life has a positive place and purpose for both parts.

LESSONS FROM THE COLORADO RIVER

I went on a two week trip rafting down the wild Colorado River. We had no professional guides, but my friends had floated the 270 mile journey before. I have wonderful memories of this experience. However, the enjoyment of these memories affects me differently than the intensity of specific experiences on the river. Some people need one trip to create memories, while other people need to go back for the experience over and over again. For these people, memories aren't what they want.

During the first part of the trip, I was fairly cocky. I sat back, enjoyed the scenery, and took pictures to remember the trip. I wanted to "create a memory". Then we came to Hermit. Here we experienced the most powerful waves in the canyon. The force of the rapids took us to the top of a giant wave, but instead of going over to the other side, the crest of the wave sent us backwards and upside down. We flew into the air and down to the deep trough at the base of the wave. Because we were upside down, the raft landed on top of us.

I was thrown deep into the river. My friend got tied up in webbing underneath the raft. Believe me, I was in the moment, giving no thought to memories. We made it to a slow eddy, and pulled the raft towards the shore to get organized. Later, a professionally-driven banana raft cruised into Hermit and got "tacoed". In other words, the front of the raft and the back of the raft folded into each other. People were caught in the middle. They weren't as lucky as we were, and several people suffered broken bones and other injuries that required helicopter evacuations.

Afterwards, I found myself at different times consciously creating memories and taking pictures. However, I spent a lot more time "in the moment" with all of my self-parts engaged with the river. Upon reflection, I loved creating memories, but I also loved the "in the moment" experiences that made me feel intensely alive. From this experience, I discovered that I was more of an "in the moment" kind of guy. We need both, but most of us favor one or the other.

I have moments of reflection about past relationships, particularly relationships that I will never have again in this life. I treasure these memories and wouldn't trade them for anything. However, life would be stagnant for me if I only lived in the memories. Like you, I need here and now relationships. But my life is enriched with great memories.

As we create our Best Life, understanding these two ways of living will help us make decisions and clarify our preferences. We will probably find ourselves wanting a combination. Our knowledge of these operating parts will help us decide "how" we engage in life. The How Strategy will guide us in identifying who we perceive ourselves to be and will help direct our course towards the Best Life.

PRACTICAL APPLICATIONS OF EXPERIENCING AND REMEMBERING

Our society takes on its own remembering or experiencing personality. Do we take our societal pulse and evaluate our well-being from a remembering or an experiencing perspective? Kahneman considers this question. "The distinction between two selves is applied to the measurement of well-being, where we find again that what makes the experiencing self happy is not quite the same as what satisfies the remembering self. How two selves within a single body can pursue happiness raises some difficult questions, both for individuals and for societies that view the well-being of the population as a policy objective."[6]

Let's take the service of psychotherapy as an example. One societal objective of psychotherapy is to help people obtain an outcome that has previously been difficult or unattainable. The client wants the therapist to help them obtain the desired outcome. The difficult part is identifying which self wants what, how to go about satisfying both, or choosing just one. Some therapists pay no attention to parts and assume that they are speaking directly to the "whole self" in a conversation. For example, perhaps the Remembering Self or the Experiencing Self, or maybe the Lawyer Self is responding. Their interests are considered, but other mini-selves are silent. The therapist isn't getting the whole picture. A part of effective therapy is getting an internal cooperation or a consensus among the parts. Therapists sometimes accomplish this objective without even noticing that it happened.

Activating or addressing our various mini-selves affects the client/therapist relationship too. This is particularly true for relational connections called transference and countertransference.[7] Transference occurs when a client intuitively transfers feelings and beliefs about someone else to the psychotherapist. The client unconsciously interacts with the therapist in a similar manner that they interacted with this other person. We can then reasonably conclude that this person has been projected onto the therapist.

On the other hand, countertransference occurs when the psychotherapist unconsciously projects the client to be someone else. When this occurs, the client brings out unconscious, suppressed feelings and actions from the therapist that are connected to this other person. The therapist is unaware of this confusion, and their professional judgment can be compromised. The therapist can be tempted to relate to the client as if they were this other person. That can compromise the client's well-being and inhibit the therapist's effectiveness.

Transference and countertransference are examples of the Remembering Self. The memories and emotions emerge into the present without conscious forethought. The past and the present are inaccurately merged together. If the therapist does not consciously identify and appropriately accommodate their projections on the client, watch out.

However, when recognized and consciously used, the dynamics of transference and countertransference can be turned into effective tools. The therapist can use these unconscious projections in order to facilitate change. If the therapist can consciously use the role projected by the client, progress can be made. The transference normally has a great amount of emotional intensity, and many of the negative and incorrect beliefs within the client are attached to the projection. The therapist can artfully take on the projected role, but respond *differently* than the client has conditioned themselves to expect.

When done skillfully, the client must search for new meanings that explain this mismatching of behavior. Old interactional patterns are interrupted during the relational interaction. The meanings are based on logical analysis of memories. In this case, the intensity of the moment helps generate the change. Reflections on memories rarely have the same intense effect.

The conscious and the unconscious minds step forward together to find new answers that allow the relationship to make sense. This is sometimes called a dialectic[8] experience. The client learns from differences rather than similarities. However, the key is that the change happens in the Experiencing Self more than the Remembering Self. Of course, this requires rational and conscious monitoring from other self-parts, and also a strategic plan. Assistance from a therapist's colleague helps ensure that the therapist is functioning skillfully and is not being unconsciously deceived.

MONITORING COUNTERTRANSFERENCE

In countertransference, the therapist's feelings and thoughts may be in the form of "intuitions" about the client. However, these intuitions are not really about the client, but about something in the therapist's past. These intuitions cannot be trusted because they originated from suppressed and unconscious sources. They are tainted with self-interest. In other words, the Experiencing Self needs to intervene. If the countertransference is overwhelmingly powerful for the therapist, it may be better for the client to be referred to another therapist. The therapist's greatest risks may be the overreliance on intuitions or impressions for two reasons. First, the intuitions may be tainted with countertransference inspired self-interests. Second, the intuitions may be a lazy attempt to pigeonhole or categorize a client by associating them with a fixed pattern. In other words, the therapists may focus on seeing the client's characteristics that are consistent with the familiar pattern, and not recognizing the differences that could make the pattern misleading.

Recognizing patterns can help guide interventions. They are important and often accurate. However, deferring to intuition without some conscious input can be misleading. As discussed, patternicity can lead to overconfidence or lazy reliance. A therapist may quickly say, "Oh, I've seen this before, so I'll put them in *this* slot." That may be a premature and inaccurate conclusion. Intuition or fast thinking can be both an effective tool and a stumbling block.

It can be difficult to distinguish between intuition for the client's benefit and intuition for the therapist's benefit. This may be especially true for therapists whose intuitive skills have historically seemed both accurate and useful. Intuitions that assist the client and the intuitions of countertransference both originate in the same unconscious memory bank.

This evaluation was not intended to be a therapist training. Rather, it demonstrates how the mind can slip into experiencing or remembering mode with varying results. These examples demonstrate the importance of checks and balances between the Experiencing brain and the Remembering brain. They each have different but equally important functions.

WHOLE SELF ENGAGEMENTS

Part of maintaining quality relationships with others requires us to engage them with our whole "selves", and not just fragments or parts. The dynamics of transference and countertransference don't just apply to psychotherapy. We all experience these projections and intuitions in our day-to-day relationships. The caution to therapists really applies to all of us. Recognizing how parts of ourselves assert themselves unconsciously can help us pause and engage other parts to show up as a whole person.

The conscious mind is normally in charge of self-control. We can't consciously review everything that we do or say. However, we can choose specific relationships and contexts as moments for "pause". We can consciously decide beforehand when we need to pause and evaluate ourselves. We can create internal reminders. For example, we can decide that while engaging certain people or entering into specific contexts, we need to pause and evaluate what is happening from an observer perspective. What are our intentions in the moment? How do we really feel about the people we're engaging?

These pauses uncover whether we are operating congruently, or if we feel internal friction and disagreement. We may wish to remind our mini-selves of the Best Life and to focus on creating quality relationships. These pauses and reminders can help us to unify our self-parts. When we can't align ourselves, we know that we have work to do. While in the moment, we can make efforts to create what we have previously decided is important. We may be lead astray from our identified priorities during a relational experience. Reminding ourselves of a Best Life direction can reorient us. We can make "pausing" a pattern in how we relate to others.

Let's review another common example. What does it mean to fall in love? Many people seem to be attracted to another person spontaneously and without any forethought. It is almost as if it was unconscious, or even a non-brain, hormonal decision. How many people refer to *both* the Experiencing Self and the Remembering Self in choosing a partner or a spouse?

This is such a crucial issue in some cultures that parents choose lifelong mates for their children. This is because they acknowledge that the Remembering Self of their child can't be trusted. The child's memory bank is relatively empty, especially about creating long-lasting relationships. Parents can use their rational, Remembering Self rather than just their Experiencing Self. However, the child's Experiencing Self rarely agrees with the Remembering Self of the parents when young love strikes.

We can also fall in love with *things*. This includes spending money, using time, obtaining education, and other attractive things. In all contexts, consulting opposing parts can help us make better short-term (tactical) and long-term (strategic) decisions. In doing this, we have a better chance of a good outcome.

Not understanding the limitations of their emotional Experiencing Self, some people just do whatever they "feel" like doing in the moment. Others experience the opposite and are afraid of their short-term, emotional selves. These people are constantly suppressing their feelings. Maturing is a process of knowing when to express our feelings, and when *not* to dwell on specific feelings. In creating a self-concept, let's notice if one of these selves dominates our decision-making? Be honest and take a moment to include all of your "selves" in making important decisions whenever possible. We don't want just one or two parts of us dominating our whole self.

STRATEGICALLY USING SELF-PARTS

We have reviewed several metaphors to explain patterns of emoting and thinking discovered through research and observation. You've had opportunity to think of yourself as having a Fast Brain and a Slow Brain. You have also considered the Heart Self and the Mind Self as well as the Experiencing Self and the Remembering Self. The self is not a simple "thing" with black and white perspectives. The self "itself" is an integration of components with varying degrees of intelligence and sophistication. The manner in which your self-parts (or mini-selves) interact with each other controls the efficiency and the quality of your thoughts.

The world of the mind is a relational world. The dynamics of these inside of self, and outside of self, relationships control decision-making. Social interactions with other people and the world around us influence our mini-selves differently. The interaction of these interpersonal *and* intrapersonal relationships shapes our self-concept.

The Best Life that you pursue requires an ongoing negotiation with other people and with your complex, internal self. You need to have quality, virtuous internal and external relationships in order to achieve good mental and physical health. Managing the interests and well-being of all these relationships seems daunting, but it is necessary to create a healthy self-concept.

By accepting responsibility for our choices, we are motivated to get to know all parts of ourselves. This also nurtures good health and well-being. By framing our life around responsibility and accountability, we are encouraged us to treat ourselves and others virtuously and empathically. Research gives us only a few clues about which part of you is the decision-maker. Making moral decisions allows us to feel a centralized self that is accountable and responsible to others or a Higher Power.

NOTES

1. McCraty R (2003). Heart-Brain Neurodynamics: The Making of Emotions. HeartMath Research Center, Institute of HeartMath, Boulder Creek, CA, Publication No. 03-015.

2. Damasio, A. (2010). *Self Comes to Mind: Constructing the Conscious Brain.* New York, NY: Pantheon Books.

3. Kahneman, D. (2011). *Thinking Fast and Slow.* New York, NY: Farrar, Straus and Giroux.

4. (Kahneman, 2011).

5. (Kahneman, 2011).

6. (Kahneman, 2011).

7. Wiener, J. (2009). *The Therapeutic Relationship: Transference, Countertransference, and the Making of Meaning.* College Station, TX: Texas A&M University Press.

8. I am using the word "dialectic" here in a narrow sense. Upon considering a fact or experience, we relate it to other facts or experiences to garner its meaning. When, upon comparing, we cannot put the new fact or experience in a known niche or category, the mind begins searching for a new meaning. This new meaning or category is the result of this dialectic process.

CHAPTER 14

Self-Stuck: Being Who You Don't Want to Be Reflecting On the Psychological Autopsy of Self

SIAMESE TWINS

Have you ever seen pictures of Siamese twins? Astoundingly, two heads actually share one body. Each head has a mind of its own, and yet the one body must serve two masters simultaneously. Imagine the confusion and frustration within the two heads when they can't agree on what to do. Perhaps it is even worse for the body—caught in the middle of two masters demanding different things to be done at the same time. Does the body sit down or stand up? Go to school or stay home? Eat now or later? Play the piano or read a book? Sleep or stay awake? That is a truly intrapersonal and interpersonal conflict of the highest order. Siamese twins take the challenge of loving self to a stratospheric level.

To make matters worse, imagine trying to figure out if the connected twins are one person or two. Two brains are vying to control one body. When the body acts, who is responsible? If the body breaks the law, who is accountable and who should be punished? Can one head be innocent and the other guilty? How can one be punished without punishing the other as well? It gets all mixed up!

MINI-SELVES

We experience a similar dilemma when one mini-self within us competes with another mini-self for control of the body at the same time. As a child, one of my daughters went through a routine with me every night for months. She imagined that at night a witch lived under her bed. So every night before she went to bed, we sat together and rationally discussed how we had looked under the bed a million times and found no witch. I explained how no one else had ever seen this witch, how no one could get into her room with the door closed and the windows locked, and so on. She agreed, sighed, smiled, and nodded her little head up and down as we went through this reasoning process. However, when the lights went out, she howled and carried on about the ridiculous witch. I went back into the room, looked under the bed, and reported to her that there was nothing there. She asked me to yell under the bed to keep the witch away, so I yelled. She would then lie down and close her eyes. We hoped that sleep would come even though her little heart pounded in her chest. I would rejoice at this and leave her room cursing the imaginary witch under my breath.

Her body was caught up in two emotions brought on by two conflicting parts of her mind. One moment she felt confident and relieved as she looked under the bed and found nothing. She thought of the months of being safe and never seeing a witch, and was comforted that her parents were close by. The next moment, out of nowhere, adrenaline pumped into her blood, and she was flooded with fear that the witch was back. One part of her wanted to sleep while the other part feared sleep would invite the witch to attack her. Like the Siamese twins, her body was being yanked in two different directions. She craved sleep, but feared closing her eyes. Nighttime had become a warzone for her. She wondered why she couldn't make up her mind one way or the other.

If you think that this is unique to childhood, think again. Somewhere a thirty-year-old woman curses herself for screaming and hitting her children when they disobey her. She vows, "Never again". And then a child breaks another rule. She screams and threatens in spite of her vows. She feels pangs of guilt for hurting her kids, but worries that they will be miserable failures if she doesn't discipline them harshly. After all, it's her job! Her body wants to hit and scream, but strains to stay composed. She can't figure it out. She's not afraid of a witch—she's afraid that she *is* the witch.

Somewhere an employee at work stares vacuously at a computer screen filled with pornography. Job performance has deteriorated and job satisfaction has evaporated. Fear and anxiety nag at the back of his mind that he soon may be unemployed and unable to support his family. He is up to 3 hours a day of viewing and ignoring his work. His body is filled with guilt and fear mixed with excitement. He tells himself that he will work harder tomorrow.

My daughter, this mother, and the addicted employee have conflicting parts in contentious conflict. Most of their conflicting thoughts show up as feelings. Somehow, they can't reason the feelings away, but continue the circle of confusion and frustration.

All of us have experienced (and probably continue to experience) this dilemma. Mini-self AB competes with mini-self CD to get what it wants. AB believes that if CD gets its way, then AD loses everything and vice versa. This win/lose mentality inflames the conflict. The mother can't quit her abusive ways without allowing her kids to be failures. My daughter can't sleep without being attacked. The employee can't have prurient, virtual experiences at work without compromising his job and family relationships.

Consciously, these people can't wrap their heads around the conflicts. My daughter is unaware of why she believes the witch won't go away. The mother is unaware of the origin of her belief that she abuses her kids to save them. The employee just caves in viewing explicit sex at work that endangers his family and employment. Outsiders are quick to dismiss my daughter as an imaginative child, the mother as an uncaring, child abuser, and the employee as a pervert. But let's get back to us. Think about what *you* want to do, but don't do in spite of your determined efforts. Or imagine what you want to stop doing that you just can't shut down. Finally, think of who you want to be, but can't fully embrace. Do you consciously understand what is getting in the way? Is it confusing that you perpetuate two opposing outcomes and end up feeling frustrated or even guilty no matter what you do?

We get frustrated when we can't "reason" the dilemma away. It appears illogical and unreasonable to risk a marriage and a job for porn, or hurt children so they can be responsible, or believe in witches under the bed that are never there. The emotional commitments to these seemingly irrational desires resist logic and affirmations. We all get stuck in these seemingly no-win dilemmas.

MINI-SELF CONFLICTS

Let me suggest an explanation for many of these ongoing conflicts within us. We previously discussed the processing or operational parts of ourselves like the Lawyer and the Scientist. Confusion amongst these parts can contribute to our conflicts. Let's focus on how our mini-selves also compete or complement one another.

We have already discussed mini-selves. They seem to have values, attitudes, and specific responsibilities. They are not complete people hiding between our liver and kidneys. When we have competing desires, values, or concerns, it is useful to attribute them to the different parts, or mini-selves, within us. Attaching desires, values, and so on to mini-selves allows us to strategize relational resolutions. Relational resolutions include using empathy, integrity, higher purposes, and virtue to solve internal problems. This helps us learn how to treat ourselves more congruently and lovingly.

We can approach internal conflicts the same way that we resolve external conflicts with other people. Identifying and acknowledging these mini-selves gives us a "hands-on" way of resolving internal incongruence. This can be very effective and efficient. Here is a list of self-parts in all of us that have powerful, dominant interests. Please note that this is a partial list. Some people have very unique and specialized mini-selves.

- Protector—Provides strategies and tactics to protect us from anything that could hurt us.
- Connector—Connects us with people so we have a sense of acceptance and belonging.
- Persona—Responsible for maintaining our image and persona in the world. It helps us fit in and find our place wherever we go.
- Recreationist—Ensures that we have pleasure and recreation in our lives.

- Equalizer—Ensures that we are treated fairly.
- Mission—Gives us a purpose and a reason to live in the world.
- Spirit—Connects with the power and direction of a divine source. We acknowledge that much of the world's population seeks connection to a Supreme Being or influence.

These mini-selves take their jobs and identity seriously. They represent critical needs that every human must satisfy, not only to survive, but also to thrive. For example, all of us need our Protector to keep us safe physically, emotionally, and spiritually. We need our Connector to create quality relationships because we are relational beings. All mini-selves have critical roles in building our self-concept.

Notice that we have included Spirit as a mini-self, and I will explain why. Some people believe that because the spirit is immaterial and the body is material—that they cannot be joined within an embodied person. This argument is speculation, because scientists do not claim to understand the nature of "spirit", and therefore they are clueless how it could coexist with a material body. Strong Relationality allows us to view the spirit as part of our multi-faceted self, because Strong Relationality recognizes immaterial things can be real. There are many worldwide belief systems based on interactions between the body and the spirit. We cannot ignore this almost universal phenomenon.

MINI-SELF COLLABORATION

Optimally, mini-selves honor and assist one another when possible. They should all be subservient to the same self. For example, Dr. Frankl explains how he survived a Nazi concentration camp during WWII1. His Protector self did not have a fortress to physically shield him from the inhumane treatment of the guards and the other prisoners. Protector was almost helpless to avoid the slave labor, starvation, beatings, and inhumanities spewed on him by his guards.

Fortunately, his Mission-self stepped up to help the Protector. Mission took its job seriously and found profound purpose in adversity. Without being overwhelmed by the oppression, it embraced a life mission of lifting spirits and caring for fellow prisoners. This saved the Protector who was failing to protect Dr. Frankl from physical abuse. As a result, the new purpose gave Protector something new to protect. It may have been helpless to protect Dr. Frankl's physical body from the prison guards, but it *could* protect Dr. Frankl's commitment of helping other prisoners.

Dr. Frankl's love and value for his fellow man became more important than breathing or just surviving. Somehow, his Mission infused life and energy into him that helped him endure the pain and deprivation of the circumstances. It created a more powerful flow of life-sustaining energy. The Protector could have easily quit when it realized that it was powerless to protect Dr. Frankl from his environment. Instead, the Protector joined forces with the Mission and found a cause that in many ways protected Dr. Frankl's life. Their collaboration made Frankl's total self stronger. These two mini-selves became wonderful, cooperative, team members. Likewise, we want all of our mini-selves to collaborate as we move through life.

HOW MINI-SELVES OPPOSE ONE ANOTHER

Unfortunately, mini-selves often oppose one another and create friction or conflict within us. Consider the harsh disciplining mother. Let's use her as an example to see how mini-selves operate. What mini-selves inside her were in conflict? Let's assume that the Persona adopted "mother" as her primary identity. Her full identity included more than being mother, but caring for little children took up most of her days and nights. She embraced this important, human responsibility. Being a mother became the primary part of her Persona.

At the same time, her Connector was responsible for her connections and relationships with others. The Connector managed her relationships with friends, family members, store clerks, motorists on the road, strangers, and everybody else. This included relationships with her children. Let's assume that the Connector wants her children to like and respect her. She wants a loving relationship. Now, we can begin to identify a conflict brewing between the Persona and the Connector.

Each mini-part has guiding beliefs that control how they approach their roles. This mother grew up with a mother of her own. Her mom was her model and example of motherhood. As it turned out, her mother and father were strict disciplinarians. She and her siblings were yelled at, slapped, and threatened whenever they broke a rule. The punishments were harsh. She got angry with her mother for the ill treatment, but ultimately she obeyed. She learned to get things done the way her mother demanded, or she learned to covertly cover up any disobedience. Her mother constantly told her to follow the rules or she'd "get it".

As we expected, the daughter modeled herself after her mother, even though she swore that she never would. Her experiences and relationship with her mother influenced the core-level beliefs that she formed in her unconscious mind. Notice that I did not say "*create* these beliefs". Her parents' behavior influenced her, but did not make her choose specific beliefs. We can assume that her beliefs about motherhood settled within the Persona mini-self. The Persona's commitment to harsh punishment came from embracing these beliefs.

When she had children, Persona insisted that she follow the model of harsh punishment because it was the "right" thing to do. Persona honestly believed that without harsh punishment, a child would go astray, get hurt, or fail in life. Therefore, Persona was responsible to keep her from failing as a mother and hurting her children. If she didn't threaten and harshly punish them, she would fail. Persona was adamantly committed to hitting, yelling, and threatening in order to keep the kids on the right path.

At the same time, the Connector knew that hitting, yelling, and threatening destroyed respectful, loving relationships with the children. The Connector gained this knowledge through experience over time. She came to know that fear is not the basis for quality relationships with anyone. Therefore, the Connector urged the mother to be more kind and to stop the abuse.

Both mini-selves believed that if the other part got its way, they failed. This created a no-win relationship and lots of emotional turmoil within this woman. Somehow, decisions had to be made about how to treat the children. In this case, the Persona mini-self won along with her deep-level beliefs about motherhood. That didn't stop the Connector from feeling guilt or urging change. This conflict kept this woman in a constant state of frustration and anxiety. The ongoing disagreement and conflict between Persona and Connector was the cause. A resolution for this woman would require a reconciliation and agreement between Persona and Connector.

Remember our discussions about who in us makes final decisions? How does that work? Did her Persona make the final decisions, and did the Connector yield to Persona? That is the million-dollar question. Let's assume that Persona got her way and that Connector's needs were ignored. In this case, Persona's strength prevailed, and any change in how the children are treated will require Persona's willing participation. That is a relationship issue between Connector and Persona. The solution is a relational intervention to bring them together. Imagine how these internal conflicts affect our own self-concepts. With two strong mini-selves competing with one another, we wonder which self-concept we are really thinking about.

Significantly, lost in the conflict between Persona and Connector is the concern for the whole self. These separate parts often wear blinders that restrict their view to only their narrow responsibility. The overall well-being of the person gets lost. An important part of the relational intervention for Persona and Connector is recommitting them to their common responsibilities to the self. This mutual responsibility to the self is the common denominator that can give them a unified objective and build a need for their interdependence.

Treating this woman's internal conflict as a relational issue reinforces the importance of empathic, quality relationships among the mini-selves that constitute her self-concept. Resolving these conflicts strengthens the self-concept and creates powerful, creative collaborations among the mini-selves (like we saw with Dr. Frankl). Approaching our internal conflicts as relational issues invites creation of relational methods to resolve our emotional pain and unhappiness. Essentially, we must learn how to virtuously get along with ourselves.

Note that Persona and Connector's conflicting beliefs created the conflict about how the children were treated. Therefore, part of the relational intervention will be reevaluating these beliefs and their compatibility. As we successfully nourish the evolution of our self-concept, we will mediate incongruent beliefs among our mini-selves. Since many of these beliefs reside in our unconscious, we are constantly searching for ways to facilitate communication between the conscious and unconscious mind.

EXAMPLES OF MINI-SELVES IN CONFLICT

To reinforce this idea of self-parts having conflicting beliefs and values, let's refer to examples in earlier chapters. Think of the urban "not-a-hiker" young man, the Native American young woman, and the "loser" homerun hitter. They all are examples of people who were limited by conflicting beliefs between their mini-selves. Each mini-self had its own cluster of beliefs. As one mini-self's belief became dominant, the other mini-self's beliefs were suppressed. Reflect on how the Native American young woman resolved her internal conflict in a dream. Her Protector's beliefs changed because of the dream. The urban hiker maintained his mini-self's belief that he wasn't a hiker. The belief itself didn't change. However, his behavior was reframed from hiking to walking, and that satisfied the mini-self's belief. We saw no change in the loser homerun hitter's beliefs.

HOW MINI-SELF BELIEFS CAN BE FORMED

Let's look at an example of how these core beliefs are formed. This explanation can help us understand why beliefs are so ingrained in us and are resistant to change. Imagine an all-American young man. He is good-looking, intelligent, and savvy. Tom met this profile. This six foot, 185-pound athlete fit the mold quite well except for one thing. Wherever he went, people picked on him. Some of the hassles were verbal, and some even turned physical. The perpetrators weren't your classic bullies. And young women were as bad as young men with their insults and jabs. This went on for years. It got so bad that fellow students couldn't resist harassing him and disrupting the classroom. He would sit quietly in class, but he controlled the behavioral atmosphere by his passive presence. Often, teachers asked him to leave the room when he had done nothing but sit quietly in his chair.

Finally, he went to a program for help. While there, he was assisted in some deep-level introspection and his unconscious mind revealed important information. His self-concept was connected to a feeling that started when he was in first grade. There was a bully in his class. He was repeating the first grade, and therefore he was older and larger than his classmates. He was methodically going through the class, beating up kids whenever he could. Tom knew that his time was coming, and he was petrified. Violence and fighting were not part of his life, and the big bully intimidated him. At home, he stopped eating and sleeping, much to his parents dismay. His mom and dad were medical physicians with busy and demanding schedules, but they loved little Tom dearly.

One night, Tom couldn't take it any more, and he crawled into bed with his parents. They were exhausted after from a long and demanding day. His mother woke up, and in her delirium, she asked, "What do you want?" Tom told her the story about the bully. Without realizing the significance of her response she replied, "You little wimp, get back in your bed. Deal with it." In addition, Tom's well-meaning grandfather wrote a letter to Tom the next day, reinforcing what it meant to be a "wimp".

A perfect storm came together. Because of the timing, the power of his relationship with his mom and his grandpa, and the accumulation of less intense, but similar experiences, an unconscious, self-concept belief was triggered in Tom. He bought it all. As a result, he completely believed that he was a wimp.

His brain formed a long-term potentiation memory. Because of the intensity of the learning experience and the significance of the belief, the neurological connections in his brain associated with this memory were more extensive than almost all other memories. In other words, this belief became deeply embedded in his brain.

Understand that the experience with mom and grandpa *triggered* the belief. However, it was not the sole cause for the creation of the belief. The "perfect storm" had been set up through earlier experiences. The interactions with mom and grandpa were the final, formative trigger. Note that the belief was not set up or triggered by what we might call a classic "trauma". The belief was not formed after Tom was beat up. In fact, the bully actually never made it to Tom.

Many of our unconsciously embedded beliefs are formed in a similar way. There is no trauma, but emerging circumstances in conjunction with a final relational interaction, produce a powerful belief. The belief may be positive, or it may be negative, as it was in Tom's case. We love the positive ones, and struggle to overcome the negative ones. Realize that at the core of choosing these beliefs are external relationships. They powerfully influence the meaning that we attach to our identity and our relationship with the world. This is another reason why the Best Life is about quality relationships.

Tom went on to live his life consistent with what he believed was true: "I'm a wimp". The belief acted as a bias, and he ignored contrary evidence. He was so committed to the belief that he sent out covert and overt messages announcing to the world that he was a wimp. He was not consciously aware that he was doing this. However, his Persona mini-self was determined to make the belief a reality. And it worked! People picked up the cues and bullied him. Being bullied satisfied the identity belief of being a wimp, but other mini-selves within his self-concept were tired of being picked on and disrespected. Ironically, his Persona was doing a great job at bullying the rest of his self-concept. The Equalizer and the Mission were particularly stifled. Consequently, Tom as a whole was not happy. He was stuck in a powerful internal conflict among the mini-selves within.

Fortunately, the program helped him consciously discover the conflict and begin a resolution. He was able to create empathy and new pathways of communication among the mini-selves. They were able to individually realize faulty assumptions supporting the beliefs that perpetuated the conflict. Correcting these assumptions allowed the beliefs to change. Again, we see the importance of mini-selves committing to a common purpose. Tom's mini-selves were committed to their own compartmentalized jobs, but they became more united to perform their jobs. This benefitted both themselves and Tom's overall well-being. As a result, they became more relational. He left the program and went back to his old school looking forward to a better life.

A couple of months later, the program director received a phone call from Tom's headmaster. The director took a deep breath and was prepared to hear that Tom had reverted to his old wimpy behaviors. The headmaster explained that Tom was now beating up the kids who had picked on him. A few phone calls with Tom helped him integrate his new identity as a normal, healthy, young man without needing to become a bully himself. His "wimpy" identity had changed, but other beliefs tied to the old wimp took a while to adjust. The Equalizer, in particular, had to give up revenge. In a sense, Tom changed his self-concept, and his life was happily different after the adjustment period.

Tom improved the quality of relationships among the mini-selves within himself. This relational improvement reduced internal conflict and created internal unity for his self-concept. Consequently, he had permission and motivation to change his behavior. The Best Life became more accessible to him.

YOUR SELF-CONCEPT BELIEFS

We all have entrenched self-concept beliefs that were formed in this manner. They either help us or hinder us from having the Best Life. We must recognize any dissonance and incongruence in our emotions and behavior. We have reviewed examples of how improving the quality of our internal relationships can change our lives. We recognize the importance of bringing unconscious beliefs to our consciousness. This allows us to identify the specific mini-selves that are either in conflict or are in positive collaboration. We must learn to understand their individual responsibilities in helping the whole person. We can create empathy and a spirit of cooperation that benefits both our mini-selves and our whole self. We can become a more unified, focused person and not suffer from internal confusion and dissonance.

By learning additional skills, we can accomplish these reconciliations and conduct internal interventions. The next chapter discusses methods to identify and resolve internal conflicts among our mini-selves. Some of the recommendations you can do yourself and others require additional assistance.

NOTES

1. Frankl, V. (2006). *Man's Search for Meaning*. Boston, MA: Beacon Press.

CHAPTER 15

Personal Strategies to Resolve Internal Conflicts

EXERCISES FOR GETTING OURSELVES TOGETHER

We've talked a lot about changing beliefs and the meanings associated with relational experiences. To achieve the Best Life, we need quality relationships, both with others and within ourselves. By upgrading and changing our embedded beliefs and feelings, we are on the path to the Best Life.

Unfortunately, millions of us have read and tried many strategies for change, with no avail. Three major stumbling blocks usually stop us. First, we assume that we can change ourselves without changing our relationships (with others and within our self). Second, we do not know how to unite our conscious and unconscious minds. Third, we aren't congruent about what we really want. We're divided.

The logic behind many change strategies is the same. Exercises may consist of positive affirmations, repetition of useful behaviors, visualizing happiness, planning tools and schedules, venting feelings, conditioning new responses to difficult contexts, and so on. These are all helpful to some people at certain times. These strategies attempt to change behaviors in order to eventually change the underlying beliefs. I embrace and recommend this approach. Give it a try. However, sometimes it doesn't work. These approaches typically fail to effectively change self-concepts and values.

Let me suggest a reverse approach to this method. Instead of changing specific behaviors in hopes of eventually changing beliefs, let's consider changing beliefs first and *then* focus on the behaviors. This approach is helpful because embedded beliefs control our motivations and permissions to think or behave. If we are trying to force behaviors that our unconscious beliefs reject, our progress can be slowed. Essentially we are swimming against the current. However, if we can change our beliefs *first* and access the permission and motivation for new behaviors, our progress will move more quickly and thoroughly.

A helpful way to do this is to engage in exercises that access both our conscious and unconscious minds. By doing so, we are able to change our embedded beliefs and emotions. However, this takes more concentration and mental effort than superficially changing our behaviors. Perhaps, this is why fewer people engage in this "belief first" approach.[1] Dr. Bruce Lipton mentions this in his book, *The Biology of Belief*, and he recommends a belief approach that he came across.

For thirty years, I have worked with various academics and therapeutic practitioners to discover the most effective strategies to change unconscious beliefs and emotions. Fortunately, I have found three or four extremely effective approaches. I will not review all of them in this book. Some exercises you can do on your own. Other ones require a facilitator.

INTRODUCTION TO SELF-INITIATED EXERCISES AND PRACTICES

For an introduction to these exercises, I have included two of these for you to do on your own. Be sure to follow the instructions closely. They explore empathy within relationships and involve both the conscious and the unconscious minds. These exercises are designed to help you discover what is preventing you from changing. They are also designed to help you remove any obstacles to your desired outcomes. Please note that some people make remarkable progress by engaging in the exercises three or four times. Others need more repetition or outside assistance.

You will need to set aside about least 30 minutes of uninterrupted time. Do not do both exercises on the same day. You will need someone to read the script to you and guide you through the exercises. They need to read it *exactly* as is written in the script. If needed, ask them to reread a sentence.

After completing the exercises, think about how you felt when the exercises began. You may or may not feel different immediately. Either way, when beliefs are changed, they affect your entire belief system. This may cause a bit of confusion as your mind reorganizes itself. These exercises may generate change in the moment and also over time. You may wish to consciously begin following a "behavior-oriented" plan after finishing these exercises. These are the plans that I mentioned above. Be aware that sometimes, individuals discover they want something much different than they thought prior to the exercise. As a result,they discover a more congruent direction for their self-concept.

EXERCISE #1: THREE CHAIRS

Before you begin, read through the exercise one or two times. This will allow you to flow through the experience more easily.

Preparation: Think of a disagreement with someone to explore.

Set up: Place three chairs together. Number the chairs 1, 2, and 3.

Duration: Approximately 30 mins.

1. Stand beside Chair 1. While standing beside the chair, think of a conflict or disagreement with someone that negatively affected the relationship. Be sure you can imagine being in the disagreement as you experienced it. Perhaps, the disagreement is ongoing and you want to find a better resolution than appears presently possible. Pinpoint the *specific* times and places that you experienced the argument with that person. What does the argument mean about your relationship with this person?

2. Sit in Chair 1 and re-experience the disagreement from only your perspective. To help ensure that you are in this "self" perspective, lean forward a little bit and slightly bend your head forward. This will help you "lean into" the disagreement and be focused on only your personal interests.

3. After re-experiencing the disagreement through your perspective, move to Chair 2. Try to remember as clearly as you can what the other person looked like during the disagreement. Imagine fully stepping into this "person". Be them in every way

possible. Change your posture, movements, extremity positions, eye positions, facial expressions, and so on to mimic theirs. This is not just a metaphor. This will actually empower you to experience empathy for the person.

4. Now, imagine going through the disagreement again, but this time experience it as they do, to the best of your ability. Notice the thoughts, emotions, and physical feelings they have. Relax and focus on what is happening. Feel and think about that person's objectives. What do they want? Be that person as completely as possible. You will know when you have experienced their perspective as much as needed.

5. When finished, sit in Chair 3. As you do so, imagine yourself as an observer of the disagreement. See yourself and the other person interacting with one another. You may even imagine standing beside them or up above them like a fly on the wall. Stay out of the disagreement. Be an observer only. Watch closely and listen carefully.

6. Notice your "observer thoughts" as you hear and observe both persons. What is happening between these two people? What do you think about each of their arguments and each of their expected outcomes? If you were they, what would you do differently? You will know when you have seen enough.

7. Take a deep breath and go back to Chair 1. Think about what you learned from Chairs 1, 2, and 3. With this new knowledge, lean forward a little bit while you re-experience the disagreement again from your perspective. Notice any changes in the disagreement as you use your recent knowledge in your interactions. Notice what happens as you continue the discussion. You will know when you are finished in Chair number 1.

8. Sit down in Chair 2. Step into this person again as fully as possible. Be aware of any changes from the person in Chair 1. Do they look or sound differently? Are they expressing anything new? Respond to any changes you may have noticed in them. Think only as the person in Chair 2 thinks. Respond as they would respond. You'll know when you are finished.

9. Now, sit in Chair 3. Observe this second round of the disagreement as it happened. What changes if any do you notice? Do they make sense? What if anything is happening in the relationship between the two people? Think about what the changes mean. Form opinions about what is happening in the disagreement. You'll know when you've learned enough.

10. Sit again in Chair 1. Notice what has changed if anything after completing Round 2. Take any new learning or feelings into the disagreement. Engage exclusively from your perspective. However, notice any changes in the other person as the discussion progresses. Notice if you are more effective in presenting your ideas. Notice if you are clearer about what you want from this person. Go to Chair 2 when you are ready.

11. Sit again in Chair 2. Step into this person and assume their posture and their feelings. Notice if it feels differently than the last time you stepped into this person. Engage in the disagreement noticing any changes in the person from Chair 1. What are your expected outcomes now? What new thoughts are in your mind if any? How do you feel about the other person from Chair 1? How do you wish to leave the disagreement? When you are ready, move on to Chair 3.

12. Sit again in Chair 3. Assume the posture and feelings of the observer. What do you notice has happened as the disagreement has evolved? What is different if anything in the person from Chair 1? How about the person in Chair 3? Where is the disagreement at this point? Where is the relationship at this point? What advice would you give both people? When you have finished, stand up and take a deep breath. Walk around for a moment and sit anywhere except in Chairs 1, 2, or 3.

DEBRIEFING THE EXERCISE

Good job! Now that you are finished, what are your thoughts and feelings? What difference (if any) do you notice from when you began the exercise? What do you notice about the disagreement at this point? What about the relationship? If something changed, what was it? What do you need to do in the future with this relationship? How does your response in this relationship affect any other relationships you have?

You can go through this sequence as many times as you wish. The more fully you step into the different perspectives, the more powerful the exercise.

Let me briefly discuss features of this experience that uniquely affect the unconscious mind. By experiencing empathy for the other person (or self-part) your unconscious mind considers thoughts and possibilities that it would not normally think through. Empathy can't occur without seeking to think someone else's thoughts. In doing so, those thoughts slip through some of the barriers of passionately held unconscious beliefs. Additionally, empathy invites feeling what the other is experiencing. Experiencing another person's thoughts allows us to be less opinionated and more tolerant. Empathy can almost immediately open up avenues of change on an unconscious level.

Experiencing the disagreement as one's self and then as an observer is a different kind of empathy. Being "in" the disagreement stimulates the same emotions and reasons that support our self-interest. On the other hand, the observer is removed from these emotions and desires. Being an observer to the disagreement allows us to be more objective about ourselves. We learn different insights about ourselves and the disagreement from an "outside" perspective. We are usually surprised about what the observer notices. As an observer, we critique what we observed, including our own actions and position.

As an observer, we notice things that we ignore when we are in the disagreement. These observations are persuasive to the unconscious mind and open up possibilities of change and resolution that may not have existed otherwise. Again, these thoughts slip into the unconscious to be seriously considered. This can't happen unless we fully step into the roles of the other person and the observer. It's in the experience of playing the role that our unconscious shifts, not just upon reflection after the experience.

EXERCISE #2: THREE CHAIRS AND A DREAM

You will engage this exercise in much the same way as Exercise 1. Read through it two or three times to familiarize yourself with the process. Find someone to read the script to you and help you through the exercise.

Set up: Put three chairs together in a line. Number the chairs 1, 2, and 3. Sit down in Chair 1.

Duration: Approximately 30 mins.

1. While sitting down, think of a dream or a hope for the future that you have wanted badly, but can't seem to get. As you think of this dream, allow yourself to see what it would look, sound, and feel like to actually have it. In other words, enjoy a daydream of having what you want as vividly and completely as possible.

2. When you finish experiencing the entire daydream as many times as you wish, get up and stand behind this dream chair. Thinking of the dream, ask yourself, "What would this dream actually get me if I could have it?" In other words, what would you *get* that is even more important than what's actually in the dream? The dream is an avenue to obtain what you truly want. What do you really want that you believe the dream will get for you? Say to yourself in one sentence what you really want. Repeat it to yourself. When finished, move on to Chair 2.

3. Sit in Chair 2. Ask yourself, "What prevents me from having what I really want?" Imagine what this looks, sounds, and feels like. Consider carefully how this reason is connected to the dream. What do I value about this obstacle to my dream?

4. What about the dream threatens this obstacle? Somehow, the thing that is stopping you has become more important than attaining your dream. Ask yourself, "What are beliefs about my dream's intention that threaten this conflicting desire?" This question is *extremely* important. Ask it several times. To help you fully understand the purpose and depth of this question, let me give you an example.

EXAMPLE: If my dream was to have an island of my own, what would it get me? Let's say it would get me more peace and less stress. What stops me from having an island or more peace and less stress? Let's say that I would have to give up my profession. At this point, think creatively. Be insightful. What are the underlying beliefs about *why* peace and stress threaten my profession? I answer, "My profession involves stressful life-and-death situations, but I'm good at it. If I seek more peace and less stress, I will be abandoning people who need me." In other words, I believe that my dream and its objective would cause me to feel like I'm abandoning people in need. Those are the type of honest beliefs that this question is searching for.

5. The obstacle to the dream had good reasons for resisting the dream. What were those reasons? This may generate some thought and discussion. Keep going until you feel that the answers are correct. Your answers will help explain *why* the dream threatens the obstacle's intentions. When finished considering these thoughts, move on to Chair 3.

6. Sit in Chair 3. Ask yourself, "What could make me have the dream's intention (like having more peace and less stress) in spite of the obstacle in Chair 2 (like the desire to continue helping people in need)? This is a difficult question to answer. Spend some time thinking through your answers.

7. When you come up with what is more important than the obstacle, evaluate this answer. You may have already tried this answer, but it didn't work. In the example, the answer to living more peacefully and less stressfully was that my health would be threatened. However, I have been saying this for years, but it hasn't been strong enough to change my lifestyle of life-and-death rescues. If you notice the answer has already been tried, (but it obviously hasn't worked to now) keep searching for what would make you have your dream's intention in spite of the obstacle. What do you value that is stronger than the obstacle in Chair 2? Can you see, hear, and feel what this valuable asset is like? Take all the time you need and engage in honest discussion with yourself and the person reading the script. Find that compelling reason.

8. Refer again to the example that I provided in Step 4. Assume that I discovered that if my life's mission required me to find more peace and less stress, then I would do it in spite of my job. This answer requires me to think seriously about my life's mission and what it requires. What if I understand that helping people with serious needs is part of that mission? Does my mission require a specific job to fulfill the life purpose? Are there other ways to

help people that would allow me to have less stress and to live longer? Can I do my present job with less stress? Think about all of these questions with the passionate feeling: I *want* to live my life purpose.

9. When you find your answer, step into it. The feeling must be strong and powerful. If there is not a strong feeling or a sense of passion, you're not there yet. Keep searching. When you finally have "it", notice the feeling attached to it, notice your breathing as you're in it, and notice your thoughts as they come to you. When you are ready, take that *complete feeling,* and move back to Chair 1.

10. Keep the feeling from Chair 3 as you sit in Chair 1. With this feeling, begin to think about your original dream. Keep the feeling from Chair 3. Notice what happens to your dream as it mixes with this feeling. If your feeling is strong enough, the dream will begin to change into something else. (If this doesn't happen, go back to Chair 3, or other chairs as needed.) Don't force it. The new dream needs to flow into your mind. As the dream changes, let it continue until you have a new dream. Notice what is different than in the old dream. Let the new dream and the feeling from Chair 3 mix together. When you're ready, stand behind Chair 1 with the same feeling from Chair 3.

11. While standing behind Chair 1, let the feeling of Chair 3 and the previous objectives of the old dream mix together. Notice the feeling and any thoughts or images that come. Notice how the vision of what the dream gets you also begins to change. Notice what it becomes. Feel it throughout your body. When this experience ends, get up and move to Chair 2.

12. Sit down in Chair 2. This chair represents the obstacle to the dream and its intentions. Take the feeling of Chair 3 into the obstacle found in Chair 2. As they mix together, something new may automatically happen. If the valuable asset in Chair 3 is strong enough, you will begin to envision new ways to satisfy the underlying needs of Chair 2. However, these new changes will not be obstacles to Chair 3 any longer. In fact, you may discover that the objectives of Chairs 2 and 3 are now compatible. Write down these thoughts and ideas.

NOTE: You may have to go back and visit the chairs more than once as you think through the questions in each position or chair. Do so patiently and let the valuable asset of Chair 3 reveal itself. Ensure that the concerns of Chair 2 are accommodated and part of future plans.

DEBRIEFING THE EXERCISE

In the days ahead, refer to the feelings from Chair 3 and continually visualize the new dream and what it will get you. New choices will present themselves to bring all three chairs together harmoniously.

This exercise combines changing perspectives with a sense of empathy. Again, fully experiencing the deadlock from different perspectives can help us access that which is most important to us. This can change our lives. All other hopes and dreams change to support that which is most important. The exercise helps our unconscious and our mini-selves prioritize (and then align with) that which is most important to us. This allows the unconscious mind to reframe possibilities, beliefs, and inconsistencies that would that it would normally resist.

This exercise can be helpful when attempting to attain parts of a self-concept that seems unreachable. Both exercises demonstrate the dynamics of changing our perspectives and being empathic. There are many more exercises that I may be able to share with you at a later time.

NOTES

1. Lipton, B. (2005). *The Biology of Belief: Unleashing the Power of Consciousness, Matter & Miracles*. Carlsbad, CA: Hay House, Inc.

CHAPTER 16

Life Experiences That Change Unconscious Beliefs: The Power of Interpretation

Powerful negative and positive beliefs are normally created through our *interpretation* of what our life experiences mean. The experiences themselves do not create the beliefs. Our minds automatically search for meanings that explain how the experiences are connected to our identity and worldview. The beliefs we choose construct and color our self-concepts. Our knowledge and imagination may limit the options that we can come up with to explain what happened. Too often, we end up conjuring up meanings that inaccurately degrade ourselves. Because these limiting beliefs were intensely imprinted on our minds, we can't just talk ourselves out of believing them. To counter these negative beliefs, we need to create intensely imprinted new, healthy beliefs.

We can do this in the following three ways:

1. Prepare ourselves to focus on positive meanings in case we have negative, abusive, or fearful experiences.
2. Prepare ourselves to emphasize positive meanings from impactful positive experiences.
3. Purposely create new, positive, impactful experiences.

PREPROGRAMMING MINDSETS FOR NEGATIVE EXPERIENCES

We rarely choose our negative, belief-forming experiences. Who wants to be abused, diseased, injured, bankrupted, lost, and so on? Sometimes a seemingly non-traumatic event (or series of events) triggers a deep, embedded belief. Remember our fearful first grader being called a wimp. He incorporated that identity into his self-concept. Name-calling isn't normally what we would consider a "traumatic" event. However, the combination of a first grader's naïveté, the bully, and the *perception* of his parents' beliefs about him, triggered the "wimp" identity. Being called a wimp itself didn't create the belief. Likewise, some of our life experiences seem non-traumatic, but are actually perfect storms for creating negative beliefs. We need to prepare ourselves to respond to negative experiences with healthy beliefs.

A problem-solving, positive mindset is one of the most important elements within our self-concept. This kind of mindset not only protects us from embedding negative beliefs, but also instigates personal growth from our experiences. It can be part of our resilience to the "hard knocks" of life. Resilience is springing back, rebounding, and recovering readily. Being resilient helps us stay on the path to the Best Life.

For our purposes, let's define mindsets as "attitudes made up of resilient beliefs". What are some useful mindsets?[1] Some people create a mindset that believes that everything happens to them for a positive purpose. That presupposes some type of unconditional outside intervention. This belief reassures them that positive results will evolve from any challenging experience. Logical or not, this mindest works for some people.

Other mindsets provide the same kind of reassurance, hope, and sense of opportunity. We should primarily focus on learning something important from every challenging experience. In doing so, we change our focus and expectations from losing, suffering, and experiencing what we cannot control. Every experience becomes a growth experience, and its meaning is another opportunity for us. This mindset resists beliefs and conclusions that demean our worth, lovability, or even our competency. We all need mindsets that can help us transcend the inevitable challenges and difficulties of life. These mindsets are part of our self-concept. A weak mindset leads to a weak self.

Religious faith that a higher power will help us, allows many people to overcome adversity and grow. We are hopeful and justifiable when we have a benevolent, powerful "partner" that shares in our experiences. Most religious beliefs are guides to engaging and maintaining this alliance.

Simply put, mindsets are deeply-embedded beliefs. They can allow us to find useful and healthy interpretations of our life experiences. But where do our mindsets come from? They are formed like the rest of our beliefs—from the meaning that we glean from life experiences. Our relational experiences with parents, siblings, coaches, teachers, mentors, and even our enemies affect our mindset. Therefore, being able to create experiences to foster healthy mindsets are critical to having the Best Life. How can we intentionally create experiences that are powerful enough to match the intensity of negative experiences? Our confirmation biases that favor our existing beliefs make the change even more difficult. Remember the discussion on patterns of thinking.

Fortunately, we can have powerful, positive experiences that contradict our negative, unconscious beliefs. We can use chance and choice to our advantage. Chance experiences surprise us because they just happen. To take advantage of them, we need to create a healthier mindset. People who transcend trauma, rejection, failure and other life challenges are often characterized as resilient. But what is resilience? For our purposes, resilience is springing back, rebounding, and recovering readily. We can learn to enhance our resilience by training our conscious and unconscious minds to reframe seemingly negative experiences as stepping-stones. We need to embed hopeful and positive beliefs about ourselves and about our lives. How to develop resiliency could be a book in itself. However, let me suggest a powerful strategy that can really make a difference in your life.

THE FUTILITY OF ASKING "WHY?"

Challenging, traumatic experiences often leave us asking "Why?". Why did this happen? Why did it happen to me? Why did it happen at this time? We can become obsessed with searching for the "why". We seem to believe that if we could just understand "why", then somehow it would fix things.

However, "Why?" is a question that is rarely answered correctly, completely, or honestly. Instead, let's condition ourselves to automatically ask useful questions. These questions will guide us into action instead of existential angst. Here are some examples of these kinds of questions:

Alright, now what?

Okay, what's the next step?

How can I do this?

Where's the opportunity in this?

How can I make this a stepping-stone?

Resiliency comes from action. *Why* can paralyze, while *what* and *how* can activate. We all seem to have a universal question that we use whenever we are severely challenged. Is it a why, how, what, or who question? Listening to ourselves and observing ourselves (think of the observer position in the chair exercise) can help us discover our universal question. Creating a question that is more useful and resilient than "why" can make a real difference. In fact, this question can automatically help us reframe negative beliefs to positive beliefs when we suffer a trauma or challenge. Let's examine some potentially destructive experiences that led to positive outcomes.

ESCAPING FROM CAMP 14

Let's first review an exceptional and miraculous example of how quality relationships can shatter negative self-concepts. In his book, Blaine Harden describes the remarkable life of Shin.[2] Shin is a North Korean young man, born and raised in a prison camp for political prisoners. I cannot describe the unthinkable, horrible conditions in the inhumane, nightmarish world somehow called a "camp". These North Korean prisons have existed for over fifty years, and continue the torture of thousands of North Koreans to this day.

Until his escape, Shin knew of no other life outside of the prison. He was born and bred there by the guards. His purpose was to labor unceasingly for the state until starvation, disease, beatings, or torture killed him. His worldview and his self-concept were brutally imprinted on him by the prison guards. His beliefs about his life and identity were continuously beat into him. I cannot imagine a more powerful environment for creating long-term imprints of degrading life values and distrustful relationships.

His mother and father were essentially strangers, chosen by the prison guards to breed over a five-day period. Their order was to produce another worker for the state. Consequently, Shin was born and was allowed to live in the same shelter as his mother. His father was confined elsewhere. The prison guards raised him. His mother was ordered to keep him alive until he was old enough to live on his own. For years, his everyday diet was pickled cabbage, cabbage, and a thin, ground-up corn mush. He was constantly hungry and suffered extreme malnourishment. He stayed alive by catching mice, rats, and insects.

He was taught that he was a "tainted" human being because of the crimes of his parents. He was told that he deserved every painful deprivation because of this identity. His primary responsibility was spying on his parents and fellow prisoners. If he discovered any wrongdoing, he had to report it. If he did not, he would be killed.

He competed with his mother for food. He often stole her food, despite the brutal beatings that she inflicted. His schooling was rudimentary. It was limited to basic reading and math skills. He was not exposed to pictures, ideas, or books about the world outside of the prison. In class one day, he witnessed a female classmate beaten to death by his teacher who was having a bad day. He helped carry the child out of the classroom. He did not think of the incident as exceptional or tragic. It was just part of life in the prison. He was only six years old.

Another time, he overheard his mother and brother discussing a possible escape plan. He reported the incident to his schoolteacher. As a result, his mother was put to death. He was required to witness the hanging. He was not saddened by her death, but rather angered because she put him at risk by planning to escape. To gather more information, the guards took him to an underground prison within the camp. They tortured him, hoping to find out more about the escape plan and his involvement in it. He denied knowing anything beyond what he told the teacher, but they beat him anyway. Eventually, they brought him back for more questioning. This time they hung him horizontally over hot coals and fire. Their intention was to "burn" the information out of him. He had nothing else to tell, and ultimately passed out from the third-degree burns on his back and legs. Afterwards, they placed him in a cell with an older man called "Uncle". Little did Shin know that his harsh worldview and self-concept was about to be ruptured inside of this cell.

The guards would not enter the cell because of the stench from the pus oozing out of his infected burns. Nevertheless, Uncle squeezed out the pus and treated the burns with a poultice created from their scarce food. Slowly, Shin recovered and he realized that Uncle had saved him from certain death. However, Shin was confused. He could not fit Uncle's actions into his paradigm of the world. Uncle gave up his food to Shin and made other sacrifices that were incomprehensible to this broken, young man. Uncle also shared his knowledge of a world outside the prison. It was a world of food and freedom that Shin could only hope to experience someday. Through his charitable care and stories of freedom, Shin's belief system crumbled. He had experienced selflessness from an old man who saved his life. This man also had additional knowledge of a world with food enough to fill his belly.

Finally, he was taken out of the prison and was placed in a sewing machine repair shop. In this shop, he met another older man named Park. Park gave him an even greater vision of the outside world. In his pre-prison life, Park had developed a dignity and refinement that Shin had never seen. The old prison paradigm of ruthlessness, selfishness, brutality, and self- deprecation was further ruptured. The pair planned a daring escape. Up until this time, no one born in a North Korean prison camp had ever escaped. The guards and the electric fences were seemingly impassable.

Park and Shin finally managed to elude the guards and get to the fence. Park tried to crawl between the first and second strand of wires. He was electrocuted. Shin crawled over his body and to the other side. As he crawled over Park, he could feel the current being conducted through Park into him, but Park's body absorbed the worst of the current. However, his legs slipped to the side and touched part of the wire. This severely burned Shin from his knees to his feet. The injury bled and festered for weeks. However, he escaped into an unknown, free world. He endured months of perilous travel throughout Northern Korea and China. Finally, he arrived in South Korea and obtained assistance. The South Korean and U.S. authorities were fascinated to have a prison-born escapee in their custody.

Shin eventually immigrated to the U.S. where he continues to receive psychotherapeutic, medical, and other assistance today. Once his stomach was filled, he began a campaign to help the prisoners he left behind. From a ruthless, selfish, competitive life of brutality and scarcity, he emerged with compassion for those he left behind. His compassion for them was strong enough to even put himself at risk.

What happened to Shin's prison self-concept and worldview? They had been intractably created under the threat of death. Incredibly, the charitable and virtuous ministrations of two older men were powerful enough to counter his long-term potentiation beliefs. His time spent with Uncle and Park was short compared to the time he spent in Camp 14. However, their charitable and virtuous acts pierced his brutal, dog-eat-dog worldview.

His life today is a struggle, but is nothing compared to the life in prison. He has difficulty trusting people, and he experiences intense mood swings. Nevertheless, he has radically changed his self-concept and the nature of his relationships with other human beings. For that he can thank two compassionate men whose kindness and connection gave him hope and new choices. The true power of virtuous relationships cannot be measured.

I am not encouraging you to experience imprisonment or torture in order to change intractable, negative beliefs. However, Shin's life illustrates the power of virtuous relationships. They can puncture negative beliefs and put us on course for a richer, more fulfilling self-concept. Receiving love when we are open and vulnerable can change our self-concept. When we connect with quality individuals during difficulties, our deepest, unconscious beliefs can change. Seeking out these individuals may sound like an overly simple strategy to change these intractable beliefs. Fine! Then keep it simple.

LES MISÉRABLES

In *Les Misérables*, Jean Valjean suffers the injustice of hard labor and imprisonment for stealing bread for his hungry family[3]. After leaving prison, he enters a church where a benevolent priest feeds and houses him. He steals the priest's silver and is quickly arrested. The police return him to the priest. And this is the pivotal moment in the story. The priest explains to the police that the silver was actually a gift, and tells them to release Valjean. Once they are alone, the priest explains that he has ransomed him from sin and desperation. This moment of kindness shattered Valjean's previous worldview. This moment changed everything for him.

The rest of the story is an intriguing juxtaposition of mercy and justice. As a result of his encounter with the priest, Valjean's heart changed. He began to sacrifice and love others. Despite the years of injustice and imprisonment, Valjean's self-concept and worldview changed because of the actions of the priest.

Perhaps, while in dire straits, some of us have been selflessly succored by a quality soul. Perhaps the experience ruptured some of our negative self-concepts and worldview. This can happen randomly in life, as in was the case of Jean Valjean. Even when it is unplanned, embrace the positive meanings embedded in these experiences. Allow those self-defeating beliefs to be ruptured. If this happens to any of us, may we be grateful.

WE ARE NEEDED EVERYWHERE

We can be like Uncle, Park, or the priest. Serving and forgiving others, even those who don't deserve it, conjure up virtuous emotions and beliefs. We can change as we are rescued, and we can also change as we rescue others. Giving and receiving love can shatter negative paradigms. We don't have to wait to be rescued ourselves to have life-changing experiences. Uncle and Park were also prisoners, but that didn't stop their compassionate service.

We are surrounded by those in need. We can increase the intensity of charitable service by seeking experiences outside of our comfort zone. For example, many charitable organizations organize trips to Third World countries where we can serve the deprived and disadvantaged. We can work shoulder-to-shoulder and hand-in-hand with those whose lives are unimaginably difficult. Instead of vicariously experiencing the lives of the starving, suffering, and hopeless through TV or a book, we can be there. Nothing replaces being there.

THE PARADOX OF BEING UNCOMFORTABLE

I know of two sisters who were brought up in a privileged world. By "privileged", I mean that they had never been without food, water, shelter, medical care, or transportation. They lived with carpeting, electricity, indoor plumbing, and refrigerators. They had clothing appropriate for every season. For the great majority of the world, that constitutes being privileged. In Third World countries, that constitutes living like royalty. They were also blessed to have wise and loving parents who arranged for them to serve in a Third World country. They worked in an orphanage and cared for the little, unclaimed, and homeless children.

The experience was life-changing for these young women. It shattered their beliefs about the worth of human beings, their responsibility to others, and the quality of their connections with those around them. The needs of the children far exceeded the hours in a day, the energy of the sisters, and the material resources available to them. They dealt with stomachs protruding from malnourishment, constant weeping, vomiting, and feces. One of the sisters even experienced losing a child while holding them. Death from abandonment was no longer a theoretical concept to her, but a reality. The resources to help the children were basically limited to their hands, arms, and voices. The sisters held each child in their arms and sang to them. Everywhere they went, children clung to them and begged them to hold them and sing to them.

They returned home with new beliefs imprinted upon their unconscious. The two sisters were invigorated by a new, passionate purpose in their lives, but were not necessarily driven to permanently serve in Third World countries. However, their eyes were opened. They saw that they were needed by others, no matter where they were. The value of life itself, and specifically the value of children, overshadowed their previous social image and physical comfort. College became compellingly purposeful, and friends of common interests were easier to identify. Changes in their self-concept and worldview occurred without much conscious thought. Connecting with and touching those in need can blow out negative beliefs in the unconscious mind. We have a choice in *how* we wish to serve.

Who knows the full impact on the children that they served? I wonder if somehow the sisters' touching, hugging, and singing imprinted a message of self-worth and hope on the impressionable, unconscious minds of these children. For many of us, we can't consciously pinpoint the early childhood experiences that helped build our self-concept. Can you remember someone in your life who gave you such a gift?

THE POWER OF KINDESS

We don't need to be Marvel Comics superheroes to make a difference. My first wife selflessly nurtured me through an illness that lasted for years. She was killed in a car accident. It was a one-car rollover down a steep hill. We were both thrown from the vehicle. Every bone in my face was broken, among other injuries. However, somehow I retained consciousness after the accident. I felt impressed to crawl up the hill to get help, rather than going to her. I could not move very well due to broken bones and a separated pelvis. Help came. They told me that my wife's condition was about like mine. The ambulance arrived and I was placed in the back. An empty bed lay next to me. The driver made sure that I was secured, and then started to close the door. I said, "Wait, where is my wife?" He said, "She's dead", and then closed the door. I believe he did not understand the shock he gave me from his blunt reply. It was a long, lonely ride to the hospital and a long, lonely helicopter ride to a bigger hospital.

Many surgeries were required. I was in intensive care for a long time. While in the hospital, my nights were long, and flooded with "what if" questions and memories. However, most nights, a nurse named Billie cared for me. There was something about her presence, her voice, and the way she cared for me that eased my emotional and physical suffering. I loved Billie. She not only cared for me, but also inspired me. Somehow, I began to transcend this horrible experience. My mission and life-purpose were intensified. Perhaps I would not have done so without Billie's powerful influence. I was vulnerable and humbly receptive to her influence. For years, I took flowers to her in that hospital. They say that timing is everything. I was fortunate to have Billie as my nurse.

NOTES

1. Dweck, C. (2006). *The New Psychology of Success*. New York, NY: Ballantine Books. Carol Dweck in her book, *Mindset: The New Psychology of Success*, reviews the ends and outs of resiliency and mind-set beliefs. She recommends creating a Mindset based on personal growth. "When you enter a mindset, you enter a new world. In one world—the world of fixed traits—success is about proving yourself smart or talented… In the other world of changing qualities—it's about stretching yourself to learn something new. Developing yourself… In one world, effort is a bad thing. It, like failure, means you're not smart or talented. If you were you wouldn't need effort. In the other world, effort is what makes you smart or talented… Mindset change is not about picking up a few pointers here and there." She speaks here to the challenges and even the potential traumas of failure. Mindset applies to all challenges and potential traumas.

2. Harden, B. (2012). *Escape from Camp 14: One Man's Remarkable Odyssey from North Korea to Freedom in the West*. London, UK: Penguin Group.

3. Hugo, V. (2013). *Les Misérables*. New York, NY: New American Library.

CHAPTER 17

The Power Of Purpose: Discovering Meaning and Mission for the Best Life

NEAR-DEATH EXPERIENCES

Another phenomenon that purges unconscious beliefs is the near-death experience. I am using these experiences to demonstrate that our perceived experiences can change us profoundly and almost immediately. Dr. Alexander was a neurosurgeon who experienced an unusual near-death experience. This experience could not have been caused by his brain, because it was completely shut down during the coma. Dr. Alexander's embedded worldview and self-concept changed after this experience. Secular scientists were shaken by Dr. Alexander's experience because he promoted the reality of life after death. Biologically influenced or not, Dr. Alexander's near-death experience was so powerful that his worldview and self-concept changed. His beliefs about his profession, his life purpose, and his relationships with family, friends, and God changed as a result of this experience.

These kinds of experiences are so powerful that they shatter embedded beliefs and create new worldviews and self-concepts. And sometimes, this is accomplished within a few moments. Thousands of people throughout the world have had these incredible, life-changing experiences. There are many studies about near-death experiences. Perhaps the pioneer of this research is Emmanuel Swedenborg. At the time, he was considered one of the most intelligent men in the world. He had his own experiences, and like Dr. Alexander, they changed his worldview[1].

Near-death experiences teach us that intense experiences, and our interpretation of them, can change who we are. Thoughts generated in the midst of powerful experiences, even unconscious ones, can turn worldviews upside down. In order to shatter deeply embedded beliefs, experiences must be profound and intense. Let's explore possible ways to create profound and intense experiences that can lead to healthy beliefs.

CONSTRUCTING LIFE-CHANGING EXPERIENCES

Part 1: Rites of Passage

In many parts of the world, rites of passage are used to generate new self-concepts and worldviews. A rite of passage refers to an event (or series of events) that bridges one stage of life to another stage. By "passage", I mean passing from one social circle to another and from one worldview to another.

Humans seem to almost innately crave rites of passage. Some cultures recognize this need and consciously create these experiences. These cultures require people to acquire specific knowledge and to prepare to enter specific social groups before they are considered a trusted member of the community. Our culture does not promote life changing rites of passage. We do not have a cultural consensus on a worldview to obtain through a rite of passage, and we have no criteria to move from one social group to another one. Instead, subcultures within our culture may provide abbreviated rites of passage for their members. This may consist of ceremonies for weddings, graduations, births, or funerals, and so on. They are abbreviated in that the experiences lack intensity, risk, and a transfer of knowledge to be gained in no other way.

We are searching for organized, life-changing experiences. Our Western culture views rites of passage as "primitive" and unnecessary. However, some social critics believe that some Western social problems are linked to a lack of these transitional experiences. Our youth seem to intrinsically desire rites of passage, and they fill this gap by creating their own. Unfortunately, these attempts often include illegal and unreasonably dangerous behaviors.

Street gangs practice raw brutality in their initiations to prove loyalty and commitment. It is considered a "passage into adulthood" for adolescents to engage in drugs or sex. Some critics say that our culture is stuck in adolescence, because our rites of passage are weak and meaningless. In our society, many middle-aged adults cling to immature adolescent values, like looking good over being good, or that sensual pleasure is more important than anything else. Like Peter Pan, they never grow up.

Effective rites of passage impart critical knowledge commensurate with entering the new social group that cannot be obtained elsewhere. In a rite of passage, knowledge is acquired from experiential undertakings rather than intellectual processing. The rites must appear risky enough to prove the initiate's loyalty and trustworthiness to the new group. Knowledge and loyalty are the prerequisites to leaving behind the old group and embracing the new group. To be successful the rites must therefore embed knowledge through experiences and prove trustworthiness by successfully facing difficult challenges.

Malidoma Patrice Some' explains African rites of passage.[2] He was kidnapped from his African village at a young age, and was trained as a priest in the Western tradition. Finally, when he was about twenty years old, he escaped, and made his way back to his village. Even though he was loved, he was not accepted as an adult member of the village, because he had never been initiated through a rite of passage. He was ignorant of ritual-based knowledge, and therefore could not be trusted. His only option was to join a large group of boys for a two-month rite of passage experience. He reveals some, but not all of his experiences. It is mind-stretching for Westerners to try and comprehend these experiences.

Let me say that I have never been through any experience even close to what he described. Who am I to judge the efficacy or meaning of what he reports? In his village, his descriptions of the experiences would be commonly understood. For anyone else, these experiences could rupture their worldview.

Some of the experiences were exhausting and even life-threatening. In fact, he claims that four boys from the group never made it home. Nevertheless, mothers and fathers viewed the transitional knowledge and the loyalty created as worth the risk. Their children could not be villagers without acquiring the knowledge and proving themselves. He learned and comprehended knowledge at a deep level that could not be acquired through discussion, pictures, or reading. The successful participants were permitted to enter an adult world with adult knowledge that they had "paid for". As a result, Malidoma was welcomed as a member of the village.

You may wish to organize or seek ways to participate in challenging rites of passage. The experience may boost you into a more useful concept and add knowledge to your worldview. Adventurists are drawn to these experiences. However, be careful.

Various organizations sponsor indigenous-type rites of passage. People feeling that urge for initiation pay money for these experiences. Some people even report a clarification of their worldview and self-concept. However, the passage to a new social group does not include the people that a participant will have long-term, daily relationships. The knowledge gained from the experience is generally insufficient to constitute a profound, new worldview. However, a person may gain new insights about life. Authentic rites of passage do not exist for most Westerners who live in a world of modernity and comfort.

Just having intense experiences does not constitute a rite of passage. If you seek out a rite of passage sponsored by an organization, carefully evaluate the "elders" who are facilitating the experience and their knowledge base. Experiencing indigenous rites of passage out of your cultural context dilutes the experience. In addition, copying another culture's rites without actual membership in that culture can be disrespectful.

PART II: PEAK EXPERIENCES

"Peak experiences" are somewhat similar to rites of passage.[3] They occur when people push themselves to their limit and beyond. The experience breaks barriers and expands personal boundaries. For example, climbing Mount Everest or sailing around the Horn are ventures requiring endurance, skill, and strength. These are intense experiences. Perhaps you have read about the blind man who scaled Mt. Everest[4], or the man with three prosthetic limbs running on a marathon team[5]. Through these peak experiences, individuals hope to discover knowledge about themselves and their relationship to the world. The key is pushing themselves to their peak, or beyond.

Remember our discussion about the Remembering Self and the Experiencing self? We are sometimes motivated to experience relatively short-term pain in order to create a long-term memory. The memory of the experience becomes a metaphor about our self, and the world. The experience is over when we physically complete it. However, the memory of the experience lives on. The memory of the experience, and what we learned from it, can rupture our worldview and self-concept. Peak experiences usually are not enjoyable. In fact, they are typically painful, gut-wrenching, and risky. We don't savor the pain of the experience, but we savor what it means to us

A successful conquest can alter one's perspective of the world and their place within it. It is valuable because it is hard to achieve, and it engages our whole mind and body (especially our nervous system). All of "us" is affected by the experience.

Think carefully about your objective for engaging in a peak experience. In many ways, the price is high, but it can pay for itself many times over. Life is full of opportunities for peak experiences. My brother-in-law hiked the Pacific Trail by himself over a five-month period when he was in his late fifties. That is over one thousand miles from Mexico to Canada. He hiked over mountains higher than 13,000 feet and into Death Valley, which is below sea level. Part of me envies his experience, although I am unsure what I would have learned about myself. It's an uneasy feeling.

WILDERNESS THERAPY

Wilderness therapy can be described as a hybrid combination of a rite of passage and a peak experience. These types of experiences have been around for thousands of years in many different places. However, the intentional use of wilderness therapy as a modality to change worldviews and self-concepts gained momentum during the 1980's in the United States. I am proud to be associated with this movement and its evolution. From less than a handful of programs in the early 1980's to a plethora during the early 2000's, they are recognized as the treatment of choice for troubled teens. Programs are also available for young adults and adults.

There are many brands of wilderness therapy, but the formula for success is fairly consistent. Wilderness therapy is not a military boot camp experience. Transplanted from an urban world of modernity and comfort, participants live in an outdoor wilderness of mountains, desert, or ocean. With only rudimentary equipment, they learn to take care of themselves and others.

Self-sufficiency, creativity, cooperativeness, and tenacity are required to succeed. Activities may include learning primitive survival skills, horsemanship, sailing, search and rescue skills, hiking, and woodcraft.

Similar to a rite of passage, participants have the equivalent of "elders" who are their guides and instructors. To meet the challenges within the experience, participants have only each other and their guides to rely upon for anything. There are no distractions of media, social groups, cell phones, hobbies, or other modern conveniences. Participants are required to dig deep into their personal resources to thrive.

Relationships with "elders" in this environment are more compelling and necessary than perhaps any relationships that they have previously experienced. The elders are therefore extremely influential and persuasive to participants. Unconscious beliefs and self-concepts can be influenced in several ways. The intensity of the experience opens up the mind to new choices and meanings. Adapting to a new potentially threatening environment requires more adaptability and effort than many people have previously experienced. As a result, the contrast and comparison of the wilderness to "home" creates real life perspectives that could not be learned vicariously.

By mixing Thoreau's contemplative Walden's Pond perspective with peak experiences, wilderness therapy is a recipe for deep-level changes. Much of the success depends on the quality of the relationships between participants and elders. Additionally, self-concept barriers are removed by the stark necessity of coping, doing, and surviving. As a result, participants grow stronger physically, emotionally, and even spiritually.

SEARCH AND RESCUE

Let me share an example. In one of my wilderness programs, the students trained to become a cohesive search and rescue team. You might call this a healthy dose of the Best Life. In doing, so they learned how to focus on the needs and the well-being of others. In fact, they came to view their own limitations of anger, depression, anxiety, or addiction as impediments to safely rescue another human being. They discovered that what used to be "my" personal problems are now risks to other people. Self-improvement and emotional healing began to take on a dual purpose. They could take the Best Life step to improve themselves for the well-being of others.

Participants in search and rescue not only want personal relief from emotional pain, but they also want to trust themselves to save someone else's life. This added permission and motivation to change, heal, or improve can rupture their unconscious resistance to let go of old beliefs and relational patterns. Additionally, the wilderness experience fully engages the participant's entire nervous system (that includes their unconscious).

Two young men enrolled in this program. Both were from broken homes and lived with their mothers. Their relationships with their mothers had deteriorated into open rebellion and dangerous behaviors. "Mom" was viewed as an impediment to freedom. Their dads were absent except for when they showered them with material gifts to demonstrate they were "good guys". Mom carried all of the family burdens. The young men slowly committed to the search and rescue team both physically and emotionally. They learned that when they were sufficiently trained, they would be "on call" with the sheriff's department, and would participate in search and rescue missions. When calls came in, they were told that they were being called to a real incident or a scenario. They were not told which one it was. The way in which they responded to each call revealed their commitment to the spirit and the mission of the team.

One afternoon, a call came. Each team member had a specific role on the team. The communication person took the radio call. They were told that a woman had been missing since yesterday and that authorities suspected that she was in the team's mountain territory. Packs and equipment were gathered and the search began. As the day unfolded, the group learned that an abusive husband had beaten the woman, and that she had fled to the mountains to escape. They learned that the husband could not be found, and that he was believed to be looking for her. A team member created a search pattern on their map that they followed throughout the day. After about six hours of intense hiking and searching, the sun started going down. They came upon a mountain road, and hiked up on it to get out of the brush. After hiking about a half a mile, they found a hat on the side of the road. That intensified the search.

Finally, a woman stood up from behind a rhododendron bush. Her clothes were torn and there was blood on her face and shirt. Her hair was everywhere and her eyes were wide open. They ran to her, and she collapsed onto the ground. The team members assumed their duties of checking her vitals and for potential injuries, providing emotional support, and stabilizing her. She tried to talk, but her crying and weeping prevented her from making any sense. However, she did repeat over and over, "No more, no more."

She couldn't walk very well because of a sprained ankle. They put her on a backboard and carried her the short distance to the road. Right when the girl with the radio started to call the sheriff, an old, Ford pick-up truck suddenly rumbled towards them. The woman went bananas, and the team just looked at each other. The truck stopped about ten yards from them, and a large, full-bearded, bear-of-a-man stepped out. His eyes were red. His words came out slurred, but loud. "Give her to me. That's my wife. She *belongs* to me." He rolled his big shoulders forward, and came toward the group. The two, much smaller, young men stepped in front of her and faced the big man. "Get out of my way, that's my wife. I want her back!"

Tears streaming down his cheek, one of the young men held up his hands and said, "Leave her alone. She's had enough." The big man responded, "I'm taking her anyway" and took a step forward. The young man answered, "We can't let you do it. You need to cool off." The big man replied, "Who's going to stop me?" Quietly, the answer came. "We're going to try." A few moments passed. The big man pointed his finger at his wife, turned around, and got back into his truck. When he sped off, the group gathered around the frantic woman. She hugged both of the young men and said over and over again. "Thank you. Thank you. Thank you."

Something happened inside these two young men that night. One wrote a letter to his mother—a letter much different than was written a few days earlier. At the end of the program, their mothers were overwhelmed by the hugs from their boys. Something had changed inside these young men about the relational meaning of "mother". Old connections were cut, and new connections were merged together. A good wilderness program can revamp relationships and change self-concepts.

TRANSFORMATIVE RELIGIOUS/ SPIRITUAL EXPERIENCES

This is a potentially controversial topic. Some readers may feel comfortable, others neutral, and others put-off by questions of a religious nature. With respect for all readers and their beliefs, I will report and comment on a universal, human quest for transformation of self. Of course, there are many religions, philosophies of religion, and spiritual perspectives. I am not comparing or critiquing any religious or spiritual doctrine, belief system, or practice. Rather, my comments are about universal, typical, religious experiences of people worldwide. We will focus on how these experiences are transformative of self-concepts, worldviews, and relationships. The desire and quest to pursue religious experiences is an extremely personal decision. I do not intend to imply that religious doctrines are unimportant, or not critical. They can certainly make a huge difference in our self-concept and worldview. Distinguishing doctrinal differences has practical, here-and-now significance about how we relate to one another. They may also critically differ in how a person establishes and maintains a relationship with a higher power

Additionally, for those who believe in an afterlife, doctrinal differences can set out different expectations about the next life and our preparation for it. In this book, we're not going there. We are not engaging in a theological discussion. Our concern is exploring religious, transformative experiences that can help change our self-concept.

Many authors and researchers have focused on the nature and the effect of religious experiences. I will continue the William James vein of thinking on this subject. He was a psychologist and scientist, not a theologian or representative of any religious institution or philosophy. He focused on the *effect* of religious experiences in the lives of people across many different cultures. From James' perspective, all religions or spiritual movements appear to address two general human characteristics[6]. He noted the following:

1. Humans have an uneasiness that something is wrong or incomplete as they naturally stand.
2. The solution to the uneasiness is making a useful connection with a higher power.

In other words, he concludes that humans are drawn to a higher power that will complete or transform them. A religious or spiritual experience occurs when a significant connection between the person and the higher power occurs. Through the influence of the higher power, beliefs and the nature of the person are changed in a positive way. Modern psychology fumbles around trying to fit in religious beliefs and experiences as a part of human nature. The problem of course is proof. Psychological research and knowledge is fundamentally based on empiricism and the scientific method that we discussed. This method of "knowing" requires the study of matter and material things whose existence can only be verified by one or more of the five senses. A higher power, its influence, and alleged origin of "spiritual experiences" don't lend themselves very well to empirical inquiry. Therefore, the science of psychology looks askance at religiosity or spirituality.

This makes it difficult for psychologists who are religious to reconcile personal and professional beliefs. People who are religious, or who have religious experiences, can be difficult clients or patients. Psychologists are torn whether to give credence to clients' religious experiences and commitments, or to view them as pathological.

James' response reflects his philosophy on the nature of truth, and what he calls "radical empiricism"[7]. Spiritual experiences are real in the sense that a person has, what is to them, a unique, distinctive experience from other life experiences. There are two ways to question the authenticity of a spiritual experience. First, one can wonder if the person actually had an experience. Are they being honest and accurate in describing the experience? If yes, then secondly, how can we attribute the experience to a higher power? James found a pattern, a commonality of spiritual incidences that happens to individuals all over the world. Most of them had no contact with one another, and often they were unaware of one another's religious belief systems. The pattern and the great number of occurrences logically suggest that people are honestly reporting real experiences.

The experiences were not insignificant or meaningless in the lives of these people, but instead they were often transformative, healing, and life-changing. In other words, these unique experiences really exist, and are difficult to explain empirically. Millions of people personally attribute their experiences to something spiritual. While debates continue about what might have happened to them, they enjoy a transformative life. We can't dismiss this phenomenon.

The experiences cannot be ignored or disregarded because of disagreements about definitions and theology. Experience equates to some type of reality. If a person is interested in exploring ways to improve the motivation and permission behind human behavior, how can religious experiences be ignored? To ignore them is to disregard a universally experienced phenomenon associated with the well-being of humankind. James's research concluded that religious experiences can arrive suddenly for some people and gradually for others. He found that some people seem to enjoy them for most of their life. James identifies three practical difficulties in seeking a religious experience[8]:

1. How does one "realize the reality" of one's higher part or power?
2. How does one identify one's self with this higher power exclusively? (This makes it personal.)
3. How does one identify this connection as part of "ideal being"? In other words, how does this connection fit into what we have called the "Best Life"?

There are many institutional and personal religions. For our purposes, they generally agree about some things. They agree that a "higher power" of some nature, actually exists (whether they conceive of it as a personal god or "an ideal tendency embedded in the eternal structure of the world")[9] They also agree that the higher power not only exists, but it can interact as well. Finally, there is agreement that when the higher power acts, something *is* improved, and your life benefits from putting yourself in "its" hands.

Major disagreements occur about how divine connections are made. Various answers are proposed, such as: pantheism, theism, nature and second birth, works and grace, karma, immortality, reincarnation, resurrection, rationalism, and mysticism. Nevertheless, people embracing each school of thought record religious experiences. This may suggest that connection and religious experience may depend as much on intent and personal preparedness as on doctrinal understanding. The ultimate higher power may respond to the cries of a humble heart regardless of race, ethnicity, or even religious affiliation.

Remember, we are most concerned with experiences that can change self-concept and limiting, negative beliefs. Obviously, distinctions in religious doctrine about the afterlife are critically important to believers. However, a higher power seems to also be responsive to the here-and-now needs and well-being of all people, in spite of doctrinal differences. Humans have transcending, healing, religious experiences, whether they are explained away as subliminally originated brain phenomena, or the intervention of higher power.

Let me use an example to illustrate a "religious experience". William James reports the experience of a well-respected "scientific man" of his acquaintance. This gentleman was not affiliated with any specific religion or religious organization. We have discussed the universal nature of religious experiences, and this example may be viewed as somewhat generic, in that no particular theology or doctrine is involved. However, the important characteristics of "feeling a need" and "reaching out" to God are present here. Additionally, the experience appears more interesting because it happened to an empirical-thinking, scientific man. Think about how he distinguishes this experience from other life experiences.

"Between twenty and thirty I gradually became more and more agnostic and irreligious, yet I cannot say that I ever lost that 'indefinite consciousness' which Herbert Spencer describes so well, of an Absolute Reality behind phenomena. For me this Reality was not the pure Unknowable of Spencer's philosophy, for although I had ceased my childish prayers to God, and never prayed to IT in a formal manner, yet my more recent experience shows me to have been in a relation to IT, which practically was the same thing as prayer. Whenever I had any trouble, especially when I had conflict with other people, either domestically or in the way of business, or when I was depressed in spirits or anxious about affairs, I now recognize that I used to fall back for support upon this curious relation I felt myself to be in to this fundamental comical IT. It was on my side, or I was in ITS side, however you please to term it, in the particular trouble, and it always strengthened me and seemed to give me endless vitality to feel its underlying and supporting presence. In fact, it was an unfailing fountain of living justice, truth, and strength, to which I instinctively turned at times of weakness, and it always brought me out. I know now that it was a personal relation I was in to it, because of late years the power of communicating with it has left me, and I am conscious of a perfectly definite loss. I used to never fail to find when I turned to it. Then came a set of years when sometimes I found it, and then again I would be wholly unable to make connection with it. I remember many occasions on which at night in bed, I would be unable to get to sleep on account of worry. I turned this way and that in the darkness and groped mentally for the familiar sense of that higher mind of which had always seemed to be close at hand as it were, closing the passage, and yielding support, but there was no electric current. A blank was there instead of IT: I couldn't find anything. Now, at the age of nearly fifty, my power of getting into connection with it has entirely left me; and I have to confess that a great help has gone out of my life. Life has become curiously dead and (65) indifferent; and I can now see that my old experience was probably exactly the same thing as the prayers of the orthodox, only I did not call them by that name. What I have spoken of as 'It' was practically not Spencer's Unknowable, but just my own instinctive and individual God, whom I relied upon for higher sympathy, but whom somehow I have lost."[10]

Notice at the end of his narrative, he struggles to identify this presence, but he adamantly believes it was with him. In spite of thousands of accounts that describe connections to a higher power, resulting in healing, inspiration, encouragement, comfort, and transformation, fewer people in our Western culture seem to reach out. Again, this is a personal matter. Nevertheless, remember that after gathering the facts and careful contemplation on both reasonable sides of an issue, we choose what is most useful to us. Seeking religious experience may be a reflection of our vulnerability, or receptivity to higher-level connections. In the example with the "man of science", we note that the man could not control the "it", and we wonder why the connections ceased. We may wonder about the reciprocity required by both parties to the connection, and whether the ceasing was related to the quality of the relationship.

In choosing whether to "reach out" for this connection, we all choose what we think is useful. However, let us not be fooled that biological determinism or genetic explanations preclude our reaching out to a higher power. Scientific explanations for religious experience do not conclusively explain the nature and origin of these experiences. Facts and sound reason exist countering the proposition that spiritual experiences with a higher power can't happen. These speculations are not conclusive barriers to seeking religious experiences of a transformative nature, unless we want them to be.

In these matters, the sincere desires of hearts and minds will rule. Let us not judge one another for whether we choose transcending religious experiences or not. However, may all our choices lead us to quality, virtuous relationships with others and within ourselves. Being grounded by loving and virtuous motives can protect us from being deceived and led in directions injurious to others and ourselves. Spiritual experiences that lead to unvirtuous behaviors should be questioned. Of course, as we have discussed, some people will question what is "virtuous". Again, I point to virtues encompassing integrity, love, respect, and empathy. There may be cultural differences in how these virtues are manifest, but the differences are insufficient to destroy the general universality of virtue. Some experiences labeled as "spiritual" do not lead to integrity, love, or compassion. For those seeking virtuous, spiritual growth, be careful of pride, ego, and exclusive self-interest. These motives can lead to a primarily selfish and non-altruistic love, that can be destructive to yourself and others.

THE MEANING OF OUR EXPERIENCES

In this chapter, we considered how life experiences and our interpretation of them form our critical self-concept beliefs—both the positive ones as well as the negative ones. We learned how to become more resilient. We explored ways to maximize our experiences to change unhealthy, destructive beliefs about ourselves and about how we connect to the world. We also reviewed experiences that can be designed to build positive, unconscious beliefs, and to rupture negative ones.

Perhaps our most significant freedom comes from *choosing* the meaning of our experiences. That includes our uniquely spiritual experiences. We must increase our availability to choices that are presently outside our knowledge or reach. We learned from our North Korean escapee that choices become more available as we gain knowledge and virtuously connect to others. Through all of this, the intentions of our deepest selves seem to unconsciously guide us on our way. Virtuous and loving desires invite the Best Life for others and ourselves.

NOTES

1. Swedenborg, E. (1990). *Heaven and Hell.* (G. Dole, Trans.). New York, NY: Swedenborg Foundation.

2. Somé, Malidoma. (1988). *The Healing Wisdom of Africa: Finding Life Purpose Through Nature, Ritual, and Community.* New York, NY: Putnam Books.

3. Csikszentmihalyi, M. (1990). *Flow: The Psychology of Optimal Experience.* New York, NY: Harper & Row.

4. Weihenmayer, E. (2002). *Touch the Top of the World: A Blind Man's Journey to Climb Farther than the eye Can See: My Story.* New York, NY: Penguin Group.

5. Montoya, A. (2013). *The Finish Line.* Mustang, OK: Tate Publishing.

6. James, W. (2008). *Varieties of Religious Experience: A Study in Human Nature.* Charleston, SC: Forgotten Books.

7. James, W. (1912). *Essays in Radical Empiricism.* London, UK: Longmans, Green and Co.

8. (James, 2008).

9. (James, 2008).

10. (James, 2008).

CHAPTER 18

Get A Grip On the Best Life: From The Good Life to the Best Life

WHY CHOOSE THE BEST LIFE?

Many people want a life of ease and comfort. They believe that ease and comfort are the best objectives in life. Ironically, people sweat and bleed for years trying to achieve the Good Life of ease and comfort. In other words, they do not truly live the Good Life while they are striving to obtain it. This so-called Good Life is rich in self-indulgence, but suffers an absence of meaning and purpose. It's plagued with the quest for satiation. To be satiated is to be full. The Good Life is a never-ending quest to get enough of feeling good. Feeling good is like fried froth—one can eat it all day and night, but still be famished for want of substance.

THE BEST LIFE STANDS APART

The Best Life offers more life substance. Quality relationships, character-building experiences, and charitable love, are filling and fulfilling. These substantive pursuits are meaning-filled. The pursuits of the Good Life are almost meaningless. The less meaning we have to live for, the less reason we have to live. The richer our life purpose, the deeper our passion will be to live and thrive. Virtuous purpose and meaning is the fuel of life's higher passions.

The incredibly courageous and brilliant Helen Keller, while blind and deaf said it well. "The most pathetic person in the world is someone who has sight, but has no vision." The iconic George Bernard Shaw said it this way: "This is the true joy in life, the being used for a purpose recognized by yourself as a mighty one; the being thoroughly worn out before you are thrown on the scrap heap; the being a force of nature instead of a feverish selfish little clod of ailments and grievances complaining that the world will not devote itself to making you happy." The witty Yogi Berra, the philosophical catcher of the New York Yankees said it in his special style. "The future ain't what it used to be. If you don't know where you're going, you might wind up some place else."

How does purposeful meaning separate the Best Life from the Good Life? Webster's Dictionary defines "meaning" as, "the end, purpose, or significance of something". "Purpose" is defined as "an end, an aim, and a goal". We now ask what is a meaningful, purposeful self-concept? Using the definitions, a meaningful self-concept focuses on the ultimate end and significance of what we are becoming. A purposeful self-concept consists of the aims and goals that we choose in life. Everyone is going *somewhere* as Yogi implies, but what is the quality or significance of that destination? What is the quality and benefit of the life we are living? After all, in spite of biological determinist's claims, we have a choice in our quality of life.

QUALITY OF LIFE

Quality living is not a function of quantity, whether that entails acquisitions or achievements. In other words, we are not equating high-quality living to having the most money, most wins, most intelligence, most beauty, most sex, or most physical pleasure. Let me clarify. Obtaining money, beauty, pleasure, etc. can be useful elements to an enriched life. However, the Best Life is not a reflection of how much we have of these things. In fact, the Best Life can be abandoned when our primary purpose in life becomes getting more and more of those things. Humans are easily deceived by the camouflage adorning these hedonistic objectives. They persuade us to believe that they are the most important things in life.

This slippery slope makes it difficult to get a grip on our best self-concept. Adolescence seems to be the time we start to search for the Best Life. Our teenage years are the time to get the Good Life out of the way, so we can get on with the Best Life. Unfortunately, some of us extend our adolescence for another ten, twenty, thirty, or more years! The Boomers want to keep on booming! Some of us never grow up. So what can we learn from our adolescence?

Teenagers are forever asking "Why?" and "What does this mean?" This can drive parents and teachers crazy. We go crazy because of the repetition. Sometimes, we get frustrated simply because we can't answer the questions. "*Why* is this right? *What* is so important about that? *Why* should I follow someone else's rules? *Why* isn't this my life?" At the same time, they are asking, "Who?" "Who am I, and who are you? What is the significance and meaning of our relationship?" These are recurring questions that we continue to ask our adult selves as we move throughout life.

MY QUEST FOR THE BEST LIFE

Let me share a few of my own experiences from high school. This was my time of asking, "Who am I?" Maybe you can relate. To me, the Good Life and the Best Life seemed mysteriously intertwined. I had no idea how to differentiate them. Nevertheless, I was curious and ready to go.

As a new freshman in high school, I had wide eyes. How do I fit in? How can I be happy here? The answer was right in front of me. I decided that I needed to watch the seniors. They were so old, wise, and *much* more mature than me. In fact, I did not fail to notice that the senior girls looked like women in every curvy way. Certainly, these old people had the answers. I could observe them and model myself after the ones who seemed the most successful. But which group of seniors? There were so many choices: the Jocks, the Social Climbers, the Intellectuals, the Partiers, and the Power Brokers. Disclaimer: I will not mention names and do not intend in any way to disrespect or disparage anyone. I will report my experience as seen through the eyes of my adolescence.

THE SOCIAL CLIMBER

What does it mean to be a Social Climber? To me, they were easy to spot. They dressed in cool, expensive clothes. Other students talked about them and were jealous of them. Most of the guys and girls were good-looking and witty. They seemed to be above it all. I constantly watched one guy in particular walk down the hall. He didn't even glance at anyone else who wasn't a dyed in the wool climber. I tried to get his attention, and I even said "Hi" to him a few times. He sauntered on by me like I didn't even exist. He seemed untouchable. He was at the top of the food chain. I envied him and his car. I thought that's what I wanted—to be envied and above it all: untouchable and in control. What a life that would be! As time went by, I accumulated a bit of a wardrobe, and I tried to hang out with the cool kids in my class, along with one or two upperclassmen. I ignored other kids and developed my own condescending walk. In the end, I doubt if anyone envied me or put me on any kind of pedestal.

After a while, I felt uneasy about ignoring other kids and not talking to them. My interaction with the cool kids seemed a bit superfluous and shallow. However, I felt protected by walking as if I was "above" the lesser beings, and by pretending I was in control. I wasn't fulfilled, but hey, I was just getting used to the lofty places I was climbing. I was getting "altitude sickness". However, soon enough I began sensing the meaning of being a "climber". I did a cost-benefit analysis. Ironically, it happened at church.

I went to a large church with a congregation of some of the most socially elite. The kids were on even higher social pedestals than the ones at my school—bigger fish in an even bigger pond. At times, I felt intimidated—especially by the girls. As I tried to rise to this challenge, I observed that climbing includes the risk of falling. Something happened to the family of an elite girl. I don't know exactly what happened, but this family lost their place and status in the community. I was too young to know what happened to the parents, but I watched their daughter tumble off her pedestal. People avoided her, and others outright excluded her. I watched her demeanor and even her walk change. Her eyes were lowered and her shoulders slumped forward. She was in pain. This whole experience was eye-opening for me.

I could see what was going on. And I wasn't very satisfied by the rewards of climbing the ladder. I realized that I could be forever lured from a small pond to a bigger pond and even higher ladders. There are always bigger ponds creating more stress to be the bigger fish. Social-climbing to an elite identity was a risky endeavor. Putting my biggest marbles in that pot was precarious.

I learned that social status is not just about material things. Social ladders can be built out of more than money. While money obviously bought status, I also learned that high achievement, high intelligence, and elite connections also created status. The objectives were all the same. They were all ways to place self above others. I saw that some people spent their entire lives scrambling to be above other people. I learned several things about identifying myself as a social climber. It is difficult to get to the top and stay there. Worse yet, the ladders are rickety and you can't trust their builders. You can't even get a 30-day guarantee. Worst of all, being above others seemed meaningless. I decided that the Best Life was not one's position on some contrived social ladder. I pretty much gave up my grip on the ladder.

THE INTELLECTUAL

I needed something more meaningful and less precarious to live for. I thought, okay be smart about this. In fact, I decided to literally be smart. Our school was intellectually oriented. I decided that I would find the answers to these questions intellectually and find my place in life as an "intellectual". This would be fun and exciting. I chose a few classes that I enjoyed and wholeheartedly focused on them. I became engrossed with social issues and world events. I was even chosen to participate in a nationwide program called "Great Decisions". We attended lectures by intellectuals chosen from universities or politics. We read papers and took copious notes. Later, we would gather together in forum discussions. I loved it and got passionate about the issues. In the end, I was even chosen as the Most Outstanding High School Contributor in our region. That was great, but I only got a little plaque—no money.

I was on a roll. My reading list broadened and I became engaged in the world of philosophy. My classmate's father was a professor of philosophy at the university. We had many discussions. I wanted answers—clear answers and solutions to tough questions. "What is the meaning of life? Does truth exist? How are thoughts fully communicated through language?" I found myself swimming in deep water. However, my resolve to intellectually figure out difficult life questions weakened. Who was I to critique Plato and Aristotle? What did *I* know?

Some of my smart friends didn't seem to care about finding the answers. They played the intellectual as if it was more of a game. I couldn't do that. I wanted answers. Finally, I got an idea. I would research the IQ's of all of the great philosophers. I assumed that the highest IQ equated to the smartest mind, and the smartest mind would lead me to the fullest truth. The high IQ would at least help them make the fewest intellectual mistakes. I planned to embrace the philosophy of the smartest philosopher. I thought that this would be a great shortcut to finding the answers about life.

I did a little research, and took my proposal to my favorite teacher. She listened intently, and then laughed heartily. I was devastated. I couldn't prove to her that being right and having a high IQ were objectively correlated. I couldn't prove that IQ measurements, especially of the deceased, were accurate predictors of finding truth. I couldn't figure out a path to truth except by IQ measurement. I guess I hadn't thought it through very well.

What the heck? The smartest minds differ and sometimes passionately. How could I figure out these tough life questions? Did this mean there were no answers? Or did it mean that the answers were unobtainable? Did being an intellectual ensure that my life purpose and values were the best ones for me? Thinking and questioning is fun and helpful, but a high IQ doesn't ensure being right, correct, or even finding the truth. Thinking intellectually is important, but it is not the panacea to making correct decisions about life. It helps, but more is needed. I continued to admire and follow great minds, but I lost faith in where they would take me. Not all bright minds come to the same conclusions. I learned that bright minds can create paths to almost anywhere, including where I did not want to be.

GOOD LIFE PARTIERS

The Best Life and self-concept require more than intelligence. I kept my eyes open for other choices. Perhaps I was too serious-minded, and just needed to chill out. Maybe I was expecting too much of life and my self-perception. With this in mind, a group of seniors barged in on my search. They were easy to spot, hear, and experience. They were the party animals—the pleasure seekers. The significantly meaningful life for them was sensually feeling good. To them, school was only the prep time for weekend fun. Sometimes, they just couldn't wait until Friday night. I saw little flasks of various alcohol blends secretly passed around. One guy in particular was always laughing and joking as if he had no cares or stresses, even during final exams. What a relief! This looked good and was so simple to me. There was no social stress or intellectual frustrations. I decided to focus my self-concept on being a "party boy"—a true partaker of the Good Life.

Life seemed simple. It was all about *feeling* good. I needed to find out what felt good and what felt the best. Alcohol, drugs, sex, and rock 'n roll had a big following, so I gave it a go. I went to parties, tried to laugh at everything, played pranks, and chased girls. Alcohol seemed to be the catalyst of it all. Kids got drunk and did things they would never do sober. Some of it was just embarrassing or disgusting. Afterwards, there was trouble with parents, school, and even the police. But the risks just made it more exciting. However, after a while, my grades dropped. I lost respect from my teachers. Then, my health started deteriorating. And my non-party times were unbearably boring. I couldn't party all the time. Nevertheless, I was caught up in the world of feeling good.

PARTYING TO A DEAD END

My home life was not happy. Without consciously understanding why, partying had become a retreat for me. It was a respite from the emotional tension and depression I experienced when I was home. In many ways, my stepfather was an exceptional man, but he had become an alcoholic. He had suffered trauma from flying bomber planes in the war. He had watched crewmembers die next to him. I have never been able to comprehend or relate to his horrible experiences. His alcohol use wasn't about having fun, but it was an escape. He was a stoic man. He was aloof, but charismatic. People were drawn to him.

One night I came home to find him alone. He was sitting on the couch staring at a glass full of vodka. He looked at me, and then looked away. I sat down next to him and tried to find something to say. We were silent for a while. Finally, he stood up, so I stood up. He pulled me into his towering frame, and he began to cry. I was shocked. I had never experienced anything like this in my life. I could hardly breathe. And then he released me. Out of his wallet he handed me two twenty-dollar bills. He then grabbed his suitcase from the closet and walked out the door. I sat down alone, but I couldn't make myself cry. My eyes were opened. Sensual distractions like alcohol and partying were not the substance of life. My dad was escaping. And I had been doing the same thing. My conscious and unconscious mind joined in agreement. Enough was enough.

POWER AND SELF-CONCEPT

Things were happening in the world, and some of my academic classes required reading and observing life beyond my provincial little space. There seemed to be crisis everywhere. The economy was shaky. International tensions threatened war. Racism was divisive. Authority was being questioned. And a few brave souls seemed to be taking on these problems. These were the movers and shakers in the world and in my little school. These were the power brokers who decided how money was spent, who got benefits and who didn't, what activities were promoted and what happened on all levels of society, even in high school. I decided that I needed to be a power broker.

I ran for student body offices, and I experienced a bit of success. I gave idealistic speeches to the student body, and I organized a backbreaking project to beautify the school grounds. The energy was contagious and invigorating. I was recognized as "somebody", and my decisions affected students in our little world. I don't know how much good I was doing, but it felt good to have us all working together.

The time came to pass the torch to the new student body officers. I was to give a speech. The night before the assembly, my Mom and Dad got into a horrible argument. I ended up having to physically intervene. Instead of working on my speech, I kept watch all night long. The next day, I got to school late. I was exhausted and extremely nervous that something might happen at home while I was gone. A teacher allowed me to use her office to write my speech. I went to the assembly, gave my speech, played my part, and before the assembly closed I walked off the stage and rushed home. While I was gone, all hell had broken loose. However, I was able to thwart another dangerous incident.

This experience left me wondering. I realized that I could not give my heart and soul to being a power broker. When push came to shove (literally), my devotion was to my family, not my ego. They somehow came first, even though I hated the role that I had to play. A part of me wanted to love something else besides family because they were the source of so much pain. And then again, as I sat on the stand during the assembly, I wondered what "power" really meant. I know I had good intentions for the students and the school, but I was also caught up in the image. I had enjoyed the attention. This was hard to admit.

IDENTITY AS A "JOCK"

I was a pretty good high school athlete. It was easy to experiment with being a jock. I actually came to the school to play basketball, all five feet, eight inches of me. Thank heavens a point guard is useful in basketball. I *loved* sports! I *loved* competition, and I *loved* winning. I *loved* basketball! I loved my teammates! I *loved* the camaraderie of being a team member with guys who sacrificed, sweated, and bled together. I *loved* the unity, the community of honest effort and joint focus. My teammates were great young men. We almost won the state championship. Our team represented much of what was important in life. We took care of each other. We squabbled, and then made up. We rebelled against the coach, and then came back together. We laughed and cried with our wins and our losses.

It was a great time in my life. After high school, some of my teammates went on to play basketball in college. However, it was the end of it for me. Yes, I loved the game and winning, but I loved the relationships even more. Nothing will ever compare to the intensity, preparation, and sacrifice that I experienced on that team in high school. But I still have an overzealous passion for winning. My Best Self has quite a time trying to keep a lid on winning even today.

TRANSISTION INTO THE ADULT WORLD

My adolescent search had a few common denominators. In each of various identities, I was looking for something. I felt empty in some way or unfulfilled. I was definitely searching for an identity that had a place in my little world. I wanted to know that life was worth living and how to "do it". At some level, we all have this void to fill. Our aim is to leave behind footprints in the world. We want to make a difference. We want to leave a legacy. There are many paths in this quest.

I mistakenly assumed that the Good Life was the Best Life. I was absorbed with the big ME. This is a normal state during adolescence. I wanted to feel good and look good. Whether partying, climbing the social ladder, or being a leader, I thought only of how it affected *me*. I wallowed in the physical sensations and emotions of my experiences. I was led by whatever sensations were most pleasant and rewarding. My motivation for living the Good Life was simply how "good" I felt.

These high school self-concepts don't end with graduation. They simply become more sophisticated as we move into the adult world. Many of us are still stuck on some identity that we hope will lead us to the Good Life. Unfortunately, we probably haven't clearly differentiated the Good Life from the Best Life. We get them mixed up. Some of us continue catering to a self-centered image or we forever chase what promises to maximize our pleasure.

AVOIDING A GOOD LIFE STEREOTYPE

Let me ask a hard, personal question. Have you ever embraced one of these self-centered identities as a pillar of your own self-perception? Are you stuck in the Good Life? Are you consciously or unconsciously hoping that a rich meaningful life comes from being a Social Climber, a Partier, a jock-like Competitor, a know-it-all Expert, or a Power Broker? Everyone feels the pull of these intoxicating identities at some point. Which one speaks to you? With which one do you struggle the most?

I endorse the title of DiSalvo's book, *What Makes Your Brain Happy and Why You Should Do the Opposite.* We struggle with our intentions—how much should be self-oriented and how much should be other-oriented. Meaningful, purposeful living comes from a constant, flowing mix of the two until finally they become the same. Remember, part of who we are is dependent on who the others are in our life. A meaningful life requires taking care of our inner self and our outer self, our connections to other people. In fact, that is who we are in total, a mix of the "us" within and our other relationships.

FILLING THE VOID WITHIN US

I noticed a common objective in each self-concept I embraced as an adolescent. I unconsciously was drawn to find meaningful relationships through each identity. Whether it was at a party, organizing an activity, or engaging in discussions, I was looking for relational connections. Even in my intellectual pursuits, I constantly looked forward to not only discovering an interesting idea, but also discussing and sharing it with other people. Winning or losing a basketball game was important, but the well-being of my team members was even more important. I was particularly disappointed at the lack of connection with others at parties. Much of the interaction was about how to use others for gain and pleasure. That gets old quickly.

What I was really looking for was quality, virtuous relationships in all those roles. I wanted to respect and be respected by those on my team. I wanted to trust and be trusted by those who I worked with in student government. I wanted to feel like I mattered and contributed to the elitists who owned the social ladder. I wanted to feel intimacy and closeness with the scholars as we shared and immersed ourselves in great ideas and personal insights. I really didn't understand at the time that was at the heart of my quest. I was more consciously focused on the activities of each identity, rather than on the relationships. I was a victim of my own naïve mind.

OUR ROLES WITHIN THE BEST LIFE

The Best Life is about quality, virtuous relationships we have in all of our life roles and contexts. At times, we may play the role of: sibling, parent, employer, professional, confidant, bridge partner, or skiing companion. The point is, caring for other people as much as ourselves (or even more so at times) enriches the meaning and purpose of our lives. Virtuous trustworthiness allows closeness and intimacy to take place. We are enriched along with those we serve. Character is built through hard knocks, effort, and sacrifice. That's why we respect and cherish those of great character.

The Best Life is not any specific activity, pursuit, vocation or sensation. We can have the Best Life in prison, school, at work or play. We and the bigger world are in a better place when we live our Best Life.

For some reason this belief is elusive and even repugnant to some people. These people prefer the Good Life. But they should not be harshly judged for their decision. Our worth is not based on our belief system. However, our personal health and well-being depends on living the Best Life not the Good Life. Think about it. We hold ourselves accountable and responsible about how we live the Best Life not the Good Life. Our conscience may speak to us about lying or stealing, but rarely does it hold us accountable for not getting drunk enough at a party.

The Best Life path is the more difficult way but the most life rewarding. For some of us it is a paradox, because obtaining the Best Life is sometimes painful and difficult, but the ends, the aims, and final objectives are wonderful. As previously mentioned, it's also healthier than the Good Life.

THE BEST LIFE OF LOVING OTHERS

In summary, our purposeful self-concept can be well served by embracing the identity of the Best Person we can be. Developing forgiveness, kindness, fairness, courage, fortitude, love, and integrity are the building blocks of the Best Person. As we frame our self-concepts these virtues are most important in developing quality relationships.

This recommendation is certainly a subjective judgment on my part. It comes from a bit of intellectual searching, experience, and observing other people. It also comes from a life of "hard knocks". You can distinguish the Good Life from the Best Life just by living life. Much of what we know comes from comparing and contrasting our life experiences. We often don't appreciate what we have or understand its meaning and significance until we lose it. The contrast of having and not having, unveils knowledge of the highest order.

FULLY EMBRACING THE BEST LIFE

Sometimes, we are fortunate enough to have something precious but unappreciated that we sadly lose only to finally reacquire. When this happens we gratefully treat what is precious as if it was precious. A more passionate and enlightened commitment to the Best Life came to me as an adult.

I have mentioned being in an automobile accident in which my wife was killed, and I was critically injured—almost killed. I was disfigured with every bone in my face broken. I lost the person that I loved the most in the entire world. She was a Best Person, an inspiration not to just me but to everyone who was fortunate enough to know her. She lived the Best Life.

I lay on the hospital bed, I wondered if I would be blind, or mentally or physically handicapped. I also wondered if I would be alone. I cannot explain the thoughts and sensations that overwhelmed me. I imagined pictures of my children having no mother and no father. I know that they were thinking of me and wondering if I would be okay. I thought of the many children who I had helped in the past. I also thought of other adolescents who were miserable and at risk for all kinds of destruction. A feeling overwhelmed me that I must live, that I *would* live, and that life was a gift to me so I could give back to them. More than ever, I *knew* that I was needed and that my life mission was not yet complete.

With this spiritual experience, I made a fast (if not a miraculous) recovery. I knew more than ever what the Best Life was for me. I knew even more clearly *who* I wanted to be. I wanted a life full of significant meaning and connections. I'm still working on it. My hope is that you might have the Best Life. My hope is that you may experience love, respectful connections to others, and have opportunities for service. I know that you have been through more challenging experiences than I have endured. I hope that by comparing and contrasting those experiences, you will be led to the Best Life. I also hope that all of us can learn from each other vicariously without suffering more than is needful. It is in that hope that I have written this book.

Life is not just an intellectual experience. It is the continual act of being in the here and now and honoring and loving the people in our life. That seems to be what is most universally needed and craved by humankind. We need each other to be at our best.

Appendix

Defining Determinism: You Have Choices Beyond "Meat"

I will not attempt to prove that biological determinism is absolutely false in this chapter. I can't. Nobody can because all of the evidence has not been uncovered. In addition, intelligent, scientific explanations of the evidence can be made for and against determinism's effect on accountability. Scientific consensus backing determinism does not exist. Likewise, nobody can prove that moral choice absolutely does not exist. This dispute has been going on for hundreds of years.

However, I will provide rational reasons to justify *not* believing in determinism. No scientific evidence exists that prescribes everyone to believe in determinism. Reasonable minds can differ, and good reason exists to believe in choice rather than determinism. In spite of the "majority's" influence, you don't have to jump on their bandwagon. You don't have to abandon taking charge of who you perceive yourself to be, or who you are becoming, because of this huge obstacle called determinism.

Let me introduce three scientific theories that **give you permission** to logically and reasonably believe that you are more than a piece of deterministic meat. You can believe that you have agentic, moral choice, rather than being a biological morsel somewhere in the food chain.

The three theories are uniquely different from one another. I will introduce each theory through a scientist who proposes that theory. Each scientist has radically different reasons for advocating a belief in choice. Nevertheless, each scientist champions believing in choice and accountability, in spite of the classic, genetic theories of determinism.

I will first summarize each of the three theories. After the summaries, we will have a general idea what each theory professes. I will then take each theory separately and explain them in greater depth. By first summarizing and then fleshing out the theories, you can understand them more easily. Each theory can assist us to rationally believe in choice, and to not be locked into determinism.

We don't want to get bogged down with scientific theory in this book. However, believing in choice is so important in creating a meaningful self-concept and the Best Life that I would be remiss in not giving you a few rational, scientific reasons to overcome the choice-destroying influences of determinism. Let's first summarize the main point of each theory. Each one provides a different reason to believe in choice and to not be bullied by classical determinism.

First, Michael Gazzaniga explains that because of Emergence Theory, we are genetically determined to believe in choice.[1] Our genes compel us to believe that we have choice. Paradoxically, we must believe in choice, even though moral choice doesn't exist according to him.

Second, Bruce Lipton interprets the Theory of Epigenetics to mean that our beliefs override the supposed mechanistic behavior of our genes. In other words, our beliefs influence whether or not a gene is activated.[12] Our genes contain the specific plans of our body's structure and functional capabilities. "Activate" means that the plan will be set in motion. Just because we have a specific gene, doesn't mean it will activate. The gene cannot activate itself. It has to be activated from a source outside the gene. Our chosen beliefs can be that outside source. In other words, our non-determined beliefs can activate a gene, or cause it *not* to activate. The power of determinism is therefore overruled by our beliefs.

Third, Daniel Coyle argues that since we don't know our genetic limitations, we should not hallucinate what they might be.[3] We can only know our limits by "doing stuff". The myelination process within each of our cells controls our efficiency in performing tasks. We won't know what our limitations are until we maximize this myelination process. In other words, we should act as if we don't have genetic limitations in our endeavors. In many pursuits, we need not worry that we are limited by biological determinism. We can act as if the sky is the limit until we have maximized the myelination process within our cells.

SIGNIFICANCE OF THREE VERY DIFFERENT THEORIES

Providing us with three different theories or reasons to believe in choice is useful. One theory might appeal to one of us more than another. The cumulative value of three separate reasons to believe in choice might be persuasive. In any event, these theories demonstrate that not all scientists believe in determinism, and for well thought out reasons. We can be rationally skeptical of determinism.

INTRODUCTION SUMMARY OF EMERGENCE THEORY

The Emergence Theory speaks to those of us who are more comfortable viewing life scientifically. Many of us may be more comfortable if all phenomena can be explained as laws acting on matter. We value reason and the scientific (empirical) process as our best source for truth. Explanations outside of science make our palms sweat and raise our eyebrows. Fortunately, we can be comfortable believing in choice because of the Emergence Theory.

Not accepting determinism does not mean we reject science. On the contrary, scientific theories can support our acceptance or desire to believe in choice. We can rely on the methods of science to help us understand why we are driven to want choice in our lives rather than being puppets. Emergence Theory provides us scientific justification for believing in choice, while also validating the biological evolutionary process. This theory also helps us understand that science is evolving, even the science of evolution.

Dr. Michael Gazzaniga's emergent-based theory amends the concept of biological determinism to explain why we *need* to believe in choice. He proposes that humankind is genetically driven to believe that we have agentic choice when we actually don't. Emergence Theory explains how this could happen. Emergence-based evolution is not just single or individual organisms genetically evolving one mutation at a time. That is a rather slow linear process. He says there is another evolutionary process that causes *group* mutations. Somehow, similar individuals within a group can simultaneously change (mutate). Mutations of groups rather than individuals, reflect a different level of the evolutionary process. He hypothesizes that humankind's need to believe in choice was created by an evolutionary level leap that occurred to protect our species. Somehow, our genes perceived that believing in choice assisted our survival. Our need to believe in choice resulted from mutations dynamically created in this "level" process.

He states that this compelling need to believe in choice evolved in spite of humans actually having no real choice. This theory may sound contradictory in some ways, but hopefully you can see his logic as I describe the basics of his theory later. The mutation to "believe in choice" was passed on to future generations because according to Dr. Gazzaniga, it assisted the survival of the species. Of course, recognizing emergent levels of evolutionary change is a major shift in the classic theory of Darwinian evolution. Nevertheless, Emergence Theory gives us permission and persuasive reasons to believe in choice. Who would have thought that determinism (the dreaded enemy of choice) would provide a deterministic requirement to believe in choice?

This Emergence Theory allows Dr. Gazzaniga to logically explain that acts of apparent human altruism do not contradict evolutionary determinism. People act altruistically because their genes are programmed to make them appear to be altruistic. Of course, construing altruistic acts as being motivated by selfishness keeps the flame of evolutionary determinism alive.

EMERGENCE THEORY IN GREATER DETAIL—DR. MICHAEL S. GAZZANIGA

Dr. Gazzaniga was impressed by a large survey of persons in 36 countries revealing that 70% of them believed that their life was in their own hands.[4] This reinforced his belief that most people want to have a sense of control in life. He discovered research suggesting that beliefs about determinism affected how people follow laws or rules. One empirical study tested students' propensity to cheat in accordance with their exposure to deterministic theory. In this experiment, one group of students was given excerpts from books biased in favor of determinism. Another group was given excerpts from a book about positive outlook. Afterwards, both groups were given a test requiring all students to answer computer-based questions. They were told that the computer software had a glitch that would allow the right answer to appear on the screen. To prevent this from happening, the students were instructed to push a particular computer key that would prevent the answer from popping up on the screen. Students reading deterministic bias excerpts cheated by not using that computer key to prevent the right answer from appearing on their screen. However, the students reading the positive attitude material did not cheat.

His conclusion was that disbelieving in free will "produces a subtle cue that exerting effort is futile, thus granting permission not to bother."[5] Believing in choice requires exertion and energy, and people do not want to waste either. Nevertheless, he observes that people deterministically want to believe in free will, and it may be crucial to control selfishness. Determinism also asserts that people are first and foremost "selfish" and cannot act otherwise. This precludes truly unselfish behavior. Gazzaniga was impressed by studies that consistently recorded human babies acting unselfishly. Arguments were made by other determinists trying to explain the babies' behavior as having some ulterior, selfish motive. Gazzaniga didn't buy it. He concluded that the babies' unselfish behavior demonstrated an inherent desire to be altruistic.

DR. GAZZANIGA'S COMMITMENT TO DETERMINISM AND EVOLUTION, BUT ALSO CHOICE AND ACCOUNTABILITY

In spite of these studies and conclusions that undermine determinism, Dr. Gazzaniga refused to abandon genetic evolutionary theory. In fact, he says, "Determinism reigns—both physical and social—and we are asked to accept it, and to move on. Einstein bought it. Spinoza bought it. Who are we to question it?" However, he was also convinced that humans really do believe and act as if they have choice. He says, "We are personally responsible agents and are to be held accountable for our actions, even though we live in a determined universe."

Paradoxically, he was committed to humans believing in altruism and acting altruistically in spite of his belief in determinism. As quoted, he thought that humans should be socially and legally responsible for their actions in spite of having no real choice. Using this theory, he continues his ardent commitment to evolution and determinism, while recognizing that humans have legitimate desires and needs to believe in choice, act altruistically, and be accountable for their actions.

EMERGENCE THEORY AND LEVELS OF EVOLUTION IN ACTION

Let me begin by recounting a study that illustrates Emergence Theory and Levels of Evolution. Certain species of ants and termites group together. When the group or colony reaches a certain number, the members begin building a huge, tower-like structure. This only happens when the group number hits a certain size. There is nothing in the ants or termites individual behavior that would indicate or predict this type of behavior. Therefore, spontaneously building the structure is not a mutation-based linear change as seen in classical evolution. Studying the single insects reveals nothing to predict this behavior. However, when the insects *together* reach a certain size they spontaneously collaborate to build the structure. Somehow their "relationship" (when numbers reach a critical mass) unleashes behavior that linear evolution can't explain very well. An emergence has occurred, a break happens in the linear evolutionary pattern or symmetry.[6]

Dr. Gazzaniga explains how an emergent level theory of evolution can account for the ants and termites "group behavioral leap". He believes that this explanation is necessary to protect the theoretical viability of the biological evolutionary process. First, appreciate how difficult it is to explain how all of the insects within a group spontaneously start building a tower because the group has reached a critical number by only using classic evolutionary theory. The old classic theory says that one member of a species has one mutation at a time *separate* from all other members of the species. One favorable mutation in one insect would only be passed on to its own posterity. The termite or ant study uncovered insect behavior that challenges the exclusivity of this linear process.

An alternative to the linear mutation theory was needed to protect the integrity of determinism. Dr. Gazzaniga describes how the "levels" within a structure can interact in such a way that individual parts within the structure have to quickly change. In this case, all of the insects had to genetically change as levels of structure interacted in a unique way. What was the *organizational or structural lev*el. He believe it was the colony's population size reaching a critical level.

In reading his theory, the definition of levels can seem rather obtuse. It's hard to picture a level. He uses the word "level" to abstractly describe a synergetic mix of dynamic factors. What are dynamic factors? I suppose they could be many things. In this case, he refers to organizational or structural dynamics. Population size was inferred to be a structural dynamic.

The relationships between these levels are called "emergent relationships". Why? He explains that emerging change (evolutionary change for the insects), can occur when an organism's organizational structural level interacts with the organizational structural level of environmental factors outside itself. **The interaction of the levels unleashes energy that changes the organism's behavior.** The nature of these structures and the source of energy are not explained clearly, because he does not claim to understand them.

In his book, *Who's in Charge?: Free Will and the Science of the Brain,* he describes what he thinks happened in human evolution. "Something like the big bang happened when mind emerged from the brain."[7] This is a new "level of organization" for the brain. The interaction of these levels unleashed an energy that led to changes in behavior or mutations programming the human mind to desire to believe, "that choice matters". He calls these relationships, "the space in between" which lead to significant, evolutionary steps being taken.

He wants to establish that emergent energy is not just an anomaly of biological evolution. Any network system of any kind relies on accountability of its parts in order to work. When levels of structure interact in a relationship their parts must responsibly step up for a new behavior to emerge. For example a human society or social group has members who possess personal responsibility. The predictable behavior of the individuals helps create the cohesion required to be a group.

Unfortunately, he does not claim to adequately understand how relational dynamics works or how energy is released during group mutation. For Gazzaniga, this phenomenon is a priority for further research. Therefore, let's not feel lost in following his logic; it needs more work. The framework is there, but obviously there are many questions to explore that may enhance the believability of his theory. He quotes another well-known scientist to encourage further consideration of his emergence theory.

"Dr. Marder's work has revealed the problem for neuroscientists. The task is to further understand how the various layers of the brain interact, indeed how to even think about it and develop concepts and a vocabulary for those inter-dependent interactions. Working from this perspective has the possibility of not only demystifying what is truly meant by concepts such as emergence, but also allows for insights on how layers actually communicate with one another."[8]

With Emergence Theory we have permission to accept our innate urging and believe in choice as well as altruism. He says it would be good for the individual as well as the species. You just "gotta do it".

INTRODUCTION SUMMARY OF EPIGENETICS

Epigenetics is another scientific theory and explanation demonstrating the evolution of gene or DNA theory. Dr. Lipton's interpretation and extrapolation of epigenetics has not emerged into the mainstream of scientific thought. Lipton's version of Epigenetics attempts to explain how our beliefs somewhat control the genetic function within our cells. The key point here is that the acting intelligence is *outside* of the gene, not inside. If the gene's action is partially reliant on an outside intelligence, the chain of determinism is broken. Logic follows that if a choice exists within a person's cells, then choice exists for the whole person that is made up of those cells. Even if we are not persuaded to completely adopt Lipton's explanation, we can recognize that he presents a logical scientific theory. The truth of this theory—like other scientific theories—has not been unequivocally proved, but its reasoning and possibilities can give us reason to question determinism.

Dr. Bruce Lipton concludes that people's non-determined beliefs can *control* the genetic process, and therefore agentic choice is preserved. This is his theory of **Epigenetics.** By "control", I mean that the genetic codes within genes are not automatically activated or manifested. They are not self-triggered. For example, a gene may contain a code for eyes to be crossed. Unless that code is triggered, the gene will not create crossed eyes. The prefix, epi-, means "above". In this case, epi- refers to beliefs being "above" the gene itself by controlling when the gene is triggered.

Dr. Lipton states that the triggering is determined by an "intelligence" that interprets whether, in its present environment, the gene *should* be triggered. There is a choice. Environmental factors occur that could potentially affect the gene and its activation. However, these factors don't always automatically trigger the gene. An "intelligence" *interprets* the *meaning* of the factors before deciding whether or not to activate the gene. According to Lipton, this intelligence includes our non-determined personal beliefs.

EPIGENETICS—DR. BRUCE LIPTON

Genetic Research Has Not Accomplished Hoped for Expectations

Currently, millions and millions of dollars are being spent on genetic research. The Human Genome Project to map all the genes in a human being has made front-page news, although the project's enthusiasm has diminished.[9] Why all the interest in genetics? Because genes hold the blueprint for an organism, including a human organism. This blueprint includes not only the anatomical structure, but also the physiological possibilities of that person. Everyone has the same number of genes, and each of them has a specific blueprint that can be activated. Theoretically, you are a manifestation of your genetic blueprint. It was thought that if we can equate each gene to an anatomical and physiological function, we could predict and possibly engineer how people turn out. This includes brain function, emotion, immune functions, as well as muscular and skeletal appearance.

This has not proven to be the case. The mere existence of a gene does not mean that it will be activated or expressed. Something else must happen *to* the gene. Scientists have found that genes are "linked" to different diseases and traits, but researchers have rarely found that one gene causes a disease or a trait. In other words, genes are necessary for the manifestation of traits or susceptibility to disease. However, the gene by itself is not sufficient to "cause" most traits or a disease. There is a difference between being a necessary link and a sufficient cause.

Our genetics is a necessary cause of our structure, biological functions, and even our behavior. It is a necessary part. However, it is not by itself sufficient to be the independent cause of all of these things. We happily acknowledge that genetic research continues to be extremely important with all types of possible uses. Nevertheless, genetics controlling the "ultimate cause", the panacea everyone was hoping for, has not come to pass.

THE GUTS OF EPIGENETICS

What does this unpredictability in gene behavior suggest? Lipton understood that the gene could not turn itself on or off; it was not "self-emergent". (Remember the concept of emergence from Dr. Gazzaniga.) Generally, there is no guarantee that the gene's blueprint will ever turn on or off. The percentage of predictability for being triggered is generally unknown. A specific environmental factor alone could not create absolute predictability in how a gene would react. The environmental factor at a particular time has to be evaluated. Something has to genetically interpret the significance of an environment factor's influence on the gene. That "something" (according to Lipton) is the mind. Consequently, the cell has a choice about whether to trigger the gene or not. His conclusion was that "[...]the fully conscious mind trumps both nature and nurture."[10] This mindful interpretation of an outside factor breaks the assumed automatic chain reaction of classical genetic determinism. For him, the scientific and personal implications of intelligent interpretation were outrageously important. He concluded, "So many of us are leading limited lives not because we have to but because we think we have to."[11]

THE IMPLICATIONS OF EPIGENETICS

Self-concept is a conglomeration of beliefs that can affect your genetics. He points out that we need to be careful about the positivity or negativity of our thoughts. I would add—especially in terms of our self-perception. He says, "Positive thoughts have a profound affect on behavior and genes but only in harmony with subconscious programming. And negative thoughts have an equally powerful effect."[12] In other words, learning to control our thoughts, especially the positive or negative tenor of them, directly affects the quality of our life, even genetically. For example, we may be genetically predisposed to some type of cancer. Nevertheless, our thoughts and attitude may influence whether the gene is triggered on or off. Having the gene does not predestine us to have the cancer.

However, this insight does not suggest an easy formula for implementation. He refers to the subconscious mind and the conscious mind "interfacing" as part of the thought process. This may coincidentally refer to the relationship of so called brain levels proposed by Gazzaniga. We need to understand and acquire skills to consciously and intelligently interface the two. The interfacing process of the conscious and subconscious minds will continue to be a highlight of this book.

Lipton's theories not only free you from the perceived limitations of biological determinism, it can also empower you to believe in the emergent "reality" of your self-concept. Your perceived self is not just an ephemeral essence floating around in space. It is couched in relationships and is integrated into your biology, your genetics, and your Best Life. He describes how this empowerment helped him move from a depressed, personal victim, to a vibrant, happy, co-creator of his own destiny.

INTRODUCTION SUMMARY OF MYELINATION

Dr. Daniel Coyle primarily writes to encourage and instruct people how to develop their talents and abilities. He does not directly address the validity or correctness of classical determinism. However, he gives you another logical, rational reason to believe in choice. Coyle may particularly appeal to those who think, "Don't tell me my life is pre-programmed. Get out of my way. I don't have to believe you if I don't want to." His theory of myelination suggests that in developing your talents and self-concept, you can personally ignore what others might consider your genetic limitations. Why? Because, some of your genetic limitations are unknown to them and yourself, and to believe in "hallucinated" limitations undermine what you can become. If you fall into this category, you will enjoy his theory.

Myelination describes the cellular process of how skill sets and abilities are created and enhanced. Myelination also describes the process of how your cells maximize your genetic abilities. Dr. Coyle proposes that your potential abilities are greater than you assume they are. He uses examples of excellence achieved by small groups of people in diverse geographic areas where genetics cannot logically explain the excellence of the groups.

MYELINATION—DANIEL COYLE

Genetics and Environment Alone Cannot Explain World-Class Talent Much Less Our Potential

Coyle has reviewed many studies about high-achievers. The following study demonstrates how more than genes and environment are needed to predict high achievement. A group of 157 randomly selected children (most were age 7 or 8) beginning music classes were studied for several years. The kids were tracked using interviews, biometric tests, and videotaped practice sessions. Predictably, as time went on some kids took off and played well, while others were in the middle, and a few barely budged. Years passed. The researchers looked for patterns linking the successful students and which distinguished them from the others. They evaluated IQ, aural sensitivity, math skills, sense of rhythm, sensor motor skills, and income levels. They could not find an explanatory pattern. Finally, they reviewed the initial interviews. A key question had been asked. "How long do you think you'll play your new instrument?" The options were: through this year, through primary school, through high school, and throughout my life. Bingo! They found a telling correlation.

"The differences were staggering. With the same amount of practice, the long-term commitment group outperformed the short-term commitment group by 400 percent. The long-term group, with a mere twenty minutes of weekly practice, progressed faster than the short-termers who practiced for an hour and a half. When long-term commitment combined with high levels of practice, skills skyrocketed." Coyle quoted the researcher McPherson. "At some point very early on they had a crystallizing experience that brings the idea to the forefront, that says, I am a musician. That idea is like a snowball rolling downhill."[13] Self concept, that's what I'm talking about.

Let's look at a few hotbeds of world-class talent. Over the last 10 years, Russian women have filled the professional women's tennis tour with star performers. Coyle discovered that they were coming from one small community in Russia. He traveled there, and found, that the "penniless tennis club with one indoor court created more top-twenty women players than the entire United States." The phenomenon had come out of nowhere, and neither genetics, nor training facilities could explain it.

The Dominican Republic on an island in the Caribbean had no player in the major leagues until the 1950's. Now 1 in 9 major leaguers is from the Dominican Republic. He found another example in South Korea. South Korean women claimed their first LPGA tournament win in 1998. Now, there are forty-five on the tour including eight of the top twenty money winners. Coyle identified what he called "explosions" of talent throughout history. For example, the city of Florence, during the Italian Renaissance had a small population of only 70,000 people. In spite of this small number, it produced a plethora of art talent unmatched before or since.[14] What could explain these remarkable anomalies? Genetics and environment are inadequate explanations.

MYELINATION BUILDS TALENT

Myelin itself is simply the outer part of a cell. All of our body cells contain myelin. He described its importance. "Every human skill, whether it's playing baseball or playing Bach, is created by chains of nerve fibers carrying a tiny electrical impulse—basically, a signal traveling through a circuit. Myelin's vital role is to wrap those nerve fibers the same way that rubber insulation wraps a copper wire, making the signal stronger and faster by preventing the electrical impulses from leaking out. When we fire our circuits in the right way—when we practice swinging that bat or playing that note—our myelin responds by wrapping layers of insulation around that neural circuit, each new layer adding a bit more skill and speed. The thicker the myelin gets, the better it insulates, and the faster and more accurate our movements and thoughts become. [...] Skill is a cellular insulation that wraps neural circuits and that grows in response to certain signals."[15]

What Coyle believes is that the athletes, artists, and musicians in these concentrated, geographical areas developed an extraordinary amount of myelin for their particular skill sets. Obviously, measuring the myelin in the living brain has mortality issues. It's hard to find volunteers. However, the morgue has been a friendly place to research myelin's characteristics on a cellular level. Postmortem evaluations of human brain material have been useful. Einstein's brain was preserved after death and evaluated for differences with other human brains. There was no significant difference in the number of brain cells, however Einstein's brain had twice as much myelin in locations tied to analytical thinking as other brains. Everyone has myelin, and it grows faster during childhood than later. Nevertheless, myelin can be developed and enhanced throughout life. The question becomes, "How can you do it?"

HOW TO BUILD MYELIN

Finding the edge of your ability is critical. If you make recognizable mistakes and then correct them, you are building myelin. This process requires a slowing down to incrementally recognize mistakes as well as implement corrections. He quotes Bartzokis to distinguish most of us from super achievers. "They send precise impulses along wires that give the signal to myelinate that wire. They end up, after all the training, with a super-duper wire—lots of bandwidth, a high-speed T-3 line. That's what makes them different from us."[16] Coyle believes that 10,000 corrections of a skill are required to be world-class. Notice that does not mean 10,000 practice sessions. Repetition is important, but it doesn't create significant myelin by itself. Multiple corrections are the key. Not everyone wants to be world-class in a particular skill. However, you get the idea, being really good at something requires lots of mistakes and corrections. Coyle has broken down the process of building myelin into three categories: Deep Practice, Ignition, and Master Coaching.

I. Deep Practice

"Deep practice is built on a paradox: struggling in certain targeted ways—operating at the edges of your ability, where you make mistakes—makes you smarter[...] experiences where you're forced to slow down, make errors, and correct them—as you would if you were walking up an ice-covered hill, slipping and stumbling as you go—end up making you swift and graceful without your realizing it [...] The trick is to choose a goal just beyond your present abilities to target the struggle. Thrashing blindly doesn't help. Reaching does."[17]

Ii. Ignition

"This is how ignition works. Where deep practice is a cool, conscious act, ignition is a hot mysterious burst, an awakening. Where deep practice is an incremental wrapping, ignition works through lightning flashes of image and emotion, evolution-built neural programs that tap into the mind's vast reserves of energy and attention. Where deep practice is all about staggering-baby steps, ignition is about the set of signals and subconscious forces that create our identity, the moments that lead us to say that is who I want to be. We usually think of passion as an inner quality. But the more I visited hotbeds, the more I saw it as something that came first from the outside world. In the hotbeds the right butterfly wing flap was causing talent hurricanes."[18]

He found these mysterious bursts, these butterfly wing flaps originating in **relationships.** Relationships of various kinds ignited these athletes and performers. He found these seeds in the hotbeds. At the old tennis facility in Russia, a young woman reached international prominence by winning a couple of tournaments. Girls who had beaten her in practice were enthralled. "If she can do it, and I can beat her, I can do it too." The same type of trigger happened with the South Korean golfers. As soon as one of them won an international tournament, her peers also began to explode on the scene. The most famous example may be Roger Bannister, who broke the four-minute mile barrier. No one thought it would ever be done. Roger did it, and within three years over ten more runners broke the barrier. He released the dam, and others wanted to be in his class. This relational phenomenon in short may be called "future belonging". It is compelling. There are many more relational triggers.

Iii. Master Coaching

Master Coaching is the last of Coyle's three requirements to building high-level myelin. A master coach is someone who can effectively help you build the myelin for a particular skill or skill set. Yes, there is some motivation provided by the coach. However, you want to build myelin, and that requires an intelligent breakdown of skill sets, repetitions, corrections, and more repetitions. A master coach can help you know how to "train" for whatever skill you are seeking, whether it is mental, physical, or social. The athletes and musicians in our examples had those kinds of coaches. In your life, how much effort have you made to find the coaches/mentors who can do this for you? Once, you are conscious of the need, you can begin to focus on who can help you. Go and make that connection. If you really want to be good at something, a master coach or mentor can make the difference. Coyle describes some of the characteristics of the coaches he found in the talent hotbeds. Rather than the "rah-rah" associated with successful coaches, he saw other important factors.

"Instead, the teachers and coaches I met were quiet, even reserved. They were mostly older; many had been teaching thirty or forty years. They possessed the same sort of gaze; steady, deep, unblinking. They listened far more than they talked. They seemed allergic to giving pep talks or inspiring speeches; they spent most of their time offering small, targeted, highly specific adjustments. They had an extraordinary sensitivity to the person they were teaching, customizing each message to each student's personality."[19]

They could not be called flashy or even charismatic, but they understood skills and skill sets, and they could break them down for their players with lots of repetitions. Additionally, they treated different players differently, understanding that personalities and temperaments matter. These coaches assumed participants already had enthusiasm, or they wouldn't be there. They needed confidence, and that comes from real progress towards mastery.

Coyle discovered when Deep Practice, Ignition, and Master Coaching were combined, world-class talent could be created. In fact, these factors were necessary. Players also needed good genes connected to strength, agility, and coordination. Technology cannot look at your genetics and your environment, and set rigid limits on what you can or cannot do or who you can become.

Coyle suggests not to irrationally place limits on yourself. By using myelination, you can ultimately reach a high level of performance in activities required by your self-concept. You don't know how high until you try.

IMPLICATIONS OF MYELENATION

What does this mean about your self-concept? First, understanding myelination creates a new world of possibilities for perceiving and creating "you". Yes, there are limitations and potential strengths incorporated into your genetics. However, no one gave you a handbook of what you can and cannot do. Your range of competency leading to excellence is unknown, only to be discovered experientially by doing. You have myelin! You can be good—if not great—at something, or many things. Knowing that you are not shackled by imagined, ambiguous genetic limitations, gives you freedom and encouragement to follow your interests, passions, and inclinations. You can grow your self-concept right along with your myelin. Does this mean you can do *anything* you want? Heaven forbid! Does it mean you have possibilities you have been afraid to believe? Most certainly! Does this mean you might fail? Absolutely! Failure is feedback, and is your best friend for progressing.

You must understand that mistakes are required to move beyond the limiting shadow of determinism. Our culture stresses looking good, frequently at the expense of being good. The ignorant and uninformed majority believes that failure doesn't look good. Somehow, we are beguiled to believe that if it looks good, it must be good, and if it looks bad it must be bad. We have forgotten the saying about the book and the cover.

A self-concept built on just looking good has grave limitations. Marrying a really "good-looking" spouse may initially feel good. However, if that spouse has limited character and capabilities, divorce may be around the corner. Are you afraid to try things because you may not look good or competent in the beginning? Is your present self-concept attempting to build and protect an image? If so you are trapped in a world of gross limitation.

Myelination joins many forces demonstrating the power of relationships. Your ignition requires inspiring and barrier breaking connections with other people. Consciously seeking those connections can help you. A coach or mentor is another important relationship that can help you break out into your self-concept. How comforting to know that when we unconsciously seek to fulfill our self-perceived destiny, we attract those people who can help us.

We now have at least three scientific theories taking us beyond the barriers of determinism. We have permission to seriously and knowledgably embrace choice. We also have insight in taking advantage of choices beyond what we may have previously imagined.

NOTES

1. Gazzaniga, M. (2011). *Who's in Charge? Free Will and the Science of the Brain*. New York, NY: HarperCollins Publishers, Inc.
2. Lipton, B. (2012). *The Biology of Belief: Unleashing the Power of Consciousness, Matter & Miracles*. Carlsbad, CA: Hay House, Inc.
3. Coyle, D. (2009). *The Talent Code*. New York, NY: Bantam Books.
4. Gazzaniga, M. (2011). *Who's in Charge? Free Will and the Science of the Brain*. New York, NY: HarperCollins Publishers, Inc.
5. (Gazzaniga, 2011).
6. (Gazzaniga, 2011).
7. (Gazzaniga, 2011).
8. (Gazzaniga, 2011).
9. Gannett, L. (2010). The Human Genome Project. *The Stanford Encyclopedia of Philosophy*, Edward N. Zalta (Ed.).Retrieved from http://plato.stanford.edu/archives/fall2010/entries/human-genome.
10. Lipton, B. (2012). *The Biology of Belief: Unleashing the Power of Consciousness, Matter & Miracles*. Carlsbad, CA: Hay House, Inc.
11. (Lipton, 2012).
12. (Lipton, 2012).
13. Coyle, D. (2009). *The Talent Code*. New York, NY: Bantam Books.
14. (Coyle, 2009).
15. (Coyle, 2009).
16. (Coyle, 2009).
17. (Coyle, 2009).
18. (Coyle, 2009).
19. (Coyle, 2009).

Bibliography

2014. In *Dictionary.com*. Retrieved May 27, 2014, from http://dictionary.reference.com/browse/religion

2014. In *Merriam-Webster.com*. Retrieved May 27, 2014, from http://www.merriam-webster.com/dictionary/illusion

2014. In *Merriam-Webster.com*. Retrieved May 8, 2014, from http://www.merriam-webster.com/dictionary/insatiable

Alexander E. (2012). *Proof of Heaven: A Neurosurgeon's Journey into the Afterlife.* New York, NY: Simon & Schuster.

Appelbaum, P. Law & psychiatry: Regulating psychotherapy or restricting freedom of speech? California's ban on sexual orientation efforts. *Psychiatric Services, 65.*

Coyle, D. (2009). *The Talent Code.* New York, NY: Bantam Books.

Csikszentmihalyi, M. (1990). *Flow: The Psychology of Optimal Experience.* New York, NY: Harper & Row.

Damasio, A. (2010). *Self Comes to Mind: Constructing the Conscious Brain.* New York, NY: Pantheon Books.

Descartes, R. (1996). *Meditations on First Philosophy With Selections from the Objections and Replies* John Cottingham, (Ed.). Cambridge, United Kingdom: Cambridge University Press.

Dickens, P. (2000). *Social Darwinism: Linking Evolutionary Thought to Social Theory.* Philadephia, PA: Open University Press.

DiSalvo, D. (2011). *What Makes Your Brain Happy and Why You Should Do the Opposite.* Amherst, NY: Prometheus Books.

Doyle, B. (2011). *Free Will: The Scandal in Philosophy.* Cambridge, MA: I-Phi Press.

Dweck, C. (2006). *The New Psychology of Success.* New York, NY: Ballantine Books.

Eagleman, D. (2011). *Incognito: The Secret Lives of the Brain*. New York, NY: Pantheon Books.

Eliade, M. (1987). *The Sacred and The Profane: The Nature of Religion*. Orlando, FL: Harcourt, Inc.

Fehmi, L. & Robbins, J. (2007). *The Open-Focus Brain: Harnessing the Power of Attention to Heal Mind and Body*. Boston, MA: Trumpeter Books.

Frankl, V. (2006). *Man's Search for Meaning*. Boston, MA: Beacon Press.

Gannett, L. (2010). The Human Genome Project. *The Stanford Encyclopedia of Philosophy*, Edward N. Zalta (Ed.).Retrieved from http://plato.stanford.edu/archives/fall2010/entries/human-genome.

Gazzaniga, M. (2012). *Who's In Charge?: Free Will and the Science of the Brain*. New York, NY: HarperCollins Publishers, Inc.

Gergen, K. (2009). *Relational Being: Beyond Self and Community*. New York, NY: Oxford University Press, Inc.

Gladwell, M. (2005). *Blink: The Power of Thinking Without Thinking*. New York, NY: Little, Brown and Company.

Goncharov, I. (2005). *Oblomov*. (D. Magarshack, Trans.). London, UK: Penguin Books, Ltd.

Goleman, D. (1995). *Emotional Intelligence: Why It Can Matter More than IQ*. New York, NY: Bantam Books, Inc.

Guignon, C. (2004).*On Being Authentic*. New York, NY: Routledge, Taylor and Francis Group.

Harden, B. (2012). *Escape from Camp 14: One Man's Remarkable Odyssey from North Korea to Freedom in the West*. London, UK: Penguin Group.

Hood, B. (2012). *How the Social Brain Creates Identity*. New York, NY: Oxford University Press.

Hugo, V . (2013). *Les Misérables*. New York, NY: New American Library.

James, W. (1912). *Essays in Radical Empiricism*. London, UK: Longmans, Green and Co.

James, W. (2008). *Varieties of Religious Experience: A Study in Human Nature*.

Charleston, SC: Forgotten Books.

James, W. (1956). *The Will to Believe and Other Essays in Popular Philosophy.* Mineola, NY: Dover Publications, Inc.

Kahneman, D. (2011). *Thinking Fast and Slow.* New York, NY: Farrar, Straus and Giroux.

Lipton, B. (2005). *The Biology of Belief: Unleashing the Power of Consciousness, Matter & Miracles.* Carlsbad, CA: Hay House, Inc.

Maclagan, D. (1977). *Creation Myths: Man's Introduction to the World.* London, UK: Thames & Hudson.

Maddi, S.R. (2001). *Personality Theories a Comparative Analysis* (6th ed.). Long Grove, IL: Waveland Press, Inc.

McCraty, R (2003). Heart-Brain Neurodynamics: The Making of Emotions. HeartMath Research Center, Institute of HeartMath, Boulder Creek, CA, Publication No. 03-015.

Mitchell, L.Jay, Slife, B., & Whoolery, M. (2004). A theistic approach to therapeutic community: Non-naturalism and the Alldredge Academy. *Casebook for a Spiritual Strategy in Counseling and Psychotherapy* (Richards, S. & Bergin, A. (Eds.). Washington, D.C: APA Books.

Mlodinow, L. (2012). *Subliminal: How your Unconscious Mind Rules Your Behavior.* New York, NY. Vintage Books.

Montoya, A. (2013). *The Finish Line.* Mustang, OK: Tate Publishing.

Religion & Public Life Project. (2012). *"Nones" on the Rise.* Retrieved from Pew Research http://www.pewforum.org/2012/10/09/nones-on-the-rise/

Richardson, F. & Slife, B. (2008). Problematic ontological underpinnings of positive psychology: A strong relational alternative. *Theory & Psychology* (39.1).

Ricoeur, P. (1981). *Hermeneutics & the Human Sciences* John B. Thompson, (Ed.). (John B. Thompson, Trans.). Cambridge, UK: Cambridge University Press.

Schick, Jr., T. (2000). *Readings in the Philosophy of Science: From Positivism to Postmodernism.* Houston, TX: Mayfield Publishing Company.

Shaw, G. (1903). *Man and Superman.* Cambridge, MA: The University Press.

Slife, B. (in press). Virtue ethics in practice: The Greenbrier Academy p. 10. *Journal of Theoretical and Philosophical Psychology.*

Slife, B. and Richardson, F. See an article in press that was a presented at the 119th Annual Convention of the American Psychological Association in San Diego. The presentation was part of a symposium entitled "Exploring and Critiquing Ken Gergen's Book *Relational Being*". Brent D. Slife and Frank F. Richardson (in press). Is Gergen's *Relational Being* relational enough? *Journal of Constructivist Psychology.*

Slife, B., & Williams R. (1995). *What's Behind the Research?: Discovering Hidden Assumptions in the Behavioral Sciences*. Thousand Oaks, CA: Sage Publications, Inc.

Smith, H. (2001). *Why Religion Matters*. New York, NY: HarperCollins Publishers, Inc.

Somé, Malidoma. (1988). *The Healing Wisdom of Africa: Finding Life Purpose Through Nature, Ritual, and Community*. New York, NY: Putnam Books.

Storr, W. (2013). *The Heretics: Adventures with the Enemies of Science*. London, UK: Picador.

Swedenborg, E. (1990). *Heaven and Hell.* (G. Dole, Trans.). New York, NY: Swedenborg Foundation.

Taylor, C. (1989). *The Sources of the Self: The Making of the Modern Identity*. Cambridge, MA: Harvard University Press.

Weihenmayer, E. (2002). *Touch the Top of the World: A Blind Man's Journey to Climb Farther than the eye Can See: My Story*. New York, NY: Penguin Group.

Wiener, J. (2009). *The Therapeutic Relationship: Transference, Countertransference, and the Making of Meaning*. College Station, TX: Texas A&M University Press.